THE TEENAGE EMPOWERMENT SERIES 3 Books in 1

From Wealth to Wellness: Mastering Health, Wealth, and Managing Social Media Effectively for Teens

E. T. Mulloney

Contents

The Teenage Social Media Detox

7 Simple Steps on How Teens Unplugged in the Digital World

E. T. Mulloney

The Teenage Wealthypreneur
7 Simple Strategies on How Teens Can Learn Money Management and Wealth Generation
E. T. Mulloney

The Teenage Healthypreneur
8 Simple Strategies on How Teens Can Learn Entrepreneurial Skills and Live Healthy
E. T. Mulloney

To Patrick, my ever-loving and steadfast spouse, you are the bedrock of my life, next only to God Himself.

This book is a heartfelt dedication to you, the constant wellspring of love, encouragement, and inspiration in my journey. With your presence, each page of our shared story becomes a beautiful and meaningful part of our life together as a family, and our cherished fur companion, Tiggy boy, is an essential character in this adventure. We are beyond blessed!

The Teenage Social Media Detox

7 Simple Steps on How Teens Unplugged in the Digital World

E. T. Mulloney

Introduction

The life of a teenager dates back to the beginning of humanity. On the other hand, social media is a relatively newer concept. What was once a science fiction idea to some has now become an extension of our personalities. Of course, teenagers from hundreds of years ago didn't have electricity, let alone access to the internet. However, a teenager just 15 years ago might've had limited time on the computer, having to share it with other siblings or whoever wanted to use the phone.

The times have rapidly changed, and now we can pull up anything we want to see at the tip of our fingertips so long as our phones are charged and we have service. Even when we don't have access to the internet, we can play games, communicate with friends, and take pictures with just a few taps and clicks.

All of the noises, sights, and options become ingratiated into every aspect of our lives, altering our thoughts, behaviors, and emotions. In a way, this is a good thing, as we have access to information and communication like never before. But when use becomes mismanaged, it can be overstimulating, frustrating, and addictive.

Teenagers and young adults today are the first to experience life in the presence of social media throughout their most developmental years. From social networking forums to business pages that could impact your career, social media is an enigma that is constantly changing history.

Navigating this is challenging for any age, but the more innovations we see, the more reliant we are on the internet as a whole. Video streaming services are replacing cable, texts are replacing letters, and emails are replacing paper mail. All of this is happening on a daily basis.

In one study, it was found that 95% of teens between the ages of 13–17 have used YouTube, with 77% of them using it daily (Gelles-Watnick & Vogels, 2023). Life with easy access to the internet can be very impactful to your health, especially during a time when your mind and body are still developing.

Research also shows that the older the teen, the more likely they are to state they use the internet almost constantly (Massarat, 2022). What this shows is that our accessibility and use might increase over time. The more often we repeat a pattern, the more likely it is to become a part of our daily life. Some teens report using social media for up to nine hours daily ("Social Media," 2018).

If you feel pressured and stressed by school and family to reduce your digital usage, you're not alone. This is a common issue for teens, but that is why it's even more important for youth to work on their time and health management. If you can learn the skills to be mindful as early as possible, you can break free from the habit of overusing social media.

Social media use is time-consuming and keeps us distracted from things we might rather be doing. It creates a sense of urgency within us that can influence our anxiety levels. It changes our thoughts which will eventually start to change how we view life itself. Most of us feel the effects of excessive social media use, but knowing how to realistically reduce it can be a challenge in itself.

There are many benefits of going through a detox that you can't comprehend until you are experiencing the process because of the hold it has over your thoughts and actions. The relief and stress reduction you will feel will help you realize just how invaluable excessive social media use can be.

Not all social media is a bad thing, though! There's a reason that we are so enthralled and entertained by these innovations. There are endless ways to connect and consume information, but enjoying the benefits of social media can be challenging when we don't have mindfulness over our habits.

By becoming more aware of our habits, taking steps to reduce usage, and finding new ways to flourish in our lives, we can take back power over these habits to build a positively impactful relationship with our phones.

Social media use is very impactful on a developing mind, so it's important to implement methods of reducing screen time for all ages, but especially teenagers. There is so much life to be enjoyed in youth, and getting consumed by the pressures of social media can make it difficult to take advantage of.

The dependency on social media is frustrating and time-consuming. It holds a power over us that can make us feel trapped by our urges to check in with what's happening on the internet. It doesn't have to be this way, however, so taking the next steps to reduce your social media use will help you declutter your mind for increased emotional management.

How to Use This Book

The readings in this book will travel between seven essential steps as seen through the seven chapters. Each one can be done in a step-by-step process, but take it at your own pace and make adjustments to the process as you see fit. The relationship we all have with our phones is an individual one, and it's not easy to transform it for the better.

The seven steps will provide guidance and practical, applicable steps to reduce the use of social media and experience the benefits of controlling this habit. When initiative is taken to reduce stress and improve the quality of life, it will make it a substantial and long-lasting trait not just for your teen years, but for your life as an adult as well.

You will find tips for reducing social media use alongside methods to replace the time spent on the internet with more productive habits. It's suggested to use a journal, notebook, or digital document to track progress and write down notes and reflections.

A Note to Parents

Many readers are likely teens themselves, but it's important for parents of adolescents alike to consider their and their child's social media use. Much of what a teenager learns is through what is seen by them. If you are a parent who struggles with social media use, your teen might be getting their habits from you. This means the tips and methods used don't only work for adolescents! By implementing healthier habits into your life as a parent, you will be able to help your child make improvements as well.

Regardless of your age, reducing social media use is *always* a good thing. Knowing the ins and outs of internet management will empower you to maintain healthy and productive habits so you can find success in whatever your goals may be.

1. Understand the Impact

Social media has become such an ingrained part of our habitual nature that it's hard to comprehend just how detrimental it's been to our lives. The use of our phones is such a passive activity that we don't even realize we're on it sometimes.

"Passive" refers to the way that we might unknowingly participate in a habit. "Active," conversely, is something that requires a bit more of our attention. For example, tapping your foot or biting your nails is something that happens a bit more passively. You might unknowingly chew on your pencil or twirl your hair. Painting your nails, using your pencil, or stretching your foot is a bit more active.

Our phone use has become second nature. Have you ever found yourself lifting up your phone and scrolling through social media without even thinking about it? Every time you leave the house, your phone might be the first thing to check and ensure you have before heading out the door. At least if you forget your keys, you can call someone to let you in!

Of course, not all phone use is bad. And not all social media is bad. We can protect ourselves and stay safe through phone use, for one. A problem arises when we lose track of just how much time is spent online, though. This time could be spent doing other things, like studying or socializing. Too much phone use is associated with a decrease in mental health. In fact, teens who are using social media for three or more hours a day are more likely to experience mental health problems (Miller, 2022).

The first step in overcoming social media use is understanding the impact that social media has had on your mind.

Why is social media so addictive? Why is it so hard to just ignore the internet on your own? What makes it so enticing to want to constantly and habitually check in with the online world?

The first step to take to reduce your screen time use is to utilize methods of noticing screen time habits and become more aware of how you are using your devices so that your usage of them becomes more of an active habit rather than a passive one.

The Addictive Nature

Using a phone can produce dopamine, so we literally become addicted to using it (Goldman, 2021). In addition, research has shown that those who depend on social media use can exhibit symptoms similar to substance abuse ("Are You Addicted," n.d.).

First and foremost, phones keep us connected. That's what they were made for! Over 100 years ago, we wanted to be able to talk to people who were not in the same physical space that we were. We wanted to be able to communicate emergencies and stay in touch with people. We wanted to be able to relay important information and provide many different services to individuals.

Nowadays, we need phones to survive.

You need to call different services when you need help or have issues. You need to call your doctor to make an appointment. You need to call 911 in the case of extreme emergencies. You need to call your school to let them know that you might not be in attendance that day.

There are so many small ways of communication that we still depend on our phones for. In addition to that, the use of a phone has become incredibly twisted and reshaped over time. Nowadays, we use phones mostly to entertain ourselves. We entertain ourselves by talking and chatting with friends. We entertain ourselves by watching funny videos or looking at what our friends are currently up to. We check in with stories of strangers and celebrities, and we also express ourselves through social media. We share our own thoughts online, and all of this helps us to stay more connected to other people.

Who would have thought that in 1876, when the phone was first invented, they would have become what they are today?

Not only do we stay connected to friends, peers, and other important officials, but we also stay connected to the world. That is more true now than ever before and it is always going to be more true the further along we get in technology.

You used to have to rely on letters to connect with someone across the world. Now, you can video chat with them or watch their live posts on social media. You can figure out what is happening at the furthest point away from you in the universe by checking in online.

This makes us feel more informed. It makes us feel more like we are a part of our world.

What we haven't realized, however, especially as teenagers, is that this different type of connection can also make us feel really disconnected.

Social media can elicit many feelings of isolation. You might see a group of people hanging out online and feel as though you don't have as many friends as they do. You might focus all of your time and energy on the internet and spend your free time in the digital world, therefore neglecting real social circles in the physical world.

Our phones help us see what other people are up to and they provide instant news updates, making this a vital part of our lives. When we're disconnected from the internet, it can make us feel as though we're disconnected from our reality.

The urge and desire to be a part of something bigger is a natural emotion that humans have evolved to have throughout time. Different animals have different survival instincts. Just think of the way a mouse habitates, eats, and lives in general compared to a spider. As humans, we prefer social settings and to be a part of a group. Think of primates in the wild and how they are seen in groups, versus a wolf, who might be seen as more of a loner animal. We rely on protection and unity to help us survive and thrive.

Thousands of years ago, we formed groups that consisted of hunters and gatherers. Some people were better at trekking out in the world and fighting and killing animals. Others were better at foraging.

The mix of different groups helped people develop the cognitive and survival skills that we have, which have made us one of the most advanced species on the planet.

This level of advancement has maintained many natural social urges within us in modern times. We want to be a part of a group. We want to be recognized and acknowledged by other people. We want others to see that we are special and unique so that they see value in us. If we don't feel valued, then it can make us feel really isolated and like we're not an important part of society.

Recognizing this natural human urge can help you understand why it feels so good to be connected, not just in your social circle, but in the world in general. This natural human instinct is also why it can be so addictive to use your phone.

In addition, we are also highly addicted to our cell phones because they are so accessible.

You can't go out to eat and party with your friends every single night. You can't go to the movies every night. You can't go to a comedy show, zoo, or other place of entertainment day after day. Whether your parents say that you're not allowed to do that or you just don't have it in your budget, it's not realistic for us to be hanging out with our friends or doing fun activities every day of the week. What we can do, however, is check in with our friends every day, multiple times a day online.

Our phones are also extremely accessible because they're small and mobile. Even just as recently as a decade ago, not everybody had a cell phone, and they likely had to share phone use or data with other people.

Two to three decades ago, the average person didn't have a cell phone at all.

If you did, it might have been a luxury in the family. You also likely had to share internet usage with other people. In the days of landlines, only one person could use either the phone or the computer at a time, so you had a very limited amount of time to spend online and scroll through social media.

Nowadays, everybody has not only their phones but other devices like tablets and laptops that help keep them connected to other people. We also have many types of gaming systems and online video games that we connect to our friends with.

In more recent years, we have developed many different types of video chatting software, allowing us to hang out with other people from the comfort of our own homes without everybody having to meet up in a physical group. This accessibility makes it even more enticing to want to sit on your phone or other devices and spend time in the digital world. There is also plenty of variety, so you can do all of these things in just one sitting.

Phones fit into our pockets, purses, and small bags, and smartwatches even allow us to have notifications and messages strapped to our bodies at all times.

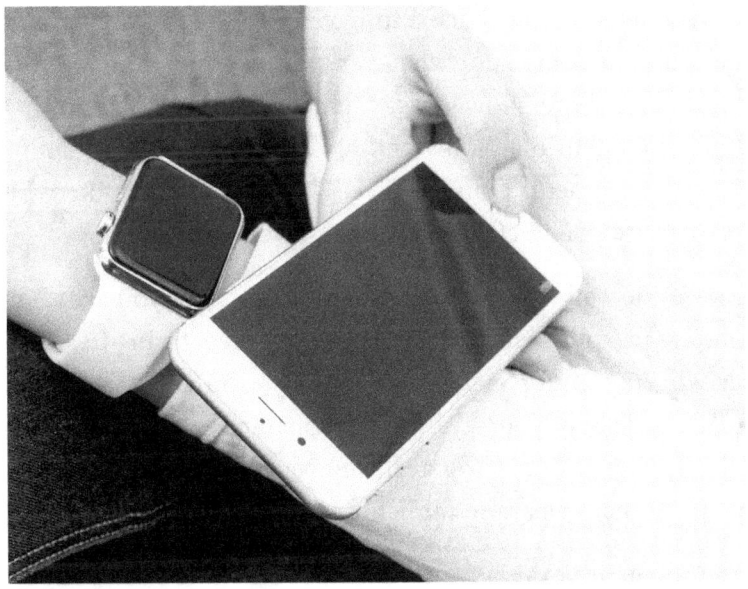

The addictive nature of phones exists because of how purely accessible they are. Consider anybody who is struggling with an addiction, whether they can't seem to give up sweets, or they're dependent on alcohol. Sometimes these things are not as easily accessible, therefore, it's easier to avoid that addiction. For example, if you're underage, you can't buy alcohol. If you don't have any money, you can buy those sweets. It's a lot harder to get access to some of these more addictive substances. However, if you have a cell phone and access to the internet, you can use it as much as you'd like.

Our phones also give us access to information all across the world. We can explore things that we never could have without technology. You can learn about interesting facts. You can watch movies and listen to music made by people across the world. You used to have to rely on whatever was on cable TV at night, or whatever you could purchase at your local video store. Nowadays, you can Google search for any type of content that you want, providing an endless amount of entertainment. This connects to the next reason why phones are so addicting: they are also very distracting.

Life is incredibly stressful, no matter what age you are. Our phones provide instant relief. If you're bored, trying to study, or working on a paper late at night, you might start to feel really bad about yourself. You feel ashamed or guilty that you didn't start sooner. You feel annoyed and frustrated with yourself that you are so far behind in your work.

You might seek out a form of instant relief. You can pick up your phone and check in with what your friends are doing. You can text somebody and complain about how much work you have to do. You can pull up funny videos on TikTok and scroll endlessly, distracting yourself from the stress of life.

This is also ingrained in our psychology. We want to find immediate relief when we feel bad. If you're hot, you might turn a fan on. If you're cold, you might put a jacket on. If you're hungry, you could eat a snack. If you're tired, you go to bed.

If you're unhappy, you find something to make you feel good.

Your phone is accessible and it's always around, so you always have something that is going to make you feel good. Anything that provides you with happiness or joy is something that your brain is going to log and remember for the future.

Next time you're feeling sad, your brain thinks to itself, *Oh, my phone makes me feel good. I'll check in on social media. I'll watch that one person's story on Instagram. I'll see what everybody is up to on Tiktok. I'll check if any of my subscriptions have posted a new video on YouTube. I'll see if there are any good deals on the food delivery app.*

Your brain associates all these good things with instant relief from your stress. Since we are dealing with stress multiple times a day, we are seeking that happiness through our phones multiple times a day as well.

Phones are there when we're bored with schoolwork or panicking about something else in our personal life. They become our best friends and biggest support systems without us realizing that they are also hurting us at the same time.

Our phones also allow us to even Google symptoms of the negative things that we're feeling. If you're stressed or anxious, you might be dealing with a rapid heartbeat or perhaps are starting to sweat. Maybe you Google signs of a heart attack thinking that your rapid heartbeat is a sign that you're physically in danger. You might have trouble breathing so you start looking up what it means to have symptoms of shortness of breath.

You can see if there is an instant answer or immediate relief from some of the things that are stressing you out and making you feel panicked. However, once you open up Google, you might close out of it, and then instinctually open up another app, distracting yourself even further.

In addition to all of these reasons that phones are so addictive, we also have to remember that *they are designed to make us feel good.*

Some apps are designed to be addictive. Think about endless scrolling. Many apps allow you to keep scrolling forever, constantly providing you with a fresh news feed. This makes it incredibly enticing because, even when you notice that you've spent an hour scrolling through Instagram, you might simply swipe up again only to see many new posts from your friends.

By the time you finish watching all of your friends' stories, more have been posted, therefore creating an endless cycle of constantly streaming content.

Phones are meant to be user-friendly. They are designed so that anybody can use them whether you're 13 or 93. They are supposed to be intuitive, so they are designed to naturally align with some of your physical and mental habits. They are colorful, they make fun noises, and they are enjoyable to use, even when you're just doing something like typing. Think about the little sounds that the clicks make or how you can incorporate emojis into what you're texting. All of this is specifically crafted so that you find more enjoyment from your experience using a phone.

We can customize the sound of our notifications so that when you hear a certain friend text you, you hear that exciting noise, making it more likely that you're going to keep scrolling online.

Like anything that makes us feel good, our brains are going to want to use this as much as possible, not just when we are seeking relief from stress. They become habitual and second nature, so before you know it, you become fully addicted to this habit.

On top of that, we *have* to use our phones. We have to check emails, check our bank accounts, and even do our homework on the internet. There's so much reliance on the World Wide Web that even when you want to escape it, you can't.

How can you tell if you are addicted to your phone? One thing to start noticing is how often you think about using social media, even when you're not using it. Do you have the urge to check in even when you can't? Do you find yourself sitting in class, wanting to pull out your phone even though it's against school policy? Do you plan and think out texts and emails when you're doing simple things like showering or brushing your teeth?

Do you find yourself constantly checking your phone even when you're hanging out and socializing with other people? Do you find that you are on your phone more often than you are enjoying hobbies, like different sports or creative activities?

As we start to unravel all of the intricacies and small details of the ways that we are connected to our phones, we can begin to improve this habit.

It's also important to note that your algorithm is set to specify what you want to look at, making it even more addicting. What your news feed looks like on different apps is going to be completely different from the person sitting next to you, even if the two of you have similar tastes and interests. There are specific formulas created to gather our personal information and use that against us so that we want to keep scrolling, make purchases, and stay connected online.

For some, this is a good thing. It means that you filter out the things that you're not interested in and can provide you with things that you actually care about. However, it can be incredibly harmful because you unknowingly get fed misinformation, hatred online, and other things that are meant to entice you and keep your attention.

When we are not conscious of our social media use and how impactful it can be to our lives, we end up becoming so addicted that it becomes a habit that feels impossible to break.

Identifying Screentime Habits

It's estimated that at least 10% of the population has a social media addiction in the US alone (Quinn, 2023). This number is even higher for teens, and it's hard to tell how great it really could be since many people are unknowingly dependent on their phones.

80% of teens believe social media makes them feel more connected to their friends (Anderson et al., 2022). When we see social media use as a good thing, though, it's hard to maintain control over it. While it's true that it does have some benefits, we still must be aware and conscious of how it is impacting our lives so that we can stay one step ahead of our use. When you do this, you allow yourself to actually enjoy the benefits while reducing the negative side effects.

It's hard to keep track of how much social media use you're participating in on a daily basis because we aren't always taught that it's something that we're supposed to track. When it comes to other addictive habits like eating, you're told that you're supposed to monitor how much food you're eating in a day. You should pay attention to how many candy bars, bags of chips, sodas, and other potentially unhealthy snacks you're consuming. When it comes to social media, there's no set limit. We're not provided with a guideline of how much social media we should be using. Of course, some people might recommend not using it at all, but for many, we understand that this is an unrealistic precedent to set.

In addition, social media use is not illegal and has actually been actively encouraged within our society. Everywhere you look, you'll see ads telling you to check something out online. Every business you go to has a little symbol or sign next to their social media tags so that you can easily look them up and follow them. When you meet new people, they ask for your social media so that they can stay connected with you when the two of you are not together.

Because of this, it's very hard to monitor just how much we're using it. As a teen, it's also difficult to stay focused on the amount of social media that you use because your brain is still developing. You are still dealing with impulse control, and that's a hard thing to manage on your own.

Parents can sometimes monitor how much social media we use, but it's very easy to get around some of those rules and restrictions, especially when they are not around constantly.

It's up to you to be proactive and to take initiative in reducing your screentime habits. The first step is to keep track of how much social media you're using so that you can get a better gauge of the way this habit is intertwined with your daily life. Start by using phone tracking software. If you have an iPhone, this is a feature that's already built into your phone and is also an easily accessible app on many other types of devices. This will keep track of how frequently you use different social media apps. It will give you a breakdown, and some apps also help you track progress between days and weeks.

It's also important after you start tracking your phone use to notice any trends. Did you notice that maybe on Sunday you spent six hours online whereas on Monday and Tuesday, you only spent about an hour each? Perhaps you were busier with other things happening on those days. Now you know that next week when Sunday comes around, it's better to have a plan for what to do that day to keep you distracted so that you are less likely to spend all of it scrolling the internet. Did you find that maybe one day you used a lot of social media after you had a particularly hard or stressful day?

Is there something that you enjoy doing that allows you to not check in with your phone at all? Whatever keeps you away from your phone is something to add more of into your life, and whatever makes you want to use your phone at an excessive level is something to monitor and reduce. Noticing these small trends and habits of your social media use will make you more aware of how you've been utilizing that habit so that you can monitor it in the future.

After you start tracking some of the social media time that you spend online, write it down in a notebook. Keep a separate record of it so that you can reinforce just how much time you've been spending online. It's easy to open your phone tracking app and see that you spent three hours on Instagram yesterday, but what you can also do is swipe away and not check in with that. However, saying "I spent three hours on Instagram yesterday," and writing it down in your journal, makes you go back over that idea again so that you can fully grasp just how much time was spent on the internet.

After you start keeping better track of your habits, it's important to set limits for how many minutes you can use certain apps a day. Use third-party apps or the built-in feature on your devices to set time limits.

This means giving each app a 15-minute daily time limit, or perhaps 30 minutes. If you only use one or two social media apps, try to keep social media use under an hour each day. That might sound hard to do, but what you will discover is that you can get just as much from social media within the hour as you might get when you are spending three hours or more on it a day.

These app limits also help you gain a better awareness of checking in on your phone without even realizing you're doing it. It gives you kind of a stop sign before you fall into the trap of endless scrolling. For example, if you use up your 15-minute time limit on Instagram, you might click Instagram on your phone, open it, and get prompted with a reminder that you've already reached your time limit for that day. It's a small reminder that helps you close your phone and put your focus elsewhere.

The last part of raising more awareness over your phone use is to go through notifications. There is no reason to have notifications for social media whatsoever. Unless you are a social media manager or that is part of your career, you do not need constant and instant updates from social media. The only notifications you should have on are for text messages or phone calls from specific people. This would include your parents, partner, or maybe some close friends. You can have notifications to get texts from a grandparent, a teacher, or somebody else whom you have to check in with. Other than that, silence group chats and turn off notifications for things like Instagram, Reddit, TikTok, Snapchat, and other social media that you might be using.

Our brains can actually start to associate phone notifications with "pleasurable feelings," conditioning us to feel a sense of urgency or excitement when one goes off ("Constant Smartphone Notifications," 2022).

You can set specific times to check in with these apps throughout the day, therefore allowing you to check in with all of your notifications at once. You can check in daily so you still stay up to date with friends, but you don't have to check it the second that you receive a notification. Is it important to respond to a meme that a friend sent you? Do you have to watch that video that your partner just sent you? Chances are you don't. The constant notifications that we get are little reminders throughout the day to grab our phone and start checking in.

Imagine if the snacks from the cupboard called your name. Imagine if all of the ice cream in your freezer made a little dinging noise throughout the day! You would be snacking on things much more often than you should.

Checking in on social media does not have to be an all-day, frequent thing. You can set aside specific time periods to stay connected with the world around you. Notifications are incredibly distracting and can pull your focus throughout the day. Even if you don't attend to that notification right away, you might start thinking about it.

For example, if you're in the shower and you hear five text messages go off in a row, you might start panicking, wondering if you should cut your shower short so that you can attend to those notifications. When you get out, you realize that it's just your friends sending GIFs and memes. Notifications create a false sense of urgency and stress when we constantly hear them.

It's up to you to go back through and identify the emotions, responses, and habits that you have as a result of social media use. There's a reason that you're here, reading this book, and seeking help. Chances are, you've already identified the ways social media has had a negative impact on your life.

List these things out. For example, you might write down the following:

- I feel anxious after spending too much time on TikTok.
- I feel tired and bored after a long day of social media use.

Once you're able to label your feelings and emotions connected to social media, it gives you greater insight into the habits that have been destructive in your life. This period of enlightenment is crucial for putting your social media addiction at bay.

Reminders

- **Step #1**: Understand the impact that social media can have on one's life.

Most of us already know that social media can be addictive— that's why we're here in the first place. But knowing the inner workings of that addictive nature is important so that we can come up with strategies to reduce screen time and take back power over our lives. Not only is excessive social media use unhealthy, but it can also be potentially dangerous.

2. Know the Dangers

Social media doesn't damage the body in the way that other addictions do, like drugs and sugar, so it's easy to assume it's not that dangerous. However, the long-term effects are certainly something to be concerned about. There are endless warnings given to teens about drunk driving or doing drugs and the severity behind these is scary, as the worst-case scenario is often death or injury. Social media is something more subtle and takes longer to show signs of overuse. You don't always get addicted to it overnight. While social media can lead to death or harm by breaking down our mental health, there aren't as many instant physical side effects, so it can be more difficult to pinpoint just how damaging it can be.

Social media use can impact our health and increase anxiety. Noticing the symptoms we've been dealing with will make it easier to reduce usage overall.

The Risks of Being Online

Your digital footprint will never be erased ("Understanding Your Digital Footprint," 2019). You can delete social media apps, change your username, and shut off your internet altogether, but remnants of your online activity will always linger on the World Wide Web.

Social media is all about sharing bits and pieces of your life online. Most of us consent to some of our personal information being shared with the world. We willingly post what we ate for dinner. We willingly share selfies. We consent to allow people to look at this content. However, there is so much that we don't understand about our privacy.

Whenever prompted with a text box that says "accept here," it's easy to click the checkmark and move on to the next stage. When you're asked, "Do you consent?", you might agree without knowing everything that's involved in that consent form. Deciphering what these all mean is confusing for a person at any age, but as a teen, it's even harder to navigate the confusing legal texts that we've already agreed to.

Just about anyone with access to the internet can find out a lot of information about you with just a quick search online. Some of this information is what you've willingly put online, while the rest is information collected by data companies and marketing agencies who track your purchase (Teague, 2019). Social media apps like Instagram track how long you spend looking at posts (Keach, 2018). This information is collected and stored, and there's no telling how big your digital footprint will grow over time.

Whether they're using your phone number, full name, email address, or even just a sibling's information, those with the right motives can find out many bits and pieces of personal information about you. The reason that somebody might want this information is endless as well. They might be complete strangers from different parts of the world who want to steal your personal information for financial gain. They might want to open up new credit cards or take out loans in your name. They might try to steal your credit card balance, your bank account information, or other very valuable monetary aspects of your life that could have devastating results.

During youth, you can't know if certain things are going to come back to haunt you in the future. When you're applying for a job or a scholarship for college, you don't know if something you posted when you were 12 years old is going to come back and make you look bad.

Even if you use fake names, don't show your face in your profile picture, and don't reveal any personal information, as there are people out there who can gain access to your personal and private information if they really want to. As much as you might feel as though you know about internet privacy, there's always somebody else who knows more and who has worse intentions.

This information is not meant to scare you. We don't have to be afraid. We don't have to avoid social media altogether, forever. It's just important that we are aware of just how much it can impact our privacy.

More than our health is put at risk when we get online. Teenagers are susceptible and vulnerable to creating a lasting digital footprint. The footprint we leave behind will never go away. It might change shape over time, but there are many websites that copy and store our information. Some of these websites do so automatically. For example, on a social media site like Reddit, you can post something online and delete it. When you go to read it, you don't see that post anymore. However, there are multiple different sites that automatically copy all of this information and save it in an archive so that you can still view certain deleted posts.

You never know if what you post is going to come back to haunt you, and you never know just how different your beliefs might be in the future. Old tweets have cost some people their jobs, scholarships, and more, so it's best to maintain a clean image online. Any celebrity or internet personality that you follow likely has some sort of scandal where past tweets or Instagram posts were uncovered, making them look bad. At the time, these posts weren't necessarily made with malicious intent, but people changed their beliefs over time. Many things that were once culturally and socially acceptable are now rightfully deemed offensive. While it certainly was offensive at the time, it was still deemed more acceptable, so people got away with that kind of behavior.

Nowadays, it's hard to tell what kind of casual language or belief systems we're using that is going to quickly become outdated and hurt our image down the line. You might post something seemingly acceptable, but later, as you age, you uncover more truths about how it really comes off.

Over time, our data is collected in every corner and stored away on the internet. It's best to make sure that what you're putting out there is something that you will always be proud of or at least unashamed of.

You likely won't regret posting pictures of your pets, and you likely aren't going to feel ashamed or embarrassed for sharing some of your thoughts or emotions. Even selfies are generally harmless. However, the frequency and amount can greatly impact your digital footprint.

Blue Light

Aside from the risks to your privacy, it's also important to raise awareness of the dangers of blue light. Blue light is a specific digital light that "can penetrate the eye's natural filters and cause damage to the retina ("Why Your Teen," n.d.)."

The artificial light that we are exposed to all day long can really mess with our circadian rhythm, which is the natural cycle that our body goes through. It's why we feel more alert during the day and more tired going to bed at night. Naturally, our circadian rhythm follows the sunlight. Humans are diurnal, which means that we sleep when it's night and we are awake when the sun is out. You've likely heard of nocturnal animals before. Well, humans are the opposite.

Sometimes we still sleep when the sun rises. Sometimes we go to bed even before the sun sets. But for the most part, humans are *not* nocturnal. Diurnal animals include ducks, bears, and whales. Nocturnal animals include owls, bats, and raccoons.

Despite our differences, we all follow a circadian rhythm that is triggered by light.

When the sun sets, that means some animals should head to bed while others start the hunt. When the sun rises, some animals scurry to their homes while others begin to awaken. Whether we are nocturnal or diurnal changes some of our biological functions. For example, some nocturnal animals have the vision to see at night which allows them to hunt better. Humans can't see in the dark because we're not supposed to be doing regular things in the dark.

Artificial light triggers these biological responses as well. When the light suddenly turns on, you might wake up. If somebody comes bursting into your room and turns the switch on, that's enough to wake you up in the morning. While you might not feel alert and refreshed, it's still a signal to you that now is the time to awaken. This is because even when our eyes are closed, our eyelids are thin enough to be able to sense the light that's around us. When it's really dark, you might feel more tired. If you're in a movie theater or cuddled up on the couch with your pet and blanket at night, you might feel a little bit more sleepy because it's dark and peaceful.

Artificial light messes with our circadian rhythm so when we are in our beds using our phones late at night after the sun has set, our bright phone can trick our brain into thinking it's daytime.

A flashy, colorful phone that is making noise is not telling your brain that it's time to go to bed. It's telling your brain that it's time to be awake and alert. Our phones also emit light even when we aren't using them through different notifications. Constant use of your phone is going to mess with your body's natural biological system and confuse those natural triggers.

This causes us stress, therefore having a greater impact on our health. Blue light can also cause eyestrain. Eyestrain alone can cause headaches but also the act of not getting enough sleep or having disrupted sleep can also increase your chance of having a headache.

As you are a teen, you're likely even more susceptible to these negative side effects since your body is still developing. Blue light also stops and reduces the production of melatonin (Summer, 2023). Melatonin is one hormone that gets released when it gets darker, especially when nighttime comes around. Melatonin helps to calm you down and make you feel more rested. When your melatonin and other hormones are messed up, then you're not going to feel tired enough to get a deep sleep.

Even if you are not using your phone and getting in bed at a decent time, excessive social media use close to bedtime can still impact your hormones, therefore impacting your sleep.

As a developing teen, getting rest is incredibly important so that you can function. If you find that you're struggling to pay attention, or you feel extremely tired throughout the day, there's a good chance that blue light has been impacting you. Our phones are not the only devices that emit blue light either. Watching TV, and using tablets, laptops, and desktop computers can all emit blue light. As you can see, it's not just the act of using social media that can have a negative impact, but also the act of using a phone or device at all.

The Impact on Mood

Aside from the basic risks and blue light effects that excessive social media and cell phone use can have in your life, these things can also greatly impact your mood. Social media use can trigger our body's natural stress response (Mastroianni, 2020).

Like the circadian rhythm, we all have a biological feature wired within us for survival. This is the stress response, also known as the fight-or-flight response. Whenever we are presented with a perceived threat, we have two common reactions: to flee the scene or to attack the threat.

The flight response is why birds and pigeons will simply fly away when you approach a group of them pecking around on the ground. The next response is to fight the threat. This is why animals like snakes or spiders might attack you when they feel cornered.

There are other types of responses to stress as well. One is the freeze response. You can think of this through the example of a deer or a possum freezing in the beam of your headlights when you're driving on the road at night.

There are other responses, like the fawn response, where the threatened person tries to please the threat. For example, a student who is bullied might try to impress their bully in an attempt to ease up the level of abuse endured.

In terms of using your cell phone, the main stress response that you will feel is going to be the fight, flight, or freeze response. For example, if you see something really infuriating online, you might start going on rants or leaving angry comments in response to help alleviate some of the stress that you feel. You might freeze by socially isolating. You might turn your phone off and then just lie in bed and not talk to anybody. You might flee by closing one app and immediately opening another one, trying to ignore any stressful feelings or emotions by immediately distracting yourself with new content.

Most living things have a stress response, which is a chemical reaction that happens in your body. When you feel stressed, your heart starts to beat. Often, sweat will start to produce at a more frequent rate. You might also notice that you have trouble breathing or regulating your heart rate. All this can lead to even more stress, therefore creating an endless cycle. The fluctuation of the content that we see online can also seriously impact our mood. At one point, you're watching something hilarious and laughing to yourself in bed, and the next moment you are crying because you just saw the saddest video of a poor little abandoned animal who no one will adopt. After that, you're enraged and infuriated because you learned about something in history that seems unfair and unjust, and then you see videos of food and artwork that you want to consume and purchase. This can all happen within a matter of *10 minutes* and that is a lot of emotions to experience all at once, especially as a developing teenager.

We also have to think about *how* we use social media and *when* we use it. If you wake up first thing in the morning and start your day off by looking at enraging content or things that make you upset, then this is going to impact your mood for the rest of the day. You might get consistently triggered throughout the day, therefore feeling stressed and tired through every hour. The stress of social media isn't something that just stays stuck in your mind either. It can start to make the rest of your body feel sick. You might grind your teeth or notice that you have really tense shoulders and even a tense jaw from the stress. You might even realize that it is impacting your digestive system. You might have trouble eating or maybe you feel nauseous before and after eating. While it feels like you're just emotionally experiencing some of the things you see on social media, it is constantly sending off internal signals in your body that are telling your brain to activate certain hormones.

When you are repeatedly activating the stress hormones, this will lead to a buildup of cortisol, and this impacts your cardiovascular and digestive systems. As you can see, the excessive social media use that we participate in is not just impacting our minds, it is having devastating results on our bodies as well.

Materialism

Excessive social media use can make us more materialistic. Studies show that an increase in social media use also increases feelings of materialism (Staloch, 2023). There are many advertisements online, and these rely on feelings of exclusivity and urgency to get you to make purchases. However, those signs have to be subtle. If a post says, "Buy this item because we want your money," you're not going to buy that item. However, consider an influencer doing a cleaning video. In one, brief shot, they show a cleaning product. They flashed the label really subtly, but it was long enough for you to see what they were using. You're more likely to purchase that item because you see it being used in a seemingly more authentic way. The methods that marketing agencies are using are very hard to catch nowadays, making us feel constantly pressured to make a purchase without realizing we're being sold something.

Seeing your favorite artists, musicians, actors, and influencers all using similar products or following a specific look creates a standard you might feel pressured to follow. When you can't access these things because they are sold out or too expensive, it's ultimately you who is left feeling as though you are not good enough.

A high level of social media use can cause an intense fear of missing out ("Is Your Phone," 2022). When we see people online with things that we don't have, it's hard to not feel as though there is something bigger, better, and more exciting that we are missing out on.

Raising awareness of these signs and symptoms does not make them go away overnight, but it can help you reduce the severity that they have on your mental health. The internet opens new doors to both good opportunities and potential risks.

Label Social Media Symptoms

Aside from social media use, the rates of depression and anxiety are still high among teens, with 40% of high school students reporting these mental health issues before 2020 (Weir, 2023). The pressures on teens, whether it's from social media or society in general, have always been hard.

One in three teens struggle with feelings of nervousness, anxiety, fatigue, irritability, and anger (Smith, 2022). Can you recall the last time you felt the same way? It's hard enough to manage school work and your social life, and on top of that, you have to figure out what you want to do with your future. Are you going to enter the workforce? Join the army? Go to college? What are you going to do once you get there? These pressures are endless, and it's a lot for a developing mind to handle.

The first thing to do to start reducing the impact of the emotional, mental, and physical effects of social media use is to label your emotions. Labeling your emotions is the act of putting a name to the thoughts and feelings that you are struggling with. Each behavior starts with a reaction. That reaction is the result of a thought or emotion that we have. If we can retrace our behavior back to those thoughts and emotions, we have better management over feelings, therefore it's easier to control our actions.

It can be hard to recognize the difference between controlling your emotions and responding appropriately. For example, have you ever had a classmate act out in the middle of class? They might have thrown something across the room or even physically harmed another student. You might have heard them say that they couldn't help it, or that they were upset. Our emotions are extremely valid. It's totally okay to be upset. It's completely normal and expected to be enraged or angry, especially when somebody does something that triggers you.

However, it is not okay to respond with violence or physical aggression. There's a difference between feeling the emotions that we have and what we choose to do with those feelings. Labeling is the way that you can stop those intense and seemingly out-of-control feelings from turning into destructive behavior.

Whenever you notice yourself wanting to participate in potentially harmful behavior, label your emotions. Having feelings and understanding your emotions are two different things. You can feel angry. You can feel annoyed. You can feel upset. What are you going to do with those feelings, though?

First, pick a specific word. Are you frustrated? Are you annoyed? Are you perturbed? When you're feeling angry, are you enraged? Are you disappointed? Are you offended? When you're feeling stressed out, are you overwhelmed? Are you overstimulated? Are you panicked?

All of these different words that were just used can mean very different things, even though sometimes those feelings can intertwine with each other and feel very similar. Labeling your emotions is a way of untangling all of these thoughts that connect them.

Once you are able to label that emotion, you then know how to respond appropriately. If you're angry and overstimulated, it's important to walk away from the situation. If you're feeling hurt or upset, it's important to talk to the person who might have triggered that feeling within you. This is the first step in increasing mindfulness over our stress levels.

Self-reflection is a powerful tool that enables you to raise awareness over how you are thinking, reacting, and behaving in general. It becomes more of a natural habit to reduce your feelings and respond appropriately when you make it a priority in how you react and respond.

Whenever you are overcoming any form of addiction, self-reflection is crucial to stay one step ahead of your most debilitating thoughts and intrusive impulses. If you're feeling stressed, sad, or overwhelmed, you might have the urge to start binge eating or snacking. You might have the urge to procrastinate and ignore your responsibilities. Social media is an outlet that we might turn to in order to alleviate emotions, but social media then causes even more panicked feelings, perpetuating a cycle of undesirable behavior.

Make self-reflection a continued practice, then start talking to others about your feelings. Talk to your parents or your best friends. Find somebody who you feel safe with and express how you feel. You are not alone in the struggle, no matter how much it might feel that way. We often feel isolated and alone because we are so afraid of talking about our emotions. Chances are, members of your family and many of your friends also feel trapped by the stress of social media. Talking it out can help you make better sense of your emotions while also gaining more insight into the things that you're struggling with the most.

After you start to gain a better sense of your emotions, it's then important to start to label triggers. What is triggering you to want to reach for your phone? For example, you might find that you're constantly procrastinating. The stress of schoolwork could be a big trigger for you that makes you want to escape into social media. Another trigger might simply be being bored at home. You might not have enough to keep you busy at home or activities and outlets that you can dive into. When you don't have a car or money to go out and do things, it can feel as though there's nothing to do other than sit online. This can be another trigger that makes you want to start checking in with the world around you.

Another trigger might be the stress and anxiety of seeing other people's lives. Seeing somebody else's accomplishments might start to trigger your thoughts of self-deprecation. You might feel as though you are not good enough or that you don't have the same things they do. Identifying these triggers will make it easier for you to take control of your mindset. Write down your emotions and your triggers. Keep a journal to help you keep track of your thoughts so that you have something to go back to. This will help you track your progress and see that you are making change, while also helping to increase awareness of the things that continually trigger you. You can also write them down on paper to make them more real. Sometimes it's hard to make sense of everything that's going on in our minds, but when we put it down on paper in front of us, it's easier to see it. Keeping track of your thoughts creates a road map of your mindset. This will help you explore what has been going on in your mind on a deeper level.

Reminders

- **Step #2**: Recognize the dangers social media has had on your life.

Social media has been such an ingrained part of our everyday life since we were young, developing children. It's hard to realize just how dangerous and damaging it can be when everyone we know and interact with is using it seemingly as much as we are.

Not all social media is bad, but, according to The Mayo Clinic, heightened use of social media (three or more hours a day) is associated with a higher rate of mental health issues ("Tween and Teen Health", n.d.). Knowing how it's been impacting you will ensure you stay one step ahead of the control that it can have.

3. Reduce Phone Usage

Once you finally understand just how damaging this habit has been, you can then start to reduce usage overall to prevent experiencing more symptoms and decrease the impact it's had on your life.

The Time We Give to the Internet

Teens spend an average of seven hours on "screen media" per day (Rogers, 2019). How are your hours allocated? Whether you're spending time online watching your friends' stories or reading threads on interesting information, chances are, much of the time you spend online is filler content that doesn't necessarily provide extensive value or elicit positive emotions.

Other People's Lives

Society is so much different now than what it used to be. Teens hundreds of years ago would have been lucky to have a couple of close friends. Nowadays, we can be a part of many different types of groups. You might have a friend group specifically from your school. You might have a wider friend group and connect with people outside of your school district. You might have a specific online group of friends who you play a certain video game with. You might have social media friends who you interact with only online, never having met them in person.

Aside from just the people that we know and connect to, we also have access to the lives of complete and total strangers. From celebrities to influencers, you can tap into the personal lives of many different types of notable figures. You can see what they're wearing. You can see what they eat. They give you glimpses into their daily life, including their morning and night routines. You might know what their favorite breakfast is, and maybe you could recite some of their favorite movies or TV shows. We know what they watch and what they do with their free time. We know the lives of their pets, and there are some people who we have watched grow over the years. You might have been following an influencer who had a child and you recall the time that they announced their pregnancy and now their child is attending school. We have access to so much information about complete strangers who we will likely never come in contact with. A lot of the time that we spend online is spent watching the lives of other people.

Alternatively, some people watch *our* lives. They spend their time on the internet, keeping up with the things that we share. Whether or not this is a good thing is completely up to you. It's nice to stay connected. It's nice to have insight into how other people live their lives. Our natural curiosities lead us to want to know what other people are up to. However, we can waste a lot of time doing this, which leads to missed opportunities outside of social media coupled with lower self-esteem.

You might follow 100 different influencers and know the details of many of their different likes and interests. When you are in a certain friend group, what other people do with their time will likely bleed into what you do with *your* time. You will likely have similar interests. You might have the same favorite band or maybe you go and see similar movies together. You might play certain games together and generally talk about the same things. That type of small social connection is expanded into the online world. Now, you might be influenced by the people who you follow. You watch what they like, you take their suggestions for food and clothing, and it can feel as though you're much closer to them than you actually are. This can create a parasocial relationship, where we feel as though they are a bigger part of our lives than they really are. Social media offers an intimate look into somebody's life. You see things that you wouldn't have been able to see years ago. Celebrities have always been a point of fascination, but nowadays we know a lot more about them. You used to have to wait for the next magazine to come out to figure out what certain celebrities were up to. The only way that we had access to what they were eating was through interviews and other types of videos. Whether you are lying in bed at night, or sitting bored in a classroom, you can open your phone and check social media to see what people are up to. This accessibility can make it hard to look away. It makes it a bigger part of our lives, so when these celebrities go through hard periods, controversies, and other stressful events, it might impact us much more than it should.

Following influencers and celebrities is not a bad thing. It's fun to have people you like and follow, and many provide us with entertainment. It's not a bad thing to have people that we like following, in general. It's also not a bad thing to be influenced. Sometimes you want to be able to trust somebody's opinion and know what types of recipes are good or where a good place to buy quality clothing might be. However, if we're not carefully navigating that relationship, it can become very influential in the way we think and the way we feel.

Advertisements

Children under three years old cannot tell the difference between ads and regular videos ("Advertising," n.d.). This means they are more likely to be influenced by subliminal messages and hidden manipulation tactics.

We are constantly bombarded with advertisements. In fact, it was estimated in 2006 that adolescents are exposed to over 40,000 advertisements every year (Strasburger, 2006). It's hard to tell just how much more that has increased over the last couple of decades.

Advertisements are what keep the internet running. Without them, everything would be far less profitable. Social media would not be a billion-dollar industry if it weren't for advertisements.

However, advertisements all have a purpose. They all have an intention. They all exist to specifically influence you to spend your money. They want you to buy into a certain lifestyle or belief.

Advertisements aren't just based on one person's idea either. There are teams filled with psychological and marketing experts that exist specifically to make a product more appealing.

There are many different types of advertisements. First and foremost, we have obvious advertisements. These are things like forced ads. You might have to watch a 30-second clip before you can continue watching a video. Then, there are very subtle forms of advertisements. These are often disguised to look like more natural product placement. You will see this mostly through influencer advertising. For example, somebody might be using specific products in their video and talking about how great they are. You'll see this a lot in makeup tutorials or cleaning videos. Some of these are still very obvious as the tone of the video might shift and there will be links to buy the product. They also have to include disclaimers on different websites if something is being sold. However, not everybody pays attention to these small, subtle cues, so it can feel a lot more natural when you see somebody using a product in their day-to-day life.

Sometimes advertisements are even disguised as viral videos. There are brands and marketing teams behind them to make them look as though they're funny or extreme videos, but ultimately, you'll end up seeing an advertisement in the background through a poster on a wall or a T-shirt that somebody might be wearing.

Teens are especially targeted by advertisements because they have a lot of spending power. Many teens have access to their parents' finances, whether they have their own credit card or a shared bank account. Many teens are also working jobs and they don't have as many financial responsibilities like rent and utilities, therefore they have more disposable income. If you're working a part-time job after school, you might be putting some away in your savings, but you still have a lot of spending power when it comes to smaller products like drinks and snacks. On top of this, teenagers have lower impulse control and media literacy. Somebody who is 45 years old might have 10 times as much money as you, but they are also a lot more aware of the manipulative and intrinsic behavior that advertisements have. As a teenager, you might not be as aware of just how tricky some of these marketing tactics are, and how obviously they're being used against you.

The best way to reduce how many ads you see is to use ad blockers. There are also paid versions of different apps that help block advertisements as well. When you do see an ad, it's crucial that you look at what the intention of it is before you let it influence you. What is being sold to you and who is profiting off of the sale? Advertisements are meant to make life look much better on screen than it is in real life, and therefore the real life around you seems bleak and boring. This makes you want to buy that product. It creates this false sense that maybe if you just purchase the thing that they are showing you, perhaps your life will look a little bit more like the advertisement you see on screen.

Advertisements also try to sell us promises. They use authority and trusting tactics so that you believe them. Aside from trying to sell specific products, advertisements also exist for brand awareness. Large companies want to make sure that their product is seen in subway stations, on billboards, in commercials, and through music streaming apps. Even though they might not be selling you a specific product, they're still creating brand awareness. Then, when you're in the store and you're looking at five different brands to choose from for a specific product, you are swayed to purchase the one whose advertising has been most prominent. You've seen that product a lot, therefore you feel as though it's more trustworthy, making you more inclined to make that purchase. It's essential that we stay ahead of the urges and temptations created through advertisements so that we don't fall for their manipulative tactics.

Upsetting News

Advertisements drive the internet. To see those advertisements, you still have to click on entertaining and intriguing content. This is done through sensationalized videos, viral headlines, and clickbait.

Sensationalized news is very clickable, and most websites know this. All it takes is a headline that reads something like, "Crazy Man Does Crazy Thing," and it gets you to want to click on it and find out what exactly it was that he did. Then, once you click on that page, you're bombarded with 50 different advertisements throughout that are typical on the right and left-hand side, as well as through pop-ups. Professionals are hired to create these sensationalized headlines, and copywriters are very skilled in making something that is a little more mediocre seem very intriguing.

In addition, not everybody is going to read the full article, so writers try to jam as much as they can in the headline, as well as in the first few sentences. What this means is that we are left consuming anxiety-inducing news all day long that has been presented in a very stressful way.

For example, you might see an article that's titled, "Scientists Discover New Life Form." They use a picture of an alien as the cover photo, and the heading underneath asks, "What does this mean for our future?" All of a sudden, your brain might start thinking about aliens or other odd creatures. In reality, once you read the article, it's a new variant of a different type of fungal microorganism that they already knew existed. In reality, they don't really know much about it, so while it's still a fascinating discovery, it's not the same thing as finding an actual alien on another planet. This is just one example of how a small news story can get inflated into a crazy conspiracy or theory.

When you see just the headlines and you're absorbing all these sensationalized things all day long, it can make the world seem very crazy and stressful. This adds to some of the panic and anxiety that you might be feeling when consuming other things. Doom scrolling refers to how we sometimes consume news and headlines in an excessive way. Even though we know it's making us feel bad and we know that it's never-ending, we might continue scrolling and reading very upsetting and triggering things.

There's always going to be interesting information out there. There's always going to be a story about somebody doing something crazy. There's always going to be stories about how the government is corrupt or science is scary. There's never going to be a shortage of stressful news because life is stressful. However, when that's all you're consuming all day long, it can make the world seem like a very scary or depressing place, and that will contribute to your mindset, even when you're not using your cell phone.

Repetitive Content

A lot of the content that we see online is also extremely repetitive. You've likely seen the same meme or funny video 10 times. After a while, it loses its humor, and you might have not even thought it was that entertaining in the first place. However, because of the way that we're able to share content, you might end up seeing the same thing over and over again.

We can also consume hundreds of images at a time or within a social media scrolling session, so you might forget that you saw it the first time around, then you see it again, and again and again, and it then becomes ingrained in your memory and loses all meaning. How many times have you had the same video sent to you by a friend? Since our algorithms are similar to our friends' and those of the people that we interact with online, chances are, they're getting served the same things that we are. When we are constantly viewing the same kind of content, it can make us feel like we are wasting time.

In real life, outside of the screen, we likely repeat the same content. You listen to the same songs that you like or you restart your favorite series once finished. However, when you see all these repeated things online, it's usually because it's simply what you're getting served and not necessarily based on the fact that you are willingly seeking this information out.

We can't always help what content we're fed, but this certainly eats away at the free time that could be better spent elsewhere.

How to Start Reducing Screentime

The average American checks their phone up to 352 times a day (Waltower, 2023). It's hard to know exactly how much everyone checks their phone, though, as screen time is tied up with work and education. We have to check emails and messages, especially if we are talking to bosses and coworkers. However, even without notifications, it's estimated that most people "check their phone every 15 minutes (D'Onfro,

2018)." Do you drink water this much? Do you get up and stretch your legs this much? There's nothing quite like phone usage, and while it is sometimes necessary to check in online, most of the time, our quick check-ins lead to distraction and wasted time.

Make It Less Enticing

One way to help reduce your screen time is to make phone usage less enticing. Phones are so addictive because, well, they are fun. They're like little video games in our hands (and often they do allow for gaming). They have colorful lights. They have fun buttons that make noises when you click on them. You can do anything that you want with a phone. They make you feel powerful.

They present you with endless opportunities, and when you get bored with one thing, you can close an app and open another. Because of this accessibility and fun usage, it's very hard to put our phones down. One way to make this less enticing is to turn your screen to black and white. Indeed, you can use grayscale, a feature that is often built into our actual phones. Grayscale will remove some of the bright colors and fun images that we see, making the phone screen's content visually less appealing.

Brains crave color. It's something that's been naturally wired into us as a survival tactic. Thousands of years ago when we didn't have access to the grocery store, we had to go out and hunt for our food. Foraging meant finding berries and seeds, as well as mushrooms and other types of fungi in the wild. All of these things are a little bit more colorful. When you're walking by a bush, you're going to notice when it has berries on it. When you're walking by a tree, you're going to notice when it has mushrooms growing off of it. When you are walking through a grassy plane, you're going to notice the flowers. These things are food sources, so we have been wired to be able to visually see color and then feel pleasure and happiness once we see this color.

When you're scrolling on your phone all day long, you're very overstimulated by all of this constant design. There are many psychological theories about color as well, and app developers know this. For example, blue is calming and supposed to be very friendly. Think about how many blue apps you might have on your phone. Colors like yellow or orange might be seen as a little bit more cheerful. Purple can be more creative. Color is used against you to elicit certain types of emotion. To block that type of manipulation, you can then turn the color off on your phone. You can still scroll through social media. You can read interesting articles, and you can watch funny videos. Once the color is removed, it makes it a little bit less stimulating and enticing for your brain, therefore helping you to slowly reduce usage over time.

Another way to make phones less enticing is to delete all of your apps except for the ones that are needed for work or school. In our modern society, many companies want you to download apps so they can track your purchases and send you notifications. They want you to have their restaurant information so you can easily place food orders. Shopping apps want you to download them so that they can track your online activity, therefore making it easier to provide you with targeted ads. The thing about these apps, however, is that they also send notifications. When you're sitting there bored at school and you get an app saying that there's a 25% off sale at your favorite store, or that there's a buy-one-get-one-free deal from your favorite restaurant, that automatically triggers you to want to consume. Deleting these apps will reduce your notifications and make them less enticing altogether.

You can still place online orders through your phone's web browser, and you can still shop online when you want. However, removing apps removes an important force of influence.

Another way to make social media use less enticing is to unfollow certain people on the internet who do not make you happy, bring you joy, or make you feel good. If anyone triggers you or causes stress, it's best to click the "unfollow" button and move on. Whether you are on TikTok, Instagram, or another social media app, it's crucial to go through who you're following to see if they're actually making you feel good about yourself and if you want to continue keeping up with them.

Unfortunately, it can be hard to let go of certain people, especially if you've been watching them for a long time, but you have to really evaluate if they are people who are making you feel good and providing value to your life. You can even unfollow people who you know in your personal life. You don't have to stay connected to somebody just because you've already established an online relationship with them. If you went to school with somebody five years ago, but you've never seen them since, it's okay to let them go. Just because they're following you doesn't mean that you have to follow them back. If you're not ready to unfollow somebody, it's also perfectly acceptable to simply block their activity so that they don't pop up in your news feed.

Another tactic to make your phone less enticing is to make it physically restricted. One way to do this is to use painter's tape. Put a piece of painter's tape across your phone screen. Put your phone in a plastic sandwich bag. Wrap some string around your phone and tie it in hard knots. When you want to reach for your phone, that small physical thing is a little reminder that you don't need to be using it right now. Our phone usage can be so automatic that we reach for it without even thinking. When you go to grab your phone and realize that there's a little piece of painter's tape over the screen, that's a reminder that tells you *Oh yeah, I'm trying to reduce this activity.* When you have a plastic bag over your phone, you can still see necessary notifications pop up if needed, so if your mom texts you to let you know she'll be late coming home from work, you can still see that text and not feel panicked when she doesn't show up on time. However, if you get a bunch of notifications about things that don't matter, it's a lot harder to navigate your phone when it's inside the plastic, therefore, you're less likely to use it.

Make It Less Accessible

On days when you really can't help but look at your phone, make it less accessible. In addition to making it less exciting, it's time to make it hard to even reach. Put it up high on a shelf that requires a stepladder, then put the stepladder away. You're less likely to want to go and reach for your phone when you have to go through the process of getting the stepladder back out. When you make a multi-step process to get the phone, then you are more likely to not want to use it. Another great way to make it less accessible is to put the passcode in incorrectly several times so that you become locked out. When you're locked out of your phone, you can still make emergency phone calls, so if something really bad happens and you do need to call for help, you will have access to that. However, you can lock your phone for 15 minutes or an hour or more, so that if you have to study or do some household chores, you will not have access to it.

This is also a great way to get you to do things like read or exercise more. You can lock your phone for 30 minutes or an hour, spend that time working hard, and then when that time is up, you have access to your phone again, and it becomes a little reward.

Consider other methods to keep you from your phone like putting it in another room or getting a timed lockbox to keep it in. You can put it in a kitchen cabinet downstairs while you work upstairs, making it harder to get to. You could also try giving it to a sibling or a parent to hide and let them know that you are trying not to use it until a specific time. Then, once that time comes, they can let you know where they hid it.

You can also consider letting the battery die so that when you're trying to study, your phone is dead, and you can't even turn it on and pick it up. This means that you won't have access to any phone calls or be able to make an emergency call, so only do this when somebody else is around just to make sure that you have an emergency contact if needed. Lastly, consider using a long and complicated passcode rather than face recognition. Make it complicated and change it weekly. Write it down and hide that piece of paper so that it's more challenging to try to get into the phone.

The less accessible and exciting your phone is, the less likely you are to spend too much time on it.

Reminders

- **Step #3**: Reduce how much time you spend on your phone.

You don't have to give up on your phone altogether. You don't have to demonize phone usage or feel guilty about the desire to stay tuned in online. The important thing to remember is to start to utilize methods of making your phone less enticing and accessible so you can put more focus on the things that really matter. One good way to help you kick-start this new period of social media reduction is to first do a temporary cleanse.

4. Take a Break

Sometimes just reducing phone use isn't enough, and while it's good to cut back on how much time you spend online overall, the next crucial step is to take a complete break from social media altogether.

Social media connects us to other people, and that's arguably a good thing. However, when we are not in the right mental head space, we might start to follow certain pages and look at specific posts a bit longer than others, and those become a part of our online profiles, impacting our algorithm. The Center for Brain Health puts it perfectly by saying:

- *"The impact of social media is minor for most people; the platform recommends friending people you might know and tailors the tone and content of posts and advertisements to suit your preferences. However, social media platforms need to be more discerning about the types of interests they use to connect with people. This can lead to severe problems when people interested in armed revolution or communal violence are automatically shown content that solidifies their beliefs and connects them with like-minded people nearby* (Chapman et al., 2021)"

Essentially, if you feel depressed and anxious, you'll get fed content that perpetuates this mindset, making those emotions worse. Each time you log on, your negative beliefs or bad mood becomes more solidified, making it harder to see anything else but the perceived truth presented on your phone. This can impact us in many different ways:

- If you like shopping and spend too much money on clothes, you're fed even more advertisements and "deals," making you feel as though you should be spending your money on these things.
- If you fall under the belief that you hate other people and the world is filled with criminals, villains, and other evil beings, you'll get fed stressful news about people committing heinous acts.
- If you believe we should all just work hard to get rich and that life is all about making money, having luxury cars, and living in mansions, you will get fed this type of content, solidifying this belief system.

When we are presented with information that challenges these beliefs, it can make us feel anxious and overwhelmed. Social media creates our belief system and then upholds it by feeding us specified algorithms. When we are unaware of this, it can have grave effects on our minds and bodies.

Your Mind Off Social Media

Research proves that when we limit social media use, it can result in (Malouff, 2023):

- lower levels of depression
- less loneliness
- improved relationships
- better psychological effects

Because everyone uses social media in their own way, we all feel these impacts in individualized ways as well. Knowing some of the benefits of staying off social media can help you recognize just how important it is to reduce screen time.

Reduced Stress

Whether you are dealing with your own conflict or just sitting in the front seat of someone else's drama, there is a lot of stress that can come from spending too much time online.

Excessive phone use can create a sense of urgency. When you receive notifications, they use sounds like dings and bells, and that makes you feel more alert. It makes you feel as though there's some sort of urgency that you need to pick up your phone and check in on. Everything that we see online can elicit different types of emotions. If you see somebody posting about an amazing new purchase they have, that can make you feel jealous. If you see somebody posting about their amazing partner or a group of friends, it can make you feel lonely. All of these emotions that we experience throughout the day can add up and really impact our level of stress. This excessive stress can make us very sensitive. It makes us more focused online and less focused on the world around us. Then, when you feel all of the natural life pressures adding up, it makes them even harder to deal with. For example, let's say you find that you've been spending four hours on social media, you finally put your phone down and decide to get to work on your homework.

However, as you're sitting there, you start to feel a higher sense of urgency, and you start to feel overwhelmed by impending deadlines. All of the good feelings you had scrolling social media have gone away, and now the rush of the stress of schoolwork suddenly floods your mindset. You're looking at your schoolwork and you've realized you haven't studied enough. You haven't completed as much as you thought you would. It makes life feel even more stressful when you're already focused elsewhere and giving less attention to the things that actually require your attention. This can also make us more sensitive to feedback. When we're feeling insecure and like we're not good enough, it makes us feel like we're inadequate. This will make it harder to take criticism. When you get a bad grade in school, it might make you feel even worse because of the excess stress that's already been built in your body through high levels of social media use. This also contributes to us being more easily triggered by stress.

Stress is triggering for anybody. It's very fair to feel over-whelmed by any of life's demands. However, when you are experiencing high levels of cortisol and other stress hormones in your body when real-life stressors do arise, it can make them feel 10 times worse. We can also feel stressed from excessive social media use because we feel bored or empty without the use of our phones. It can be harder to focus in the real world and stay present on the things that require our attention when we feel as though the internet is more interesting, and like we are missing out on things happening online.

This leads to a lack of focus, therefore, you might start to struggle with your schoolwork, and you might find that it's difficult to pay attention in class during lectures. Because of this lack of focus, you don't retain the information as well or comprehend the lessons when you're actually trying to do your homework or research papers.

You might find that it's really hard to focus on assignments and studying when you are outside of the classroom. Then what happens is your grades start to fail, and all of this homework becomes even more difficult to complete, therefore, you feel even more stressed out because of your lack of focus or excessive demands from school.

This can lead to procrastination. It's easier to want to avoid the stressors and do something more exciting or interesting rather than deal with all of the difficult things in life. All of this stress impacts our developing minds. Stress can also be triggered by the types of things that we see online. Even if you're not actively participating in fights or conflicts on the internet, you are still witnessing that stress from other people. For example, you might see a controversial video, and then in the comment section, there are many other people discussing this conflict. They might even make reaction videos and response videos and before you know it you are in a rabbit hole of some corner of the internet, learning about the intricacies of this drama. Though you might not be an active participant, you're still likely having arguments in your mind or going through conflict internally. You might be just witnessing the aggression from other people and that can bleed into your life and increase stress levels.

When you start to feel stressed out or even aggressive online, that will carry with you to the real world. You might find yourself having short tempers and more conflict with the people around you. Going through a detox from social media will help you reduce stress. It will help you clear your mind and become more focused on the things that matter.

More Free Time

There's often this feeling that we never have enough time. What you might come to discover is that once you are offline, you have plenty of extra hours in the day that you can dedicate to the things you love and have more passion for. Excessive social media use can result in decreased cognitive abilities, attention, and focus (Fotuhi, 2020).

It takes a lot of time to scroll through all of our social media platforms and profiles. By the time you're done checking one, another one has loads of new content, allowing you to endlessly scroll and be entertained through just the use of your phone. When you cut down on phone use, you'll then free up a lot more personal time, therefore, you have time to give to hobbies and things that actually interest you. This will lead to excessive amounts of productivity. Whether you are trying to get in shape, improve a physical skill, or want to study more and learn, you will find that you have more time to give to your passions and interests when you unplug.

On the one hand, you simply have more time because you are spending less time on the Internet. 30 minutes of social media time can become 30 minutes of reading. On the other hand, you will also save time because you will be more focused, therefore boosting productivity.

When you are less stressed out and you are thinking more clearly, it's easier to be productive when you're actually sitting down and reading. Trying to read in the middle of using your cell phone could mean only getting through a certain number of pages within 30 minutes. However, when you detox from social media and completely shut off from the internet, you might find that you're reading twice the speed. When you are more productive, you save even more time. There's also less urgency, meaning you can actually take things slowly and at the right pace. For example, if you're spending two hours on social media at night and then you have to study for an hour afterward, you might feel this great sense of urgency. You are trying to rush through all of your homework and get studying done as fast as you can. Then tomorrow when the test comes around, you realize that you didn't actually retain any of that information because you were speeding through the book. However, if you're able to actually sit down for those three hours and study, you find that you get your work done earlier, and you retain that information effectively because you don't have the panic and stress looming behind you. You'll also have more creative thinking skills and the ability to think more logically. This is because you will become less dependent on your phone. When you're sitting there and trying to figure out a problem, you might reach for your phone and Google the answer. You don't even have to think about the solution because your phone just has it for you. However, if you are less dependent on your phone, then you force yourself to use your thinking skills and try to come up with a solution on your own. If you are an artist and you're trying to think of something creative, you might use AI or other forms of inspiration online to help you think of ideas. When you are forced to think creatively, your perspective is going to be a little bit more unique.

Increased Health

Social media can reduce cravings and urges to binge and increase our sleep quality. Extra time spent reducing stress, taking care of hygiene, and even exercising are all additional benefits we might experience once we take the plunge and unplug.

All of these benefits that happen mentally are going to physically impact us in a positive way as well. When you are more focused and more productive, that decreases your stress level. When you're actually getting your homework done and participating in hobbies that you enjoy, you will be happier. You'll be more focused, therefore, you're going to start getting better grades and realize that you're more successful in your endeavors. You'll have more time to exercise. You'll have more time to hang out outside. You'll have more time to spend with friends and create stronger and more meaningful connections. All of this will lead to alleviated feelings and more inner peace and clarity. This will impact your health. You'll notice that it's easier to take care of yourself when you feel good about yourself and you're taking good care of yourself. This increases your body image and you'll also start to see yourself in a more positive light.

As a teenager, your body is still developing. You're growing. You're changing shapes. You're changing appearances. If you're not taking care of yourself in the right way, then as an adult you might find that you struggle with your health. You might struggle with maintaining a healthy body weight. You might find that you suffer from headaches, joint pain, and body aches because you're not getting enough physical movement. You might find yourself feeling depressed and lonely because you're not spending enough time outside or socializing with your friends.

There are many different layers to our health and social media absorbs so much of our time we start to neglect our physical anatomy. By reducing the time that you spend online, you will start to have more attention and care that you can give to taking care of your body and maintaining your physical health.

The 7-Day Detox and 30-Day Challenge

The first challenge to do is to take a 7-day detox. Sometimes it's hard to take the plunge because we feel as though we have to give up a big part of our life. One way to help this mindset is to shift your way of thinking to see it as a chance to regain lost time (Green, 2023).

If you can't do a 7-day detox, then it might be a sign that something more serious is going on. It's okay to reach out and ask for professional help if you believe it is needed! There is more at stake than just wasted time if you don't learn to reduce social media use. Your health is at risk when too much time is spent online.

Steps to a 7-Day Detox

Social media elevates our dopamine levels. For this reason, we might struggle with negative side effects as our bodies adjust to the lack of dopamine (Schubert, 2021). While that can be scary in itself, it's proof of just how important it is that we begin to reduce our social media dependency. Now is a time to find new sources of dopamine that will become long-lasting parts of your daily routine.

The first step to a 7-day detox is to identify your emergency source of contact. Many homes don't have landline phones anymore, so if there was some sort of emergency, you would need to be able to have a point of contact. Whether you need to call 911 or just check in with your parent, you will need to find some sort of emergency source that you can use to make contact during those seven days. If you have a parent who is frequently home, or even a sibling, then this can be the emergency contact. You can also enable voice-activated services on your phone, so if you are really in danger, you can put your phone somewhere nearby so that you can still call for help by voice prompts. You will likely not need to use your emergency contact, however, having one will provide peace of mind and reassurance that you do not need to check your phone.

The next part of the detox is to make your phone inaccessible by using one of the methods that was mentioned before. A great way to do this is through a timed lockbox.

Whatever you choose to use, the focus should be on simply making your phone inaccessible so that you can't reach for automatically.

Another great way to make it inaccessible is to simply make it unusable. If you make it unusable, then it's even easier to avoid reaching for it and automatically using it without you even realizing that's what you're doing. If you find that you are getting a new cell phone or device soon, and trading your old phone in, now might be the time to do that. You can simply deactivate your phone, delete all the apps, and then wait to reactivate the new one until you're done with the detox.

You can also consider trading your phone in for one that doesn't have as many smartphone features or purchase something like a flip phone so that you only have access to emergency services.

Another great way to make your phone less accessible and less enticing is to delete all your apps. Backup all of your information like any notes or photos, and then do a factory reset on your phone. You'll then be signed out of all of your devices so that you can't easily log into different apps. You can also consider changing your password to something that you don't remember. Do this for your email as well, write it down, and give it to a parent or a trusted friend for a temporary time so when you are ready to come back to your phone after that detox, they give you the password, therefore you can log into all of your apps once again.

You don't have to delete your social media accounts to do a detox. You can simply delete the app. You don't even have to deactivate the account. You simply have to remove the app from your phone so that you don't have the ability to open it. Then once you have figured out your plan for how you make your phone inaccessible, it's time to do the actual detox.

Make sure that it is a full seven days. This means Sunday night, put your phone away, and don't reach for it again until the following Sunday. The only time that it should be used is for emergencies only. If you are dependent on rides from your family members, talk about this plan with them and set up a very strict timeline so that they can pick you up after school and bring you home. Unless you have a job where you need your cell phone, then there really isn't another reason why you might have to check in online. You can use tablets or laptops to do schoolwork if necessary, and then after that, give your source of the internet away to a household member.

One important thing about doing the detox is to ensure that you have a plan in place for how you're going to replace the urge to check your phone. We become very dependent on our cell phones, so it can be hard to suddenly remove them. You might experience feelings of panic or stress. Your body is used to the use of your cell phone. You're used to those levels of dopamine and you're used to the habit of picking up your phone and holding it. If you lay in bed every night and watch TikTok, you're used to grabbing your phone and holding it with you before you fall asleep. You might find that it is hard to fall asleep at night because you don't have that routine in place anymore. When this difficulty arises, it increases the urge to break the detox. Resist impulses and know that this feeling will eventually pass.

Have something in place of that urge. When you remove something from your life that makes you feel good, your body is going to seek that out again. Your body wants to feel good, so suddenly now that source of good feelings is gone, you might start to panic and seek out other forms of instantly gratifying sources and substances. Having something in place means knowing exactly what to reach for when your social media impulses start to grow.

For example, this might be something like an exercise routine. You can download exercise videos to your desktop or laptop so that you can easily open them without having to navigate the Internet. You can go to the library and rent movies or books so that you have sources of entertainment that don't depend on the Internet. Have a craft or project that you want to work on. Buy some crochet books and crochet needles and try new patterns. Buy some paints and some blank canvases and explore your creativity. Get a notebook and a pen and paper and write down how you're feeling when you have the urge to reach for your phone. Start going on walks. When you want to just reach for your phone, instead, open your front door and go for a walk. It's still important to ensure that you let somebody know where you are going, and what time you expect to be home.

Invest in a record player so you can still listen to music without needing one of your electronic devices. Buy audiobooks on tape, or better yet, go to a live show where you can see performers share their art in person.

If you remove your phone from your life cold turkey, you find that you're going to struggle with impulsivity even more, so having a backup plan in place is always important to keep you focused through your downtime.

Steps to a 30-Day Free Challenge

Once you've completed your seven-day detox, you can participate in another challenge. This is the 30-day free challenge. All of the same rules apply. Make your phone inaccessible, have a point of emergency contact, and find somebody that you can depend on if you need rides or other forms of help throughout the process.

Going without social media for 30 days can be a lot harder, so in this case, you will likely want to deactivate your social media for the time being and make sure that everything has been deleted to reduce the urge to check-in. You can factory reset your phone and still use it for sending simple texts or making phone calls, but remember to try and make those only as needed. 30-day challenges are much easier if we have accountability partners.

Accountability partners are safe people with whom you can talk about this challenge, and they can help ensure that you stay on track with your goals. The best person to do this with is somebody who also wants to detox from social media. You and a sibling could even potentially share a phone for the time being so that you still can contact your parents or other relatives if needed, but you can hold each other accountable to make sure that nobody's checking in online or on their social media.

If you can challenge not just yourself but also another person who takes a break, it will be easier to stay true to this 30-Day Challenge. Having an accountability partner will also help reduce your fear of missing out. You can rest assured that you are not the only one who isn't tuning in online.

Another way to hold yourself accountable is to share it with the world. You might make a quick announcement saying, "Hey everybody, I'm going to be gone for 30 days. If you need me, contact [insert accountability partner]." You've likely seen it said before on social media posts about how someone is deleting their social media. While it might have induced an eye roll at the time, it can actually help you stay more accountable so that you're less likely to log right back on after taking a break. The more that you can stay consistent with this detox, the more likely you will see positive and beneficial results.

Reminders

- **Step #4:** Take some time away from social media.

Everyone can participate in a 7-day detox. You can set a 15-minute time period a day to check in with anyone you have to, like a parent that you might not live with. Other than that, you should challenge yourself to go a full week without social media use so you can discover the benefits on your own. Once you log back in, you'll find that you didn't really miss much of anything. Making social media breaks a regular part of your life can help you increase self-love.

5. Learn Self-Love

Social media can make us hate ourselves, so learning how to form healthy steps to self-care will increase self-love.

In life, when our phones come first, it's easy to let the negative thoughts and emotions that come with excessive screen time take the driver's seat in your mind. When this happens, it becomes even easier to neglect your health. Stress from social media combined with poor self-care results in even further negative side effects.

Understanding the importance of self-care begins with the acknowledgment and realization of all the ways it can impact your self-image.

Social Media and Self-Image

Social media can be very destructive to anyone's self-image, especially teenagers since they are still learning how to view the world and themselves.

Self-image is how we view ourselves. It's the opinions and beliefs we hold around our worth, whether that's through our intelligence, body, appearance, or skills. When you are constantly scrolling through social media, your mind is infiltrated with perfectly curated images presented by people who are only showing you what they want you to see. On top of that, there are many positive comments hyping up these unreal and edited images. Then, on the opposite end, you might see excessive hate and bullying. If someone looks remotely similar to you or is getting bullied for a similarity you both share, those words can hurt you just as much as the person whom the hatred is directed toward.

The constant comparison, reminders of what we don't have, and edited images can leave us feeling isolated and unskilled. As such, these are all things that can damage our mental and physical health.

Comparison

Social media has been proven to lower self-esteem, especially in teens 14 and younger (Bergman, 2023). Over 30% of teens felt shame toward their bodies, with some even stopping eating because of their level of worry ("Millions of Teenagers," n.d.).

Social media is incredibly damaging to a teen's developing mind because it provides an endless opportunity to compare themselves with others. Often, what ends up happening is that we make unfair comparisons, positioning our worst qualities against somebody else's best qualities. Comparison is hard because what it does is create a standard for how we think we should exist. When you are online and you see that somebody is living a certain lifestyle, it can make yours seem not as glamorous.

The thing is, when somebody takes a picture of their beauti- fully decorated apartment, they're not showing you the dirty garage. They're not showing you the other side of that room, where there is an unfinished paint job or stained furniture. They're only showing you the exact things that they want you to see.

Most humans are focused on their negative qualities in life. We are wired to pay attention to the small things that only we can see. Because of this, when you're scrolling online, you create this juxtaposition of *your* bad versus *their* good. A juxtaposition is the way that two things are positioned next to each other. When your worst qualities are positioned next to somebody else's best qualities, that can make you feel incredibly inadequate.

There's no one else to blame for our shortcomings but ourselves, so we end up hating ourselves and being resentful of our own appearances or lifestyles because we don't have the things that we feel as though we should have.

Comparison is also how advertisements are able to prey on our insecurities. When you see a perfectly filtered person holding up a certain type of makeup, suddenly you compare your own flaws to this very beautiful person. You think if you purchase that cover-up, you're going to be able to have a beautiful appearance just like them. In addition, we're also able to easily fixate on our flaws. When you take a selfie, you can zoom in on every little wrinkle, blemish, or other perceived flaw that you have. You can open a selfie you took on your phone and stare at it for hours, zooming in and cropping the picture, only focusing on the things that you don't like about yourself. When somebody else is scrolling through social media and they see your selfie, they likely just look at it for a few seconds and then scroll away. They're not sitting there zooming in to see that little crease you have next to your eyelid or that acne scar on your chin.

Do you do that to other people? Do you scrutinize somebody else's appearance in the same way that you do your own?

Chances are you likely don't. If you do, it's a sign that your body image issues have become so intense that they've shaped the way you perceive others as well. This comparison never helps us. It always leaves us feeling inadequate.

Comparison in general isn't always a bad thing. After you take a test at school, and you see that most of the class got an A while you barely passed, you might compare yourself. You think to yourself, *what did they do that I didn't?* This can help encourage you to study more next time. However, social media takes comparison to a whole new level, where we consistently focus on our shortcomings, leaving us feeling like we are never good enough.

What We Don't Have

Social media causes us to feel inadequate because of the things that we don't have. Since social media thrives off sales, we are bombarded with ads for things that we feel pressured to purchase, all while they are convincing us that we need them. When you see an ad over and over again telling you that you need a specific type of shoe or even a specific type of water bottle, of course, you're ultimately going to feel like you are not good enough because you don't have this thing that everybody else has. This includes products, clothes, and other things that make us believe they will give us the body image or lifestyle that we desire.

Humans are naturally wired to focus on inadequacies, flaws, and things that they don't have. This taps into our basic survival skills. When you're walking through the woods, you want to notice the spiders or snakes that are crawling around so that you stay protected. You're not as likely to pay attention to the beautiful sky or the intricacies of the leaves on a unique-looking tree. You're focused on negative aspects as a way to survive. We also fixate on blemishes for survival. If you notice that you have a rash or a bruise, you want to investigate what caused that to make sure that your health is protected.

However, that fixation on our flaws is taken to the extreme because of social media. When you are constantly focusing on the things that you don't have, you lose sight of all the amazing things that you actually do have.

One method to reduce this fixation is gratitude. Gratitude is a great way for us to appreciate the things that we actually have. Do you have a bed to sleep in every night? Do you have a bathroom where you can take a hot shower? Do you have a fridge with food that you can eat at any time you want? Do you have two legs to walk with or do you have two eyes to see with? Do you have two lungs to breathe with? Do you have a heart pumping blood? Do you have a brain that allows you to think logically? All of these things are things that we can be grateful for.

You can still have the desire to purchase certain things or live a certain lifestyle. However, when that desire becomes your focal point, you will always feel dissatisfied. You can still want to have certain clothes or other products: that's natural, and that's expected. You are human, after all, and you want to feel like you fit in and like you're a part of a group. However, when that is all you fixate on, it will leave you continually feeling inadequate and like your life is not worthy. Gratitude is a way to keep you balanced so that you can still emphasize the things that you are appreciative of. Do you have a family? Do you have parents who support you? Do you have siblings who you can hang out with? Do you have friends who make you laugh? All these things create an amazing life. We have to remember that some people don't have the things that we are grateful for, and those things we are grateful for can also get taken away at any time for reasons outside of our control.

You can log in to social media and see somebody post their beautiful house and luxury cars. But maybe they don't have anybody that they can feel safe around. Maybe they don't have anybody who loves them the way that your family and friends love you. Maybe there's something else going on in their life that we will never know about, so making a comparison to their life is very unfair to you and to all of the things that you have to be grateful for.

False Ideas

Now more than ever before, it is so easy to make fake content and put it online. Social media has built-in features so that you can smooth your skin and filter out any flaws. You can easily crop images so that you can make your life look more beautiful and appealing than it really is. This is harmful in two ways, though. The first way is because we are fed false information online. We are presented with fake images. We see beautiful people and we think we want to look like them, but even those people don't actually look like the images they're presenting online. They look much, much different.

In another way, it allows us to create our own false sense of reality. You can edit your body and your face to look much different than it actually does. You see that picture online and it makes you feel good because you believe that you are beautiful, as, now, you look like everyone else. Then, when you look in the mirror, or somebody else takes a picture of you and they don't edit it, it makes you feel even worse.

You start viewing the natural way that you actually look and thus you start feeling very inadequate. Anyone can take a selfie and put it through multiple different filters, highlighting their best features and erasing the rest. Ultimately, this leaves the photo editor and everyone else who sees it feeling as though they are inadequate. It also makes us lose our sense of reality. As mentioned in the last section, you don't know what is truly going on in somebody's life. You don't know what they truly even look like. Most celebrities don't even look like the images that they post. They have professional teams who use very expensive software to make their skin look smooth and their facial features look more appealing.

Aside from photo editing, you can also use different angles. You can use perfect lighting to make your teeth look whiter than they are. You can make your body look different based on the position that you're in. Not everybody discloses all of the little tricks that they're using to make themselves look different, and social media is getting tricky when it comes to telling the difference between what is real and what is fake. You can even edit both prerecorded videos and live videos, so it's very hard to tell whether or not somebody actually looks like the images that they are portraying online. When you are comparing yourself and your life to a life that doesn't even exist, you will never feel satisfied. This increases your stress and makes it harder to appreciate yourself and love yourself for who you are.

Isolation

Because of the constant feelings of inadequacy and our shortcomings, it can be very easy to isolate ourselves from other people. Social media can make us feel very lonely. When you are alone in your room under the covers and in the dark, it can be very lonely when you see somebody's social event. They might post a picture of themselves in a party setting where there are many people around them. You might see pictures of a group of friends all tagging each other, living experiences that you question if you'll ever have. This makes us feel very isolated, contributing to a negative self-image. When you isolate from other people, you start to get stuck in your own head. When you're stuck in your own head and constantly repeating negative things to yourself, you will ultimately be left feeling like you are not good enough. When you isolate, you start to lose out on opportunities. You might become distant in your friendships and check out of reality. However, just like we discussed in the previous sections, many people are portraying a false image online. For example, one trick that some influencers use is taking many different kinds of pictures on vacations or at a singular event. Then, rather than posting them all at once, they'll post them throughout the next month or two to make it look like they are doing something fun every weekend when, in reality, they took all of their pictures just within a couple of days.

You also have to consider that some people aren't actually enjoying these events. They are simply taking part in them because they want to have content to post online. It's important for us to stay checked in with reality so that we resist the urge to isolate and withdraw from others. It's okay to be alone. It's okay to not do everything that you see your friends doing. You are very young. You have a lot of life left to live. You will have plenty of experiences in the future. Just because it feels like your life is boring now or that you're not doing enough does not mean that this will be the case forever. Stay grounded in reality and focus on real life rather than the fake images that you see on the internet.

Successful Steps to Self-Care

It's so important today for teens to learn how to take care of themselves. Excessive social media use can negatively impact body image, and research shows that those who struggle with body image can be at a higher risk for suicide (Morin, 2022). The best way to combat poor self-image is through practical methods of self-care.

Our parents have to provide us with plenty of care. We can't pay the rent or mortgage, and they're also usually responsible for ensuring we're fed. However, beyond that, we are still responsible for many personal decisions. We are the only ones who can bathe or brush our own teeth, and it's our job to make sure we are picking the right foods and getting some healthy movement in.

Eating Right

Social media can contribute to disordered eating habits. What this means is eating in a way that doesn't promote a healthy relationship with food. One example of disordered eating is binge eating. This involves eating past the point of hunger. Usually, it involves eating mindlessly, without much thought. Binge eating can also be followed by periods of purging. Purging is either accomplished through periods of starvation or, in some cases, vomiting. Binging and purging are incredibly dangerous, especially to a developing teen's body. It can wreak havoc on your digestive system as well as your heart health. Healthy eating involves listening to your body and recognizing the different cues of hunger and feelings of fullness.

Seeing someone online with the perfect body can trigger the urge to participate in disordered eating. When you are feeling insecure about your appearance or inadequate, it's common to want to take drastic measures to achieve a certain body type.

You might feel the urge to skip meals as a way to starve yourself in order to fit into a certain body type. Alternatively, binge eating can help alleviate feelings of anxiety or depression temporarily. However, there is usually an extreme emotional crash involved after that period of eating, coupled with physical symptoms of overeating like nausea or stomachaches.

The effects that social media can have on a developing mind are very harmful, especially the mind of someone still growing and changing. As a teen, you are going to change so much over the next few years. There is no rush to get the perfect body, especially if it means potentially hurting your body's development. You already have the perfect body for you. We are all born with bodies that do their best to try and promote health. Some bodies look different than other bodies, and that is a truth of life that we will have to accept.

What's important is ensuring that you provide your body with proper nutrition.

Often, eating is seen as a means to look a certain way, and over time, we lose sight of the real value of having healthy and nutritious meals, as the focus is placed on achieving a specific body type through our meals. It's easy to compare yourself to different bodies on social media, especially when certain body types are more likely to be promoted on social media apps like TikTok and Instagram. You will constantly see people wearing perfect clothing that accentuates certain body features. They have perfect skin and very few wrinkles. When you are constantly bombarded with specific body types all day, and then you look in the mirror and see that you don't have the same one, it can be very damaging to your self-esteem.

We also have to remember the lengths that people go to to achieve these certain body types including surgeries, injections, and other types of expensive or potentially damaging treatments. On top of that, many individuals have personal trainers and workouts to sculpt their bodies as a part of their everyday job. We simply do not have the same access to resources that those who are professional influencers or celebrities do.

As a teen, it's important for you to focus on intuitive eating. This means listening to your body and recognizing different hunger cues. Intuitive eating involves eating simply when you are hungry and stopping when you are full. There are many different hunger cues that you can listen to. The most obvious one is a grumbling stomach. We all know what it feels like when we are hungry. Beyond that, look for other signs in your body that it might be best to have a snack or eat a healthy meal. This involves things like having a headache or maybe even feeling nauseous or lightheaded.

When you're feeling stressed out or you find that you're having trouble focusing, this could also be a sign that you should consider eating something to help make you feel better.

It's also important to stop eating once you feel like you are full. If you do decide to eat even after you're full, then it's also important to let your body and mind know that this is okay. Attaching guilt and shame to your eating habits will only make it harder to follow a routine of healthy eating.

It's also important to focus on meals that are balanced. Balanced meals include a diverse range of foods from different food groups. This means eating healthy carbohydrates, vegetables, fruits, and protein sources. If you are going to be eating something like pizza, or greasy fried chicken, there's no shame in that. All food is good food if it makes you feel full. The important thing is to pair it with something nutritious as well. This might mean eating some sauteed spinach if you're going to have fried chicken or eating a side salad filled with tomatoes, onions, lettuce, and mixed greens. The most important thing to focus on in your developing years is balance, and to have a good relationship with food.

The guilt and shame that are attached to unhealthy eating habits can be just as damaging to your mental health as unhealthy eating is to your physical health. If you start repairing that relationship, you'll notice that it is easier to make healthier decisions for your body in the end.

Getting Movement

On top of healthy eating, it's important that we get enough physical exercise in our routine. Just like eating, exercise can often be associated with physical appearance. Exercise can give you certain aesthetic results, but the most important thing to focus on is exercising in order to help your body function properly. Exercising keeps everything moving through your systems. This means your digestive, neurological, and cardiovascular systems are all worked out through the various movements that you do with your body.

Social media contributes to a sedentary lifestyle, so it's essential that we incorporate more methods of healthy movement into our lives. It's recommended for teens to get at least one hour of physical activity daily (Mathe, 2022).

Exercise can be broken up into small parts throughout the day. While an hour might be recommended daily, it doesn't necessarily have to be consecutive. You might go for a 30-minute walk and then do small bits of 10-minute exercises three other times throughout the day.

If you're in a gym class, then you are likely already getting a good chunk of your workout in. There's pressure to go to the gym or exercise in a certain way, but you don't necessarily have to do that. Do small things like running up and down the stairs a few times in between study sessions. Stand up and do a few squats or push-ups against the wall. Try doing a wall sit while you are listening to an audiobook. Before you hop in the shower, consider doing some jumping jacks or another exercise that you can do in place. You don't have to go to the gym for three hours today to stay healthy. As long as you're moving your body consistently throughout the day and feeling a little bit of muscle strain, you will still be able to get some of the benefits of exercise.

The more regularly you make movement a part of your life, the easier it will be to do it throughout your adult life as well. Do more active things with friends. This means going on walks and jogs with them.

Go to your local nature walks or national parks in your state and explore nature with somebody else. Take your family dog on a walk. Play with them outside in the backyard. Come up with games with your friends, your pets, and your siblings. When you can make exercise a fun activity rather than something you feel pressured to do, you are more likely to participate in it. Dancing is also a great way to get more movement in. You can dance alone in your bedroom or you can dance with friends in social settings. Invest in some small forms of exercise equipment like resistance bands or even a stair stepper that you can do when listening to audio-books or watching educational things so that you can multi-task by getting in physical movement and learning at the same time.

Staying Hydrated

Sometimes we feel terrible simply because we have not drunk enough water!

Hydration is just as important as proper nutrition. Drinking enough water and staying hydrated throughout the day is important to help with digestion. It also helps with your energy levels. If you feel sick or tired, or you're struggling with a headache, try drinking a glass of water. It's powerful in helping you calm down, stay focused, and feel better over-all. Invest in a reusable water bottle so that you always have it on you. Most classrooms allow you to have water bottles because educators know the importance of staying hydrated.

Add more hydrating foods to your diet like lettuce, strawber-ries, watermelon, or peppers. Hydration isn't just absorbed through water but also through healthy foods. Try to aim for six to eight glasses of water a day and make sure that you sip them slowly and consistently. Chugging five glasses of water in a row is not going to give you the hydration that you need. This can also be very damaging to your internal organs as your kidneys and liver will have to filter that out and can become overwhelmed with the amount of water that you're drinking.

It's important to stay hydrated up until you go to bed and also ensure that you hydrate first thing in the morning. When you're sleeping for 10 hours, that's a long time for your body to go without water, so sip a glass of water slowly in the morning along with your breakfast. Drink water with every meal and every beverage that you have as well. Things like sugary soda and even diet sodas can be very dehydrating on the body, so it's important to drink water along with other beverages. Hydration is just one important part of maintaining your health overall.

Getting Sleep

One of the biggest contributing factors to a lack of sleep for teens is social media use. The CDC recommends that teens between 13 and 18 get between 8 and 10 hours of sleep per night ("Sleep," 2020).

When it comes to getting proper sleep, consistency is key. As mentioned previously, we all have a circadian rhythm. This is a pattern that naturally occurs in our body and helps to regulate our hormones. When getting proper sleep at night, it's important to stay consistent so that you can help maintain your body's natural rhythm. Try to wake up and go to sleep around the same time every day. This means that if you have to wake up at 6 a.m., it's important to be asleep by 10 p.m. the night before, or even 8 p.m. if you can swing it.

Some teens might see this and feel overwhelmed. They might believe there's no way that they could get that much sleep because they have schoolwork and after-school activities along with trying to maintain a social life. Napping is also helpful, so if you aren't able to get 8 hours of sleep a night, it's important to try and get a little nap in at some point in the day when you have the time. If you're feeling overwhelmed and like you're struggling with focusing, it might be because you're not getting enough sleep. Once you start to actually properly energize your body, you'll find that you're more productive and able to focus easier, therefore lightening your workload.

Make sure that you're falling asleep around the same time every night and not just getting into bed around that time. If you do have to fall asleep by 10 p.m. at night, try getting into bed by 9:30 p.m. so that you can give yourself plenty of time to fall asleep. You can also try catching up on sleep on the weekends. Just ensure that you aren't depending on this catch-up period. It's something to simply do on weeks when you might not have gotten proper sleep during the weekdays.

When it comes to using social media, it is incredibly important to not use it in your bed. Our minds have a sort of muscle memory where we get used to the habits that we have. This is why tying your shoes and brushing your teeth are both second nature. Our bodies store our activities so that they take less energy to participate in them. When you are getting into bed every night and reaching for your phone and scrolling on social media, this creates muscle memory that tells you that as soon as you get under the covers, you should probably reach for your phone. Break this habit by not using your phone in bed at all. You can still check up on social media before you go to bed. Just try doing it in the living room or another area of your home so that you don't have the muscle memory associated with late nights on social media. If you can, it's best to keep your phone in a different room altogether and use an external alarm clock.

You might also have your parents wake you up if you don't want to rely on an alarm clock. When you can keep your phone outside of the room, you'll be much less likely to be up all night on social media.

If you have to sleep with a nightlight on because you don't like the dark, then make sure that you pick one that is timed and doesn't stay on all night. It's okay if you have a light on for 30 minutes as you're trying to fall asleep. Many people don't like complete pitch-black darkness. This is why many people also sleep with the television on. However, lights like this, especially ones that change throughout the night, are very disruptive to your sleep. Even if you are falling asleep, that TV on in the background might have some noise or flashing lights that keep you from reaching the really deep stages of sleep that you need for restoration. Put a timer on your TV or invest in a nightlight that has a timer so that it goes off within 30 minutes of you falling asleep. This way, you can be in the pitch-black darkness and able to reach those very crucial restoration stages at night.

When you are able to ensure that you're giving your body proper nutrition, hydration, physical movement, and sleep, you are connecting all the corners of your health, making it easier for you to stay focused and reduce feelings of stress, anxiety, and depression.

Proper Hygiene

When we feel down about ourselves, it's hard to keep up with our hygiene. Of course, styling hair and putting on clean clothes is often done for aesthetic reasons, but it can also change how we view ourselves in general.

The last thing to focus on when it comes to self-care is proper hygiene. Having clean hair, brushing your teeth, and getting dressed in the morning is something many of us do because we feel the pressure to do so. When it comes to weekends or days that you're not doing anything, you might not get dressed up. You might stay in your pajamas most of the day, or maybe you don't style your hair. You might skip the shower and avoid putting yourself together at all because it doesn't seem as important if you're not going to be seen by other people. However, hygiene is still something important to participate in every day, beyond just for reasons associated with the way that we look. We need to focus on the way that it makes us *feel*.

Getting dressed and out of your pajamas is important so that you feel more prepared for the day. Brushing your teeth and washing your hair is a way to cleanse yourself and feel like a new person. You can wash the day away in a hot bath or shower. Brushing your teeth gives you a more refreshing feeling, and doing things like washing your face and maintaining your fingernails can make you feel more confident, even when you aren't seeing other people. It's important for us to separate the pressure of participating in hygiene based on the way that we look and instead rework our relationship with it so that we can focus on taking care of ourselves and making ourselves feel like our best versions.

Follow the tips below to help you maintain your hygiene:

- Shower daily. Whether you want to shower when you wake up in the morning or shower before you go to bed at night, that is completely up to you. Daily showers help us to wash away potentially harmful bacteria while also feeling refreshed. You don't have to wash your hair every day. You can wash your hair two to three times a week. However, a quick, brisk shower can be very rejuvenating. Make sure that you clean every part of your body from the top of your head to the tips of your toes. Use a loofah to help really scrub away some of those dead skin cells and make sure that the soap is very lathered.

- Brush your teeth twice a day. If you forget or you only decide to brush once a day, then it's more important to brush at night before you go to bed, as this helps ensure that you don't have food and sugar sitting on your teeth all night while you're sleeping. However, brushing twice a day is incredibly important because bacteria can form in our mouths overnight, especially when sleeping with our mouths open. As such, brushing your teeth in the morning is just as important as at night. Make sure that you're also scraping your tongue. Having good tongue hygiene is good for maintaining clean and fresh breath.

- Make sure to style or at least attend to your hair daily. This means brushing it, combing it, or tying it back. Make sure that you get rid of the knots that are in it. When you do wash your hair, make sure to focus on your scalp and wash away the dirt and oil there. Don't overlook your nails when maintaining proper hygiene. A lot of bacteria can get trapped under your fingernails, especially if you have really long fingernails. Keep them trimmed. This will also help you avoid biting your nails if you find that you're somebody who has issues with biting and picking.

- Lastly, don't overlook skincare. Even though you are youthful and have plenty of natural restorative processes in your skin, it's still helpful to make sure that you're washing your face daily to keep acne at bay and moisturize so that you feel like your best self.

Reminders

- **Step #5**: Take care of yourself.

You only have one mind, one body, and one life to live. Whenever you run into something online that makes you feel inadequate or like you are not good enough, remember to stay grounded in reality. Check the facts. Who posted this? Is there any way that this could be edited or inflated to look better than reality? What is the intention behind what is being posted? Social media can be heavily influential over our mindset, so it's important to stay proactive about caring for your mental health as you navigate the online world through your teenage years.

6. Replace Old Habits

The urge to constantly check our phone is deeply embedded in our psyche because it's a habit, so understanding how to break apart a habit will enable you to turn it into something more useful.

Many people have bad habits that are hard to break, like procrastinating. However, procrastination isn't necessarily something everyone does. Those who do procrastinate are usually alone when they are doing it. When we use our phones excessively, we do it consistently and out in the open. We do it in settings where everyone can see, and phone use is normalized. For this reason, it can be hard to notice when a habit is turning into something that is destructive to your life. Raising awareness is the first step in breaking a habit.

The Power of Mindfulness

The pressure to reach for our phones often happens automatically and without much thought. By encouraging a stronger sense of mindfulness on a day-to-day basis, we will be able to stay one step ahead of these impulses.

What Is Mindfulness?

Mindfulness is a powerful tool that has been known to decrease anxiety and depression, as well as other health issues like sleep disorders, excess stress, and chronic pain (Mandriota, 2022).

Mindfulness is a mental process that helps ground you in the moment. When we are struggling with anxiety, depression, or other forms of unwanted emotions, we can use mindfulness as a tool to keep us in the present. This involves noticing your sensations and raising bodily and spatial awareness. Why is it important to be mindful? If we are not mindful, then we lose sight of reality. We get stuck in our own thought process. If you are somebody who struggles with social anxiety, for example, then you will end up getting stuck in your own head. You will start to replay past scenarios and see them in a darker, more anxiety-inducing way. You will start to go over a situation that you've already lived through and feel very negatively about it. You might hyper-fixate on all of the little things that you said while overlooking the reality, which is that most people aren't as fixated on the little things you said as you are.

Our phones also strip us of the ability to be mindful because they transport us to another world. Not only do they provide a distraction, but they also bring up unwanted emotions that are easy to ruminate on. Rumination is the process of going over the same thoughts or feelings in your head repeatedly.

Most of us know that people edit their pictures, so we shouldn't make comparisons to what we see online. However, in reality, many of us still end up struggling with comparison and ultimately feeling bad about ourselves, even though we know deep down we shouldn't be making these types of comparisons. Increasing mindfulness means we are more present in the here and now, therefore, we have more control over our thoughts and actions. You can use mindfulness when you're stressed about life in general, or feeling triggered by social media.

Right now, grab something small that's sitting next to you. Whether it's a lip balm, a coin, a pencil, or something else small, hold it in your hand and get a sense of how it feels. Notice the textures and the sensation that it has in your hand as you're holding it. Trace your finger along the outside edge of this object. Notice the way that your thoughts might be trying to convert back to anxiety as you're doing this. You might still feel that anxious feeling deep in your stomach and in your core, and it can be hard to look past. However, as long as you keep focusing on this object here and now in the present moment, then eventually those anxious feelings will dissipate. Below are a few more examples of mindfulness activities we can participate in to help reduce anxiety and increase presence in the moment.

Five Senses

One mindfulness activity to participate in is the five senses activity. Most of us have five senses. These include the ability to see hear, touch, taste, and smell. When you are feeling anxious, it's important to notice all these sensations. The five senses activity is as follows:

1. First, identify five things in the room that you can see. What is around you? What shapes do you notice? What colors do you notice? What objects are around you? What people or animals are in the room with you? Where are you? What place are you in? What setting are you in? Identify all these different types of things.

2. Second, notice four things that you can touch. This includes the chair you're sitting in, the cushions that you're using, and the texture of the clothes that you're wearing. What do you feel under your feet? What do you feel with your hands? What do you feel with your entire body? Notice four things that you can use to help you feel connected to your touch sense.

3. Third, pay attention to three things that you can hear. Do you hear the air conditioning or heating system running? Do you hear birds or animals outside? Do you hear kids playing? Do you hear somebody talking in the next room? Do you hear your own feet fidgeting around underneath you? What three things are in the room that make noises?

4. Identify two things that you can smell. Do you smell an air freshener? Do you smell food cooking in the other room? What kinds of scents are surrounding you at this moment? If you can't identify any smell, then you can identify the sense through certain objects in the room that might have a scent. For example, if you see a picture of flowers hanging on the wall, try to visualize the scent of the flowers. If you see an unopened bag of chips sitting across the room, think about the smell of the chips.

5. Lastly, identify one thing that you can taste. The same thing might happen with your taste sense where you can't identify something that holds an actual flavor, but try to identify objects that you can associate with this sense. For example, if you're sitting in the doctor's office waiting room feeling anxious, there might not really be anything around that has a flavor. However, there is still likely something that you can visualize the taste of. If you see the sign for the bathroom, think about water coming from the faucet, and think about the taste of water. It's also helpful if you carry mints on you so that you can actually physically taste something at the moment to keep yourself more present. Even if you can't visualize something actually edible, consider the taste of things around you. What might the wall taste like? What might the carpet taste like? It seems really silly to think about, but it's still a way that you can stay more focused at the moment and help your thoughts get distracted from a place of anxiety and instead focus on the present.

Identifying your five senses is a way to ground you in the present and make you more aware of some of the bodily sensations that you are experiencing.

Color Identification

The second mindfulness activity is the color identification one. This involves looking around you and identifying all of the objects in a room that are specific colors. Let's try it right now. Consider the color yellow. This is a very common color. How many objects do you see in the room with you that are yellow? Perhaps this is a book or a throw pillow. Maybe there's a yellow candle or something yellow in the portrait hanging on the wall. This feels like a really simple activity, but it can be enough to bring you into the present moment so that you stop ruminating over some of your thoughts and anxieties. Try going through the rainbow and identifying everything in the room that's red, orange, yellow, green, blue, and purple. Then, identify the colors that aren't in the rainbow like black, gray, pink, and white. Once you have gone through all of these types of colors, you'll likely find that your thoughts have stopped ruminating and cycling through your anxieties and it's easier for you to stay present in the moment.

Take it a step further and identify different textures or materials. What in the room is made out of wood? How many objects can you identify that are made out of metal? Do you notice any plants? Consider anything soft or fuzzy. Paying attention to these types of spatial elements brings you back into the present moment. This is something really important to do, especially after we use our phones to scroll through social media. Once you hit close on your phone and set it down, take a moment to be mindful and pull yourself back into the present. It's really easy to see something triggering online or to be struggling with your thoughts and let that spiral. This thought spiral can end up affecting your behavior and what actions you take next, so it's crucial that we stay present in the moment after using our phones.

Body Scan

The last mindfulness activity to try is a body scan. This will help you connect with your body and really feel better and more present in the moment. Social media is something that happens first mentally. We stare at our phones and we think all these thoughts that come along and are triggered by our cell phone usage. It's crucial that you connect back to your body so that you can become more aware of all the ways that you're feeling. A body scan involves literally scanning our body by using our minds from the top of our heads down to the bottom of our feet. To do a body scan, take a moment and focus on each part of your body while taking deep breaths. This means starting on your head and taking a big, deep breath in. Hold it for a moment and then slowly let it out.

Pay attention to your head and everything on it. Notice your forehead, your eyebrows, your nose, your eyes, your cheeks, your tongue, your lips, your chin, your ears, the back of your neck, and so on. Scan down to your torso next. Notice your arms, your elbows, your fingertips, your wrists, your chest, your belly button, your abdomen, and your hips. Lastly, focus on your legs. Think about your butt, your thighs, your knees, the back of your knees, your calves, your shins, your ankles, your feet, your heel, and your toes.

Once you scan from the top to the bottom, scan again from the bottom to the top, each time taking a moment and lingering on that specific body part as you deeply breathe in and out. You can also pair this with muscle relaxation. This involves tensing the muscle that you're focusing on and then releasing it before moving on. If you pair this with deep breathing, you will find that your anxiety decreases instantly, and the more that you repeat this practice, the easier it will be to have mindfulness become an active part of your life.

Exploring Your Passions

With all of the free time and motivation you have after reducing screen time, it's important to discover greater passions in life. Passions are good for taking up free time and providing you with value, and there's science behind that. Studies prove teens who find their passion are less likely to participate in "risky behavior," including things like drugs, crime, and sex ("How and Why," 2016).

Some research also suggests that finding a passion is better for your future than trying to choose a career due to the consistent changes in the job field (Bridges, n.d.). If you are able to be more mindful of what you actually want to do versus what you feel pressured to do, it will be much easier to carve out time to explore your passions.

Growth Mindset

During your teenage years and even as a young adult, your brain is going to continue to develop. During these times of brain development, it's important to focus on fostering a growth mindset. What does it mean to have a growth mindset? To understand this, let's first start by discussing what a fixed mindset is.

A fixed mindset is one that follows the same types of thinking patterns without stepping outside of the box. When it comes to solving problems, there are usually multiple different types of solutions that you can utilize to help you resolve an issue. A fixed mindset is one that only sees life in one singular way. Indeed, a fixed mindset is one that follows everything that it has been taught without questioning some of these rules and regulations.

One thing a fixed mindset does is follow cognitive distortions. A cognitive distortion is a pattern of thinking that can lead to bad or unpleasant emotions. Cognitive refers to the way that we use our brain and how our thoughts develop to shape our actions. A cognitive distortion is a pattern of thinking that is a little more unhealthy.

Think of it like eating chips versus eating carrots. Both are foods. Both are things you shouldn't feel guilty about eating or not eating. However, if you only ever eat chips and never eat carrots (or other vegetables), then you might end up feeling sick and unwell. A cognitive distortion is a pattern of thinking that will always keep us feeling very sad. While everyone has cognitive distortions from time to time (like chips), too many of these thought patterns can hurt your health.

One type of cognitive distortion is black-and-white thinking. This is when you see a situation as being either entirely good or entirely bad. Sometimes we try to put things into specific boxes and make categorizations to help us understand their meaning. For example, some people might think if you are good at sports, maybe that means you're not very good at schoolwork. Other people might think if you are good at schoolwork and you love reading, you're not going to be as athletically talented. Black-and-white thinking can take the shape of more "traditional" thinking as well. For example, you might assume that when you go to see a doctor, it's going to be male. Despite the fact that the medical industry is filled with intelligent women, if you think traditionally, you might associate certain positions with gender. Think of construction workers. You might assume that one is going to be a man. However, there are plenty of female construction workers. When you think of a stay-at-home parent who cares for the children, black-and-white thinking might lead you to believe that this is usually a mother. However, a more open mindset can help you see that no specific role is attached to a specific person. This is just one example of how we might get stuck in our thoughts and fail to see all of the other complex and realistic situations that exist.

Another type of cognitive distortion is personalization. This refers to when you might assume that a situation is about you. If you are walking by a group of people and you hear them laugh, you might think to yourself that they're making fun of you, or that they're laughing because they're teasing you. In reality, they're just laughing about something funny that happened earlier, or maybe one of their friends in the group shared a joke. Personalization can make us feel as though the world is out to get us and that we are very isolated from other people. It can make us feel really insecure and scared to be ourselves. Another example of personalization is how we might feel embarrassed after social situations. If you are to go to a friend's party, you might say something silly or maybe you even do something a little embarrassing, like spill your soda. After the party, you go home and feel really embarrassed about that small moment. Even though it was only a few minutes, you still can't help but think that it ruined the entirety of the party. In reality, most of the people forgot about what happened and they were more focused on their own embarrassing moments as well.

A growth mindset is a way that we can utilize mental challenges and obstacles to explore new parts of our brain. After you walk by that group of snickering people, rather than thinking to yourself, *Oh, they must be laughing at me,* instead, you can challenge that thought and think, *Actually, they're probably just laughing at something else.*

One way to help foster a growth mindset is to try new things and explore areas that you maybe thought you didn't like. Social media makes it easy to cater our worldview into something that serves us and revolves around the specific things that we like. It's easy to create a box that you feel safe inside of, and you might only surround yourself with the things that you and your friends like. However, when we follow the same ways of thinking over and over again, that can eventually lead to cognitive distortions. It's important to break free from this box and think in new ways to reduce feelings of anxiety and depression.

Hobbies to Try

To help you keep exploring your passions and the things that you like, it's essential that you try many different hobbies. Hobbies are great things to help fill the time that you have once you start to detox from excessive social media use. Let's discuss a few different categories of hobbies that you can try to help you foster a new mindset.

The first is crafts. Consider artistic crafts that you can do on your own. These include things like knitting or sewing. These are great things to do while you are listening to an audiobook, watching TV, or even hanging out with friends. Crafts like these help keep your hands busy so that you're less likely to reach for your phone. Continue exploring your creativity through other artistic hobbies like drawing, painting, or pottery. All of these types of artistic hobbies let you explore different parts of your brain. Whenever you are creating something, you have to think of an idea and then you have to actually execute that idea. After you're done with the creation, you have to look at what you made and evaluate it. You can see the things that you like, which makes you feel good about yourself. You can also see areas of improvement, helping you to build your skills so that you are even more talented the next time around. You can also try other crafts like woodworking.

Aside from creative hobbies, consider different hobbies that involve nature. This includes gardening, horticulture, or environmentalism. Head to your local library and check out books on birds in your area, or trees in your area, and walk around your neighborhood to see how many different varieties you can identify.

Lastly, it's important to explore literature outside of an educational context. This means having a relationship with books and writing that doesn't involve schoolwork. Academics can make us feel very pressured to read and write in a certain way. When you are forced to read assignments and work on different papers, it can make you feel really disconnected from the act of reading and writing. However, both of these skills are very important not just for your professional life in the future, but also to help you explore your mind and grow your knowledge. Find different books of genres that you like. Consider young adult, horror, or science fiction novels. You can also explore nonfiction books in areas that you are interested in. Writing is also important to try outside of school. When you don't have the pressure of getting graded for what you're writing, it's easier for you to explore your mindset and let your words flow freely.

Lastly, consider volunteering. Volunteering is a great way to help you build up your experience. Find volunteer work in your area, especially in subjects that you feel passionate about. This might mean heading to your local animal shelter to help volunteer by taking care of the animals. Perhaps you can volunteer through the park district to help keep nature clean. You can volunteer through your school or local sports if you are an athletic person who wants to work with a specific sport more frequently. Volunteering not only looks good on a future job application or college application, but it's also a great way to meet new people and stay connected. When you fill your free time with hobbies, volunteer work, and other activities, you are less likely to spend excessive amounts of time on social media.

Reminders

- **Step #6**: Increase mindfulness to reduce social media habits.

Our phones are like new limbs in modern society. They are there first thing in the morning and we often check them right before bed at night. We rarely leave the house without them and we make sure to check in with them multiple times throughout the day. The best way to ensure we are staying aware of social media use is through the act of mindfulness.

Phone use isn't all bad, so learning how to utilize mindfulness with it will ensure you can maintain a healthy relationship with social media.

7. Repair Your Relationship

Social media doesn't have to be entirely demonized and banished from one's life in order to have beneficial results. Rather, rebuilding a stronger relationship with it will help you thrive in the future without perpetuating an all-or-nothing mindset.

An all-or-nothing mindset is another cognitive distortion. This means that you either have to use *all* of something or none of it at all. For example, dieting can perpetuate an all-or-nothing mindset. Some believe that if they have just one slice of cake or one piece of candy, then they've broken their "diet," therefore they should just give up on healthy eating altogether. That's not the case at all! It's fine to focus on healthy foods while still enjoying a treat every now and then.

Social media isn't something to approach with an all-or-nothing mindset. You can still enjoy it in a healthy way without feeling like you have to give it up altogether.

The Healthy Benefits of Social Media

Social media is much like a tool, and tools can either be used to destroy things or build something amazing. Knowing how to use social media to your advantage will ensure that you maintain a healthy relationship with it.

Most of the adverse effects of social media reported through studies and research are associated with a high amount of use as well as the type of content viewed (Cullen, 2023). If you are able to reduce how much you are using it while focusing on more positive aspects of social media, you will then be able to take advantage of the benefits rather than suffering from the negative effects.

Stay Connected

Over half of teens reported that social media was actually beneficial to their friendships according to one study, and around a third believed it improved confidence (Gordon, 2022).

The reason social media was invented in the first place was to help us stay connected to other people. This was established so that we could reach out to others and share our interests online. Socialization can be difficult for some. Finding a place to meet up with other people and actually taking the time out of your day to get ready and go out and chat with others can be very tiring. It's easy for us to isolate, especially when we live in areas where it's not easy to get together with other people. If you live in a very rural area and don't have access to transportation, you might find that you spend a lot of time at home, not necessarily by choice, but because you don't have many other options. Social media is a great way for us to stay connected and to feel more close to other people. We can meet new people and we can chat with them whenever we want.

You are no longer limited to just the people in your area either. You can connect to people across the world. Social media is a great and powerful tool that you can use to stay connected; you simply have to know how to use it. One important thing to do is to ensure that you cut out those who are toxic and bring you down. Instead, focus on filling your online presence with those who inspire you and lift you up. It's okay to unfollow people who you're not friends with. One good rule is that if you wouldn't approach them in public to have a conversation, then you shouldn't follow them online. Sometimes we see people who we simply have curiosities about. It's not necessarily that you like that person or that you're friends with them, you might just follow them because you're in an athletic activity together or because you both go to the same school. You don't need to stay connected to these people if they make you feel self-conscious, insecure, or like you are not good enough.

When you cut out people who you're not that interested in, it also provides you with the freedom to express yourself, making connections even easier. If you have 2,000 followers and you only know 20 of them personally, then when you post online, you're curating your presence to people you don't even know. This can lead you to feel pressured to make specific posts and present your life in a certain way, which can add a lot of stress and anxiety to your social media use. When you have a small network of people following you, it's much easier to post things that you actually care about, therefore making it easier for others to reach out and stay connected.

Professional Development

Consider using social media for professional development. This is a great way to create a professional network and stay connected to those who could potentially help us in our careers. This might mean staying connected to certain teachers or other educational individuals in your life. You can stay connected with people so that you can ask for letters of recommendation later in life. You can also stay connected so that you can share different parts of your work and maintain aspects of career development.

Consider having a strictly professional social media that you can develop over time and use to get a head start in your career. When you're posting things, you can use hashtags to help you connect with other professionals in the area. When you create a network of people who could help you profes-sionally in the future, social media becomes an excellent resource to have. This means connecting with people who can provide you with job opportunities, or at least inspire you within your career.

We don't have to know exactly what we want to do with our lives as teens, but if you start a professional social media account, it can help you get a greater sense of what area you might be interested in exploring. For example, if you're really passionate about writing, you can start a writing-specific account where you share your work and connect to other writers. You might be very business-minded and you want to open up a business in the future. You can connect with people who inspire you and create a network of role models so that you are exposed to valuable insight. You might be very passionate about cooking and one day you want to open your own restaurant or even have your own cooking show. There are plenty of resources online for you to connect with others, helping you to build a strong portfolio and social media presence over time.

Learning Opportunities

Social media is great for endless amounts of learning oppor-tunities. We just have to ensure that we are following the right people who are educated on these topics. For example, one great learning opportunity through social media is social justice issues. You might be interested in learning about inequalities between different demographics. You might be a passionate environmentalist, so you can connect with activists in your area to learn about how you might be able to help. You can follow educational pages and those that provide realistic and practical tips. Just ensure when you do this, you know the ins and outs of fact-checking and you're able to find sources to back up what people are sharing. You can do this for career purposes, or you can simply do it to help fill your free time. You can follow science pages that share interesting information, or entertainment pages that share interesting facts about your favorite shows and movies. There are endless amounts of learning opportunities on social media, so if you start curating your online presence around this, then you'll be getting fed even more types of educational pages, therefore crafting a perfect algorithm of helpful resources rather than one that makes you feel bad about yourself.

Keeping Addictions at Bay

Knowing the benefits of social media will keep you focused on creating a productive and helpful online presence. When you are focused on mindfulness and using social media in the right way, it's easier to keep addictions at bay. However, because social media can be so addictive and habitual, it's easy to fall back into old ways. Below are a few more tips to help you manage social media use.

Make Anonymous Profiles

One tip to help you navigate social media is to make anonymous profiles. Consider creating a separate account outside of who you know in your personal life. This way, you can use social media without the pressure to create a certain image online. You can simply have an Instagram account where you follow different meme pages or other profiles and follow people who you're interested in, without the pressure to post or have a presence yourself. You can use social media as a way to watch others and entertain yourself without feeling the urge to perfectly curate an image. You can simply log on and use social media in whatever way you want without anybody knowing what you're doing online. Sometimes we feel hesitant to follow certain people or to share certain posts because of what others might think. When you remove other people from your social media use, you can then just simply enjoy it for what it is. This also helps protect your privacy.

Another important tip is to avoid liking or saving things on social media. Liking can also add a lot of pressure and can be a part of your image. Some people simply like everything. It doesn't matter who posted it, or what the post actually is. If it's somebody that they follow, they might simply like that post. Other people might feel a lot of pressure about what to like. You might even have a time in your past when you liked a post and then decided to go back later and unlike it. It's good to have a rule to simply not like anything at all.

The same can be said for saving different things online. For example, if you are constantly saving videos that you want to go back and watch later, chances are you likely won't end up watching them later. Keep your social media clutter-free just in the way that you would your home. This can help reduce feelings of being overwhelmed and other pressures that social media can bring on.

Use Other Social Media

Going forward, consider changing the types of social media that you use altogether. What platforms do you currently have an account on? Chances are you likely have a TikTok, YouTube, or Instagram account. Consider deactivating or even deleting some of these and instead creating new types of social media. For example, you might create an account on something like Goodreads or Letterboxed. These are websites that can help you track different movies or books that you read and watch. This is a great way to stay connected to other people and also help you develop some of your interests. You can still log on to see what people are up to without the pressure of posting your body or other aspects of your lifestyle. You can still have some insight into what others are interested in without the anxiety and stress that can come along and have a perfectly curated image. There are many different types of social media that are specific to the interests that we have. If you find one that fits what you are passionate about, consider focusing on this as your main social media.

Screen-Free Day

To help you keep up with healthy social media use in the future, consider having a screen-free day every single week. Screen-free Saturday has a nice ring to it, don't you think? Perhaps you want to do screen-free Sunday. These can be self-care days so that you can focus on doing things that make you feel good about yourself rather than spending excessive amounts of time on social media. Not only will this help you cut back on unhealthy use, but you will be even more aware of your use later on. In addition, you can also increase gratitude over social media use on the days that you are actually using it. For example, if you go every Saturday without social media, then when Sunday comes around, you might be more appreciative of it since you went without it for 24 hours.

Having a screen-free day every week is a perfect way to ensure that you keep any potential addictions at bay. You can still use social media throughout the rest of the week. What you will find is that having one day to set aside for productivity will make every other day of that week feel even better. You can use social media without feeling guilty or like you are doing it too much. Consider this challenge for at least a month. That means you only have to go four days without social media in a month! What you might find is that you feel so much better that you want to do multiple screen-free days a week. Whatever you decide to do with your free time is completely up to you. The most important thing to remember is to pay attention to how you're using social media and then how it makes you feel. Staying mindful and creating a level of awareness with social media use will ensure that you make the most of it without feeling the many negative side effects that could come along with excessive screen time.

Reminders

- **Step #7:** Rework your relationship with social media to use it for good.

Social media is here to stay, and it's not going away anytime soon. For some, it's how they met their partners. For others, it's how they make a career. As long as you focus on using it to your advantage, you will be able to free yourself from the restraints of addiction to live a more mindful and peaceful life.

Conclusion

Can you remember the first time you got on social media? For many, it's become such an ingrained part of our lives that it's hard to remember life without it.

Going forward, it's important to remember that social media doesn't have to be a bad thing. The main focus should be on how it makes you feel rather than giving in to the pressures that it can create.

Remember to follow the seven steps laid out throughout the book to help you on your social media detox journey:

1. Understand the impact that social media can have on your life. We're glued to our phones, so lacking awareness can mean failing to realize just how much stress and anxiety it can cause.
2. Recognize the dangers social media has had on your life. Social media is filled with funny videos and goofy memes, so it's easy to lose sight of how

dangerous and damaging it can be to our privacy and personal lives.

3. Reduce how much time you spend on your phone. The best way to start changing social media habits for the better is to incorporate small ways to reduce phone usage over time.

4. Take some time away from social media. Doing a total detox will help you realize just how dependent you are on this habit, while simultaneously freeing up your time so you can focus on the things you're interested in.

5. Take care of yourself. The intense emotions that social media brings can lead us to neglect our health and our needs, so remember to focus on self-care going forward.

6. Increase mindfulness to reduce social media habits. Raising awareness of the present moment will make you less inclined to mindlessly use social media.

7. Rework your relationship with social media to use it for good. Don't think of social media as a bad thing or feel like it should be demonized, as there are many benefits to gain from it.

There's no telling what your personal life will look like in the next decade, and most of us can't even fathom what the future holds for technology and social media. The best way to stay one step ahead of the hold your phone can have on you is to decrease use and maintain awareness in the present moment.

You only have one life to live, but the internet will be around forever. Taking care of yourself is the best way to ensure you're taking good care of your future.

References

Advertising: how it influences children and teenagers. (2022, December 10). Raising Children. https://raisingchildren.net.au/toddlers/play-learn ing/screen-time-media/advertising-children

Anderson, M., Perrin, A., Rainie, L., & Vogels, E. (2022, November 16). *Connection, creativity and drama: teen life on social media in 2022.* Pew Research Center. https://www.pewresearch.org/internet/2022/11/16/ connection-creativity-and-drama-teen-life-on-social-media-in-2022/

Are you addicted to social media? (n.d.). Lee Health. https://www.leehealth. org/health-and-wellness/healthy-news-blog/mental-health/are-you-addicted-to-social-media

Bergman, M. (2023, September 18). *Social media's effects on self-esteem.* Social Media Victims Law Center. https://socialmediavictims.org/mental-health/self-esteem/

Bridges, C. (n.d.). *5 research-backed techniques to help teens develop passion.* Hello World. https://www.helloworldnetwork.org/post/5-research-backed-techniques-to-help-teens-develop-passion

Cassell, D. (2020, November 13). *Feeling more stress and anxiety? Your smartphone may be to blame.* Healthline. https://www.healthline.com/health-news/feeling-more-stress-and-anxiety-your-smartphone-may-be-to-blame

Chapman, S., Eyre, H., Keller, A., & MacRae, I. (2021, December 5). *Social media is changing our brains.* Center for Brain Health. https://centerfor brainhealth.org/article/social-media-is-changing-our-brains

Clifton, T. (2022, April 13). *Exercise for teenagers: A complete guide.* Healthline. https://www.healthline.com/health/fitness/exercise-for-teenagers

Cullen, K. (2023, January 28). *How to use social media without losing your mind.* Psychology Today. https://www.psychologytoday.com/us/blog/ the-truth-about-exercise-addiction/202301/how-to-use-social-media-without-losing-your-mind

D'Onfro, J. (2018, January 10). *These simple steps will help you stop checking your phone so much.* CNBC. https://www.cnbc.com/2018/01/03/how-to-curb-you-smartphone-addiction-in-2018.html

Fotuhi, M. (2020, September 21). *What social media does to your brain.* NeuroGrow. https://neurogrow.com/what-social-media-does-to-your-brain/

Gelles-Watnick, R. & Vogels, E. (2023, April 24). *Teens and social media: key findings from Pew Research Center surveys.* Pew Research Center. https://www.pewresearch.org/short-reads/2023/04/24/teens-and-social-media-key-findings-from-pew-research-center-surveys/

Gelles-Watnick, R., Massarat, N., & Vogels, E. (2022, August 10). *Teens, social media, and technology 2022.* Pew Research Center. https://www.pewresearch.org/internet/2022/08/10/teens-social-media-and-technology-2022/

Goldman, B. (2021, October 29). *Addictive potential of social media, explained.* Stanford Medicine. https://scopeblog.stanford.edu/2021/10/29/addictive-potential-of-social-media-explained/

Gordon, S. (2022, November 2). *Surprising ways your teen benefits from social media.* Verywell Family. https://www.verywellfamily.com/benefits-of-social-media-4067431

Green, M. (2023, January 9). *10 tips for a social media detox.* Pickard Properties. https://pickardproperties.co.uk/talking-points/10-tips-for-a-social-media-detox/

Health advisory on social media use in adolescence. (n.d.). American Psychological Association. https://www.apa.org/topics/social-media-internet/health-advisory-adolescent-social-media-use

Healthy social media habits. (2022, September). NIH. https://newsinhealth.nih.gov/2022/09/healthy-social-media-habits

Holmquist, J. (n.d.). *Social networking sites: consider the benefits, concerns for your teenager.* ICI. https://publications.ici.umn.edu/impact/24-1/social-networking-sites-consider-the-benefits-concerns-for-your-teenager

Horwood, S. (2022, December 11). *Constant smartphone notifications tax your brain.* Neuroscience News. https://neurosciencenews.com/smartphone-notifications-cognition-22048/

How and why teens should discover their passion. (2016, February 22). Middle Earth. https://middleearthnj.org/2016/02/22/how-and-why-teens-should-discover-their-passion/

Is your phone affecting your mental health? (2022, January 14). Butler Hospital. https://www.butler.org/blog/phone-affecting-your-mental-health

Keach, S. (2018, October 16). *Instagram tracks how much time you spend gawping at people's pics – and there's a good reason why.* The Sun. https://

www.thesun.co.uk/tech/7508508/instagram-time-spent-photos-look
ing-stalking/

Lightman, A. (2021, January 15). *Teens have never known a world without data sharing, and it's creating a false sense of security.* NBC. https://www.nbcnews.com/think/opinion/teens-have-never-known-world-with out-data-sharing-it-s-ncna1254332

Malouff, J. (2023, May 29). *What are the long-term effects of quitting social media? Almost nobody can log off long enough to find out.* The Conversation. https://theconversation.com/what-are-the-long-term-effects-of-quitting-social-media-almost-nobody-can-log-off-long-enough-to-find-out-205478

Miller, S. (2022, June 2). *The addictiveness of social media: how teens get hooked.* Jefferson Health. https://www.jeffersonhealth.org/your-health/living-well/the-addictiveness-of-social-media-how-teens-get-hooked

Millions of teenagers worry about body image and identify social media as a key cause – new survey by the Mental Health Foundation. (2019, May 15). Mental Health Foundation. https://www.mentalhealth.org.uk/about-us/news/millions-teenagers-worry-about-body-image-and-identify-social-media-key-cause-new-survey-mental

Morin, A. (2022, January 6). *How exposure to the media can harm your teen's body image.* Verywell Family. https://www.verywellfamily.com/media-and-teens-body-image-2611245

Ortiz, C. (2022, June 30). *7 mindfulness exercises for teens and tips to get started.* Psych Central. https://psychcentral.com/health/the-benefits-of-mind fulness-meditation-for-teens

Quinn, D. (2023, May 17). *Social media addiction: 4+ signs you're addicted to social media.* Sandstone Care. https://www.sandstonecare.com/blog/social-media-addiction/

Rogers, K. (2019, October 29). *US teens use screens more than seven hours a day on average – and that's not including school work.* CNN. https://www.cnn.com/2019/10/29/health/common-sense-kids-media-use-report-wellness/index.html

Schubert, A. (2021, March 30). *13 things that could happen when you quit social media.* The Healthy. https://www.thehealthy.com/mental-health/quit-social-media/

Sleep in middle and high school students. (2020, September 10). CDC. https://www.cdc.gov/healthyschools/features/students-sleep.htm

Smith, K. (2022, October 21). *6 common triggers of teen stress.* Psycom. https://www.psycom.net/common-triggers-teen-stress

Social media and teens. (2018, March). American Academy of Child & Adolescent Psychiatry. https://www.aacap.org/AACAP/Families_and_Youth/Facts_for_Families/FFF-Guide/Social-Media-and-Teens-100.aspx

Staloch, L. (2023, February 4). *Exposure to social media can increase adolescent materialism but can be tempered with high self-esteem and mindfulness.* PsyPost. https://www.psypost.org/2023/02/exposure-to-social-media-can-increase-adolescent-materialism-but-can-be-tempered-with-high-self-esteem-and-mindfulness-67557

Strasburger, V. (2006). *Children, adolescents, and advertising.* American Academy of Pediatrics. https://publications.aap.org/pediatrics/article/118/6/2563/69735/Children-Adolescents-and-Advertising?autologincheck=redirected

Study shows habitual checking of social media may impact young adolescents' brain development. (2023, January 3). The University of North Carolina at Chapel Hill. https://www.unc.edu/posts/2023/01/03/study-shows-habitual-checking-of-social-media-may-impact-young-adolescents-brain-development/

Summer, J. (2023, October 12). *How blue light affects kids' sleep.* Sleep Foundation. https://www.sleepfoundation.org/children-and-sleep/how-blue-light-affects-kids-sleep

Teague, K. (2019, May 21). *Google tracks your purchases. Here's how to see what Gmail knows.* CNET. https://www.cnet.com/tech/mobile/google-tracks-your-purchases-heres-how-to-see-what-gmail-knows/

Thiefels, J. (2019, March 27). *Understanding Your Digital Footprint.* Net Nanny. https://www.netnanny.com/blog/what-every-teen-needs-to-know-about-their-digital-footprint/

Tween and teen health. (2022, February 26). Mayo Clinic. https://www.mayoclinic.org/healthy-lifestyle/tween-and-teen-health/in-depth/teens-and-social-media-use/art-20474437

Waltower, S. (2023, October 23). *How much time do Americans spend online and texting?* Business News Daily. https://www.businessnewsdaily.com/4718-weekly-online-social-media-time.html

Weir, K. (2023, September 1). *Social media brings benefits and risks to teens. Here's how psychology can help identify a path forward.* American Psychological Association. https://www.apa.org/monitor/2023/09/protecting-teens-on-social-media

Why your teen needs to worry about blue light. (n.d.). Vision Source. https://

www.mccormickvision.com/eyecare/why-your-teen-needs-to-worry-about-blue-light/

Image References

Geralt. (2017, March 22). *Artificial intelligence, robot, ai* [image]. Pixabay.https://pixabay.com/photos/artificial-intelligence-robot-ai-2167835/

Kaboompics. (2015, May 30). *Lipstick, lipgloss* [image]. Pixabay. https://pixabay.com/photos/lipstick-lipgloss-lip-gloss-lips-791761/

Koch, A. (2022, January 28). *Student, man, desperate* [image]. Pixabay. https://pixabay.com/photos/student-man-desperate-depression-6976999/

Leninscape. (2017, April 12). *Yoga, woman, nature* [image]. Pixabay.https://pixabay.com/photos/yoga-woman-lake-outdoors-2176668/

Pexels. (2016, November 20). *Woman, Smartphone, Technology* [image]. Pixabay. https://pixabay.com/photos/woman-smartphone-technology-1847044/

Sammmie. (2016, March 17). *Friends, together, hugs* [image]. Pixabay. https://pixabay.com/photos/friends-together-hugs-back-view-1262152/

Sankowski, D. (2015, November 9). *Iphone, 6s, Plus* [image]. Pixabay.https://pixabay.com/photos/iphone-6s-plus-iwatch-apple-white-1032783/

Sasint. (2016, November 17). *Tired, young, laptop* [image]. Pixabay. https://pixabay.com/photos/tired-young-laptop-beautiful-1822678/

Stock Snap. (2015, September 3). *Shibuya crossing, Tokyo, Japan* [image]. Pixabay. https://pixabay.com/photos/shibuya-crossing-tokyo-japan-asia-923000/

Visual Worker. (2015, August 10). *Girl, t-shirt* [image]. Pixabay. https://pixabay.com/photos/girl-black-t-shirt-female-woman-882336/

The Teenage Wealthypreneur

7 Simple Strategies on How Teens Can Learn
Money Management and Wealth Generation

E. T. Mulloney

Introduction

When I was 10, summer meant pure joy and endless exploration for me. Living on an island with my single mother, I cherished the simple pleasures of life—playing with cousins and immersing myself in nature's wonders. But, out of the blue, the weight of adulthood settled upon my shoulders. I was confronted with the challenge of navigating my finances and creating wealth, all without any guidance. There was no manual to follow, and school didn't equip me with the necessary knowledge. I had to figure it all out on my own, step by step.

I don't want to give the impression that my childhood was a breeze. Coming from a single-parent household meant we didn't have unlimited resources. I couldn't rely on my mom to fulfill all my material desires. The success I enjoy today is the result of my own hard work and determination. I take great pride in the journey that brought me here. Resilience, perseverance, and a strong sense of purpose were key elements of my story, teaching me valuable lessons along the way. You might be facing similar circumstances or come from a slightly more privileged background.

Regardless, as a teenager, we often neglect to consider our future and our financial well-being. It's easy to push these matters aside, thinking they only concern adults. But the truth is, our beliefs about money and finances are often shaped at a young age.

Starting early can be the key to success. You have a unique advantage—learning from the mistakes of others. By avoiding major financial mistakes and making smart investments, you can build wealth and thrive. Leave behind the struggles that others faced. Consider it a cheat code for becoming a financially savvy teen and achieving success.

My purpose is simple: to share the practical wisdom I've learned and help teenagers like you navigate the challenges of life. In this book, you'll discover valuable advice and insights to guide you toward financial independence. It's not just about knowing how to handle money; it's about developing a positive mindset and discipline toward handling your finances.

Discovering the key to something extraordinary—a task so simple that even a child can accomplish it. Prepare to unlock its hidden power and witness the remarkable impact it can have on your life. Are you ready to embrace this empowering secret? Don't let the complexity of numbers and terms overwhelm you; it's simpler than you think. Together, let's embark on this journey of discovery and unlock the keys to a brighter, more secure future. Get ready to witness the incredible results that await you.

In this book, we are going to be talking about seven strategies that can help you empower your financial future. We will be covering everything from creating a plan to budgeting and all the way to investing. These are things that you can start implementing right now so you can build up the habits that will take you into your future. Rest assured, your future self will be immensely grateful that you devoted this time to learn and develop. It will be a gift that keeps on giving throughout your adult life.

As we enter Chapter 1, we'll begin exploring essential financial concepts and principles. This lays the groundwork for the rest of the book, making everything easier to understand. From there, we'll delve into practical strategies to enhance your financial literacy. So, without further ado, let's dive right in!

1. Understanding Financial Concepts and Principles

"I am one who believes that all 10-year olds should have the competencies in reading and writing, and computation, which give them the potential to be lifetime learners. And I see financial education as an important part of that foundation of learning that children need to have in a world that is ever more complicated and requires that all of us understand computation and finance, and the implication of savings, because they are key to participating fully in what life has to offer in the United States."

— Paul H. O'Neill, U.S. treasury secretary

Why Financial Literacy Matters

Financial literacy is one of the most important skills any teenager and young adult could have. When you are financially literate, it means that you understand finances and how to use it. If your dad were to give you a toolbox with all the tools you could ever need and told you to build a house would you be able to? Probably not. Even though you have everything you need, you don't know how to use it. The same thing applies to finances. Just because you have money doesn't mean you know how to use it properly. Understanding how money works and how to use it will help you to make better financial choices so you can build up your future. There are so many benefits to mastering finances that it is simply a must for every young person.

You Will Start to Understand the Value of Money

We all know that money has value. However, you can't fully comprehend the value of money unless you are managing it on your own and earning it for yourself. I'm sure you have heard your parents say something along the lines of, "Do you think money grows on trees?" At least, that's what my mother used to say to me. This was usually the staple response when I asked for something. At that time, I didn't understand the value of money. My single mother understood the value of money because she was working and earning it.

As you get older, you will need to understand how money works and how to manage it for yourself. Many young people tend to spend too much money on unnecessary items because they don't fully comprehend how to manage it properly. Earning your own money through doing small chores and jobs can really help you to see what it takes to earn money. When you are earning your own money through hard work, it puts more value on that money. You know that it doesn't just materialize in your wallet; you need to earn it.

This is a valuable lesson because it helps you to plan and spend your money more wisely.

You Know What Is Really Important

There is a big difference between what you want and what you need. Your needs are things like food to eat, a place to live, and clothing to wear. The things you want would be things like a new phone, vacations, and the occasional Starbucks drink. You don't really need these things, but they are definitely nice to have. When you are an adult, you'll have many expenses. You will need to decide what are the most important things for you to spend your money on and what is least important. The things you need to survive will always be the most important things for you to spend your money on. Once you have all of your needs sorted out, you can then focus on spending your money on a few things you want.

When you are managing your own money and purchasing your own items, you will be able to see what is most important to you and what really isn't. This helps you to prioritize and learn about finances so that you are completely prepared for the most important things. It also helps you to see how the smaller things in life don't really matter as much.

Financial Independence

At some point, you are going to be financially independent. This means that you have to handle all your finances by yourself. Most people are just thrown into the deep end when they become adults and move out of their parent's home. This is why you find tons of young people getting themselves into debt and ending up in bad financial situations. It's not because they are bad people; they just didn't have the knowledge needed to manage their finances properly.

If you learn how to manage your finances at a young age, it is so much better. You have all your needs taken care of by your parents, so they are your safety net. You have a safe place to learn about your finances and make some mistakes if you need to. It's a lot less pressure, and you will be ready for adulthood.

Avoiding Debt

Debt is probably something you are not all too familiar with. This is actually a good thing because these days, debt is so common, and people tend to struggle with it. Debt is when you owe the bank or another financial service provider money because you borrowed from them. You can borrow in the form of a loan or by using a credit card. When you borrow this money, they put an interest rate on it, so you have to pay back more than what you borrowed. If you are not able to handle credit or loans properly, then this could get you into a very sticky situation. Some people end up in hundreds of thousands of dollars of debt. The number keeps increasing because of the interest they owe. It's not that taking out credit is a bad thing, but you definitely need to know how to use it.

Dodge the Scammers

There are so many scams out there, and it's only getting worse. Online scams are the most common, and since you're probably online all the time, you definitely will be faced with a scam or two at some point. Scammers try to get your information so they can steal or misuse your money or account. The scammers have gotten so good that most people don't even know they are scammed until it is too late. All you have to do is accidentally click on the wrong link, and all your information could be gone. This is why it's so important to never fill out your personal information unless you are 100% sure of who is sending the request. Most banks and other financial service providers do not request you to put in your account information and passwords on emails and other types of communication. It's better to be safe than sorry. It is also wise to call your bank with the phone number they gave you to verify with them that the message or phone call you received is true. Never use the phone number in the message if you think it's a scam.

There are also other ways that someone can get scammed out of the money. This can happen in the real world and is not limited to online. For example, someone might be offering you an item at an escalated price so they can make more profit. You would be buying something that you could get from someone else for much cheaper; this will result in your losing out. Being savvy with your money also means doing research on the things you want to buy for yourself. This way, you know what the going prices are, so you are not scammed when you are trying to purchase something.

You Get a Head Start on Your Future

When you are a teenager, there's a lot of thinking about what you're going to be when you grow up. Your whole life is planning for your future, but the truth is the future is closer than you might think. One day you'll open your eyes, and you will be in your mid-20s and need all the skills necessary to build financial success. The earlier you start building the skills, the better it's going to be for you. You will have a lot of practice by the time you hit adulthood, and you will be able to trust yourself to make the right decisions.

Basic Financial Concepts and Terminology

One of the biggest reasons finances seem so difficult to understand is that there are a lot of difficult words and terms that are used. These can seem overwhelming, but it's just because you're not familiar with them yet. The more you start seeing these words and understanding them in context, the more you will understand other types of financial concepts. Below are some of the most common financial concepts and terminology. This should help you understand the book a lot better.

Savings Account: This is where you will save your money for future use or for specific items. If you earn a salary, have it deposited into a savings account. It is best to transfer the money you need from your savings into your checking. Keep in mind you may be required to maintain a minimum amount in your checking account. Many savings accounts also have higher interest rates, so you can gain interest while you leave your money in the account.

Checking Account: This is a transactional bank account. It is easy for you to access your money and pay for things, so you can use it whenever you want. Just keep in mind to never write a check for more money than is in this account, or the check will "bounce," and you will be charged a fee.

Bounced Check: This is a check you write for which there is not enough money in your checking account to cover the purchase price. The bank does not approve the transfer of money, and the check "bounces" back to the account holder. Then the account holder will likely be charged a penalty fee for non-sufficient funds (NSF).

Debit Card: This allows you to have access to the money in your account. You will only be able to spend what is in the account, so always make sure you have enough otherwise, your purchase will be declined.

Interest: This is a percentage that a lender charges the borrower for borrowing money. You can either gain interest or owe interest. If you put your money in an investment or in a savings account, you will be earning interest. If you borrow money, take out a loan, or are using credit, then you will owe back interest.

Loan: This is when you borrow money at a specific interest rate. You will need to pay back the money by a specified date.

Credit Card: This is a specific type of loan where you get a card and can spend an agreed-upon amount of money each month. You also have to agree to pay back a minimum amount each month. This is called revolving credit, as you keep getting a renewed amount each month as long as you are paying back the minimum. An interest rate is also imposed upon you, so the longer you do not pay off the full amount, the more interest you will owe back.

Credit Score: This is how banks and other financial service providers can tell whether you are good with debt and credit or not. Your credit score is worked out based on your history, current debt, how much available credit you have, the length of credit and loans, as well as a few other factors.

Investment: This is an asset that will hopefully generate income for you or increase in value over time.

Stock: This is a piece or a share of a company that you can purchase on the stock market. This way, the company can raise funds in order to expand and grow. As the company expands, the value of the stock will increase, and you will be able to sell your share for more money than you purchased it.

Bond: This is a way for corporations and governments to raise more money for themselves. You are essentially loaning them money, and they will pay you back a specified interest rate. The bond is locked in for a certain amount of time, and once the time has elapsed, you will get back the original money invested and the interest earned.

Inflation: This refers to the overall increase in price for services and goods. The cost of living increases over time, so you cannot purchase items for the same price as you did a few years ago.

Taxes: This is a portion of your income that you are required to pay to governments (federal, state, county, city) in order for them to fund government-based services and activities. This can include running public schools, military operations, and maintaining public spaces.

Setting Financial Goals

Most people set goals and don't even realize it. A goal is something you want in the future, and then you make a plan to get it. Even saying that you want a new pair of sneakers could be a goal. You might not be able to afford them right now, but you can save toward them until you have enough money to buy them. Being able to set financial goals throughout your life is so important. It helps you to put your money to work and create good money habits. In order to reach your financial goals, you will need to be disciplined in the way you handle your money and make sure the habits you have in place will help you to reach your end goal.

There are many different categories when it comes to financial goals. These usually indicate how long it will take for you to get there. Short, medium, and long-term goals all need different strategies in order to get to the end. A short-term goal is something you can accomplish in a few months to a year. A new pair of sneakers would be a short-term goal. A medium-term goal will probably take you between 1 to 5 years to accomplish. Things like a down payment on a property, an overseas vacation, or a wedding could fall into this category. Then we have the long-term goals, which will take you more than 5 years to accomplish. One of the most common long-term goals is to save enough money to have a comfortable retirement.

You can have multiple different goals running at the same time. However, it is important that you track all of your goals and understand where your money is going. You don't want to overcomplicate things or overcommit yourself to too many goals because then it becomes difficult to reach any of them. It's important to understand how much money you have and how much each financial goal is going to cost you. This way, you can better plan and prepare for all of it.

Start Small

If you have never actively set goals before, how you start is going to be incredibly important. It is always better to start with a small goal so you can get the hang of it. If you set a goal that is too big and too far off, it might be difficult to stick to the plan. Once you start reaching the smaller goals, you will gain the confidence to set bigger ones and will have a higher chance of actually reaching them. When a baby starts learning how to walk, they don't sign up for a marathon. Small baby steps first, then they learn how to get faster as they grow. The same principle applies here.

Your small goals can be anything related to finances. You can decide you want to open up a savings account, save $100 for an item of clothing, or commit to writing out a budget. These are all small things that shouldn't take up that much time, and once you have reached those goals, you'll feel a lot more motivated to start planning other goals to reach.

Weigh the Costs and Benefits

Being able to reach your goals will come at a cost. This may not be a monetary cost; it could also be your time and your energy. Being able to think through every goal you set is going to be crucial so you can set the right ones. Let's say you want to be an actor or on Broadway when you are older. This is something you are super passionate about, so your plan is to take steps toward that long-term goal. You hear about an acting camp that is taking place over the summer.

They are bringing in some amazing and talented actors to speak to the campers and help them to hone their skills and build connections. This would be an amazing opportunity, and it's something you really want to do.

There is a cost to go to this camp. Firstly, you will need to have the money to pay for the camp itself as well as spending money for when you get there. You will also be giving up most of your summer and won't be able to spend time with your friends and family. Before hearing about this camp, you were planning on getting a summer job to earn some extra cash, but now that you want to go to this camp, it's going to be taking up all of your time, and you won't be able to get the job. With all of this information in mind, you have to ask yourself whether or not the camp is actually worth it. Does the cost of going to the camp over the summer match the benefits you will be getting? For every person, the answer to this question will probably be different. It is important to understand where you stand so you can decide whether or not this camp is a good idea.

With any financial goal, it helps if you write down the pros and cons. Write down what you need in order to fulfill the goal and what you will be giving up in order to reach it. You can also highlight some of the benefits that will come from reaching the goal. All of this will help you to decide whether the goal is worth it or not. Remember, a goal might not seem worth it right now, but it could totally be worth it in the future. While you may not be able to reach it at this point in your life, you can save the goal and re-look at it at another point in time.

SMART Goals

A great method for goal setting is SMART goals. Each letter stands for a specific part of the method. Every goal you set should be specific, measurable, achievable, realistic, and time-bound. If you look at every goal through this lens, you will be able to set goals that you can achieve. Many people set very basic goals, and it doesn't actually help them come up with a plan. For example, if you want to be rich one day, this isn't a good goal. It is way too vague, and you can't see the steps in order to get there.

You can use this as an inspiration to set your goals. Instead of it being so vague, you can say you want to be in a high-paying job by the time you are 30 and have $20,000 in your savings account. This is way more specific, and you can plan to reach the goal. You will be able to look at different job opportunities and see which ones are going to be the highest paying. Then you can see what the requirements are for these jobs. Once you graduate high school, you can go to college and study for a degree that will put you in line for the career path needed. You can then start saving toward the goal by budgeting correctly and making sure you are not blowing all of your money.

This example is a long-term goal, but you can do it with short-term goals as well. Once you have written down a goal, go back and ask yourself those five questions. Is it specific? Is it measurable? Is it achievable? Is it realistic? Does it have a timeframe or due date? All of these things are going to help you set goals that are more easily achieved.

In Real Life

Sarah had graduated college about two years ago, but in order to graduate, she had to take out a financial aid loan for $20,000 at 7%. After graduation, she got a great job but still continues to pay for the $20,000 debt she incurred, which continues to grow at 7% annually. At this point, Sarah is feeling completely overwhelmed because this is not the plan she had for herself. Being in debt is holding her back from her other financial goals and from being able to live freely.

She knows that she needs a plan in order to pay off her debt. Otherwise, she's never going to be able to live the life she wants. What she needs is a budget. Not knowing where her money is going and how it is working means that she can't actually put together a plan to pay off her debt. Building a budget will allow her to see how much money is coming into her account and how much is leaving. Then she will be able to set financial goals based on how much money she has. She already knows that the number one thing she needs to do is pay off her debt. Once that is done, she can start saving toward things like traveling or buying a property.

She takes all of her debt statements and sees how much she actually owes. Then she looks at how much money she needs to pay in order to pay off the minimum each month. If she's going to keep paying the minimum, she will never get rid of the debt. Debt is sneaky like that. They always tell you that you only have to pay off the minimum, but the truth is that if you do that, you will pay way much more than the original debt. Instead, you keep having to pay back interest for the rest of your life. The only way she can get out of debt is to pay back as much as possible.

When Sarah wrote down all of her expenses, she realized that she spent quite a bit of money on her daily Starbucks drink. On top of that, she eats out about three times a week. Even though she loves going out to eat and can't live without coffee, she decided she was going to cut out these things for the next year. Instead, she would make her coffee at home and try new recipes. This frees up a lot of extra money that she pays toward her debt. Now she is able to pay back more than the minimum and is quickly paying off her debt. All she needed was a plan and a goal. When she had that, everything started falling into place and working for her.

The thing that really helped Sarah was creating a budget. A budget is a powerful tool that helps you to plan and see where your money is going. In the next chapter, we are going to dive deeper into creating a budget so that you can have full control over your money. I know you might be thinking that you don't even have a job and don't have that much money to budget with anyway. Even if you just earn $10 a month, it is still a good idea to have a budget. Remember, you are building a habit, so any small amount of money counts as income.

2. Strategy 1—Creating a Budget and Managing Expenses

> *"Budgeting is not just for people who do not have enough money. It is for everyone who wants to ensure that their money is enough."*
>
> — Rosette Mugidde Wamambe

I magine you purchased a brand new desk. You've been eyeing this piece of furniture for a long time, and it just went on sale, so you quickly clicked "add to cart." Now you have your dream workstation ready to go, and you know it's going to help you be so much more productive. When the pack is delivered to your home, you realize that it doesn't come with any instructions on how to build it. It seems easy enough to put together, so you decide you're just going to do it yourself. After about an hour and a half of work, the desk looks pretty good. There are a few screws left over, but you have no idea where those go, so you just ignore them. The desk seems sturdy enough, so maybe they're just extras.

You decide to put all your stationery and supplies on your desk and set everything up. The next day you get home from school, and you plop your backpack on the desk and hear a crash. The whole desk has collapsed! Even though it looks good from the outside, there was something going on that wasn't working. Your desk wasn't as strong as it looked, and now it has caused some damage, and you need to start all the way from the beginning. It would've been so much easier if you had the instructions.

You might be thinking, what does this have to do with managing your finances or budgeting? Well, budgeting is just like creating a blueprint for your finances. You create instructions and a plan, so you have full control of your money. This will help you to create a strong foundation for your finances so it doesn't collapse later on. This way, you're not going to be stressed out about money or run out in the middle of the month. Even though it might take a little bit longer to work on a budget, it is definitely worth it.

Understanding Your Income and Expenses

Before you can start working on your budget, you need to know what you are working with. This means you have to have a good idea of your income and your expenses. Your income is everything that comes into your bank account or is given to you in cash. This could be money earned from a part-time job, your allowance money, or money that has been given to you as a gift. It is a good idea to write all of the various forms of income you have and how much you make each month. Now you know exactly what you're working with and how much you can budget for.

Step two in the process is to figure out what your main expenses are. There are probably a few things that you have to spend your money on each month. When you are older, you will have bills that you will be paying for, and this is a necessity each month. Things like utilities, rent, and insurance will be coming out of your account every month. This makes it very easy to plan for it. You probably don't have any of these expenses right now, but you might have a few things like your Spotify or Apple Music account or you know you spend $50 per month on transport to get to your sports club. Whatever your expenses are each month, make a list and write down how much you are spending.

Once you know what your income is and what your expenses are, then you can find out the difference. Subtract your expenses from your income and see how much money you have left. If you realize that you don't have any money left this means you are probably misusing your money in some way. Right now, you might be asking your parents for a little extra when you run out, but this could set you up for creating a bad habit. When you are an adult, and you want to purchase something that you don't have the money for, you will have to take out debt. It might seem like a small amount at the moment, but it can really add up. It is always better to make sure your spending matches or is less than your income.

Creating a Budget

Now that you have the base layer for your budget, you can start working on creating a detailed plan for your money. You can use a spreadsheet on your phone or computer, or you can do it old school with a pen and paper. It doesn't really matter; you just have to pick the method that will work best for you. There are also some amazing budgeting apps that you can download. One of the most popular ones is called Mint. Some of these apps do come with a fee, so make sure you understand that because it will be an expense that you will need to add to your budget.

You already have a list of expenses written out, but sometimes this doesn't reflect your true spending. The truth is that most of us are really bad at estimating how much we are spending. The best way to get a good idea of how much you spend each week and each month is to track it. In order to do this, you will need to have a notepad or a spreadsheet that you fill in every time you spend money. Even if you buy something for a few cents, you will need to write it down. Write down what you spent the money on and how much it costs you. At the end of the week or the month, you can add everything up and see how much you are truly spending. It might actually surprise you how much money you're spending on things that might not be as important. There are also many good spending tracker apps that you can download.

You can start categorizing you're spending so you know where your weak spots are. We all have weak spots when it comes to spending money. These are things that we just love to buy or spend money on, even if we don't need them. Some people spend a lot of money on snacks and candy. Others will spend it on mods for games. Some people prefer spending money on clothing and accessories. If you know where most of your unnecessary spending is coming from, then you can pay attention to those areas and avoid them as much as possible.

Tracking your spending is something that's going to take at least a few weeks. This will give you the best idea of how you spend your money. Track your spending for a few weeks, and then you can move on to the next step of creating a budget. This is where you look at your spending and see what is important and what is not important. One of the most important things you can do with your money is save it for the future. Having an emergency fund, investing, and saving for important financial goals is essential. Since you have already worked out a few of your financial goals, you can take that into account when you are budgeting. Decide how much you are going to save toward each of your goals every month. These will be your priorities because they are very important to you.

Since you know what is most important to you and what is least important, you can start cutting out the things that are least important to make more room for the important stuff. This might mean that you have to cut down on buying soda from the vending machine at school every day or only buy one upgrade for your video games each month rather than two or three. These small cutbacks will help you to free up extra money so you can do the things you really want to.

It is also important to remember that not every month is going to look the same. There will be some months when you have extra money and some when you might need to cut back a bit more. If you have a friend or family member who has a birthday this month, then you are going to need to save up more money to buy them a present. In a month when there is no special event, you might have more money to spend on yourself. This is why it is so important to look at your budget every month. Plan for whatever is happening in that month and adjust accordingly. It is going to take some time to get used to doing this, but after a few budgeting cycles, you will start to realize how your money works. It will get a lot easier to budget, and the time you spend budgeting will get shorter.

Tips for Reducing Expenses

Now that you have your budget written out, it is time to start looking for ways you can reduce your spending. Believe it or not, we all tend to spend way more money than we actually need to. We live in a world that pushes content and consumerism at us all the time. Scrolling through TikTok, you see dozens of influencers showing us the new gadget they bought or reviewing brand-new clothing items. It becomes very difficult not to want those things. This means we end up spending a lot more than we should, and it becomes difficult to reach financial goals that are important to us. This is why knowing a few saving hacks could be super helpful.

Keep an Eye on Subscriptions

Overtime subscriptions can really pile up. You might need a subscription to something for a short time, but forget that you even signed up in the first place. I remember a few years ago, I was going through my subscriptions and realized I had over eight subscriptions that I was paying for, but I wasn't even using them. Sure, I needed it at the time, but eventually, they became redundant. Now I was paying for something that didn't have any benefit to me anymore.

This is why it's important to keep track of your subscriptions. Maybe you signed up for Google Cloud but don't need it anymore because you also have a subscription to iCloud. Do you really need that many cloud services? Every time you sign up for a subscription, write it down and write down how much you are paying for it. You can make this a section in your budget. Then you always know exactly what subscriptions you are signed up for, and when you no longer need it, you can go and cancel it.

We Have Food at Home

Parents love to tell their children that they can't eat out because there's food at home. This can be incredibly frustrating when you are a teenager, but when you have to spend your own money on food, it starts to make sense. Eating out all the time really does take up a lot of your money. Cooking at home is a lot cheaper because you can buy a lot more ingredients and cook multiple meals.

Since you are probably still living with your parents or a guardian, they will be taking care of all your food needs. You don't really need to buy your own food, and any food you do buy, it's just because you feel like it, not because you're actually starving. Telling yourself that you have food at home will help you to save a ton of money. This doesn't mean that you can't eat out once in a while; just make sure it doesn't turn into a habit.

Make a Checklist

Impulse buying is a real trap. This happens when you see something that looks really cool, and you want to buy it immediately. I'm sure you have bought quite a few things that aren't being used right now. Every home has a junk drawer where everyone puts the random stuff they bought but never use. This could've been money saved for something more important.

The best thing you can do when it comes to spending is plan. If you see something that you really want to buy, write it down on a list. I have a list on my notes app, and when I go out to the store, I only allow myself to buy things that are on that list. This could be clothing, shoes, technology, or literally anything else. If I notice that I need another jacket for winter, I will put it on the list. When I'm going to go shopping, I will specifically look for that winter jacket. I might come across some other items of clothing that look really nice, but because it's not on my list, I will avoid buying it. This way, I stick to the plan and make sure I only spend money on things that I actually need and are important.

If you are at the stage where you are buying your own groceries or helping your parents buy groceries, make sure you have a list. Throughout the month, as things get finished, you can add them to the shopping list. Then at the end of the month, you know what you need. You won't be tempted to buy something because it's on sale or because it just looks cool. This also helps to prevent food waste because you only have the items that you're actually going to use.

Use Cash Over Card

Sometimes, it's a lot easier to save money and spend wisely when you're using cash. This is because you can feel the physical money in your hand, and you can see it going away when you pay for something. When you just swipe or scan your card, you can't really see the money being deducted from the account, so it doesn't feel that bad. Only when you go back and check your account will you notice that you have less money.

Using physical money also helps you to spend less and stick to your budget because you only have a limited amount. You won't have access to all the money in your account. If you are going out somewhere or going to spend your money, you can withdraw the amount in cash. This way, you know exactly how much you are spending and what you have left. It will be a lot easier to plan and stay on budget.

Choose Cheaper Activities

We all want to go out and have fun with our friends, but sometimes these activities can get pretty pricey. If your friends always want to do things that are on the expensive side, it might help to start suggesting activities that are cheaper. You don't have to pay an arm or leg to have fun.

Let's say your friends want to go to the movies. These days going to the movies can cost a lot of money. You aren't just paying for the movie ticket but also the snacks and food you'll be eating when you get there. You could suggest having a movie night at your house. Everyone can bring their favorite snacks, and you can sit in your living room in your pajamas. It's a lot more comfortable, you will have a lot more snacks, and you can watch more than one movie.

There are always ways you can choose a cheaper activity. It might just be a case of doing some research and finding a similar activity at a cheaper price. Maybe there could even be a deal for large groups, and you can invite more people in order to cut down on the price. You don't have to do this all the time, but if there is a way to spend less money, then you should definitely go for it.

Sticking To Your Budget

Now that you have your budget all written out and you have figured out some ways to reduce your spending. You have to focus on sticking to the budget. Just because you have a budget doesn't mean that it's going to be easy to follow it all the time. You will probably be tempted to spend a bit more here and there, and this could lead you to go way over budget. Thankfully, there are a few things you can do to help rein in your spending and stick to your budget.

Give It a Day

Most of the useless things we buy are a result of impulse spending. Even if we have a certain amount in our budget for something like clothing, we can still end up buying something we regret. Instead of simply buying something because you saw it and you liked it, take some time to think about it.

When you see something you like, the emotions rise up in your body and make you want to buy it. This means you are buying some things based on emotions and not using logic. Most of the time, finances are all about logic. Taking a day or two to pause and think about it is going to help you.

Budget to Zero

There are many different ways to budget, and most people choose to budget based on category. If you struggle to stick to a budget, you can try budgeting to zero. This is when all your expenses and your income are exactly the same. Instead of leaving some money spare, you make sure that every dollar is doing something in your budget.

This doesn't mean that you have to spend every single dollar on something. Budgeting to zero also takes into account you're saving and investing. It just helps you to ensure that your money is doing something productive and that you aren't wasting any leftover money.

The No-Spend Challenge

If you are someone who loves a challenge, why not try a no-spend challenge? This is when you decide not to spend any money for a certain amount of time. People usually do this for a few weeks or a month. If you have important things to pay for, like subscriptions or bills, these will still need to be taken care of. The no-spend challenge is more about not spending your money on things you don't need. You won't buy any new clothes or any unnecessary food items or even spend on fun activities. Doing this helps you to see that you can actually survive if you're not spending your money, and it helps you to save a huge chunk toward your goals.

Meal Planning

Planning out your meals is a great addition to grocery shopping. If you plan out your meals for the week, then you'll know exactly what ingredients you need to make that meal. This means you only buy exactly what you need, and it really helps you to cut down on how much you spend at the grocery store. You will also cut down on food waste because you will not be buying anything unnecessary. It also makes sure that you always have food available so you're not tempted to order takeout.

Shop Online

Buying groceries online and online shopping, in general, can actually help you save money. This is only if you do it smartly. When you purchase things online, you only have certain items in front of you. You have to search for the items you want, and those are what will be pulled up. This way, you only buy what you need and aren't tempted by aisles and rows of other items. You are less likely to see other things you might want because you are just focused on the things you need. If you are going to shop online, make sure that you don't scroll endlessly on the stores' pages. Know what you are planning on buying and only search for those items.

Pay Yourself First

Paying yourself first is the concept of saving your money before you spend it on anything else. Many people spend money first and then save whatever is left over. This isn't a good plan because you are not prioritizing yourself and your goals. Instead, plan on saving first and then use the rest of your money toward other things. Remember to save your money in a separate bank account from your regular checking or transactional bank account. If it is out of your regular bank account, you'll feel less tempted to use it. A great plan is to decide that 10% of all you earn is yours to keep.

Compare Before Committing

It is a good idea to compare different stores and different items so you can find the cheapest option. This can actually help you save a lot of money because some stores will have sales on certain items while others don't. Simply taking the time to research the item you want to buy and looking for cheaper options will help you to save so much money.

Do It Yourself

Now is the time for you to create your own budget and do it yourself. Creating a budget can be a trial-and-error experience. You will get a lot better with it as you learn more about your spending habits. The main goal is to get started and commit to doing a budget every month. This will help you to create a habit, and once this is set in stone, things will be a lot easier for you.

- Write down your total income for the month.
- Make a list of your expenses and add them up to get the total.
- Track your spending to find out what you actually spend. Find your weak spots.
- Make a list of your priorities and goals, and write down how much you want to spend on each.
- See how much money you have left over.
- With the leftover money, put it toward other things you might want during the month.
- Look at your budget each week and adjust if needed.
- Repeat!

Budgeting Template:

<u>Income:</u>

Income Source	Planned Amount	Actual Amount
Totals		

Expenses:

Expense Name	Planned Amount	Actual Amount	Left Over
Totals			

Savings:

Savings Name	Amount Saved
Total	

3. Strategy 2—Saving and Investing for the Future

Being able to invest is a great way to grow your wealth. Investing in the stock market is risky, but if you know what you are doing, it's a great place to try to grow your investment because you can get a high amount of returns. About 56% of Americans own stocks and 92% of the highest-income families own stocks (Financial Samurai, 2021). This shows that people see the value in investing in stocks. Many people believe that you need to be earning a lot of money in order to start investing, but that is not the truth. You can start investing with a small amount of money.

The Benefits of Saving Early

If you are planning on starting to invest, it is always good to start saving first. Building a savings habit is the first step to investing. You might not feel it now, but not having enough money in your savings does come with a lot of stress. As an adult, there could be many different types of situations that pop up and result in you not having enough money for something. If there is an emergency that you have to deal with, you might need to take out a loan or use your credit card in order to pay for it. This can put you in debt and can stress you out. In life, we can never plan and prepare for everything, so it is always good to have a little extra money to use when you need it.

Saving money also helps you to work toward long-term goals. Some of the things you might want in your life are going to be more expensive than you can afford in one month. If you have already built the habit of saving, then saving toward your goals is going to be a lot easier for you.

Learning how to save as young as possible is essential. If you are used to using up your entire salary for the things you want now, then it's going to be very difficult for you to learn how to save later on. However, if you start saving early on in your life, it will already be a habit for you. You will already have savings in your budget, and it's not going to be a huge stress for you to start cutting down on your spending. Saving is a lifestyle, and it is well worth it.

It is good to think of saving as paying yourself first. When you are buying items and spending your money, you are essentially putting money in other people's pockets. This means that other people are profiting from the money that you spend. This doesn't really have much benefit to you and your future. Paying yourself first means that you think of your future before you think of putting money into other people's pockets. When you save, the money goes directly back into your pocket, and you get to grow your savings with any amount of money you have. Most savings accounts will allow you to earn interest, and this means that you can make extra money just by saving. It is always a good idea to look at the interest rate so you know how much your money is going to grow over time.

If you are saving in an account that grows with compound interest, you will be making a lot more money. Compound interest is the type of interest that you earn based on the amount in your account. This means that you can earn interest on top of interest. Let's say you deposit $100 into a compound interest savings or investment account. The interest you will earn is 5%. After the first month, you will have $105. The following month you will have $110.25. The next time your interest is compounded, you will have $115.51. This will keep growing, and eventually, you will start making a lot of money very quickly. The more time you let your money grow, the more money you will have in the end. This is why it is so important to save and invest as early as possible. You don't have to start with a huge amount of money. It's just important that you start somewhere.

This may sound like a great thing, but when you look at how compound interest increases your money, you might think a bit differently. In comparison to simple interest, if you deposited that $100,000 into an account earning 6% annually that uses compound interest, you would have $179,085 at the end of the 10 years. The difference in total earned is more than $20,000 just by compounding the interest. Let's look at the chart below to compare the growth over time.

	Simple Interest (6%)	Compound Interest (6%)
10 years	$160,000	$179,085
20 years	$220,000	$320,713
30 years	$280,000	$574,349
40 years	$340,000	$1,028,572
50 years	$400,000	$1,842,015

Do you see the power of compound interest? There is a massive difference in the amount you make through compound interest than through simple interest. Not only that, but time also works for you when you invest with compound interest. The longer you leave your money to grow, the faster it will increase. In the last ten years, between

40 and 50 years, the amount almost doubled! The sooner you start taking advantage of compound interest, the better it will be for you.

When you make saving a priority, it helps you to avoid getting into debt. Because you already have the money available, you don't have to borrow it from anyone else and can buy the things that you want or need. This helps you to be a lot more financially independent, and you don't have to rely on banks or get loans in order to purchase the things that are important to you. It is also a lot more satisfying when you work toward a goal you really want. Saving allows you to work toward your goals in a healthy and sustainable way.

The "Pay Yourself First" Principle

Acquiring wealth is no secret. It is practical and simple. However, it does take discipline, and it is a good habit.

The very first thing to begin to acquire wealth is to pay yourself 10% out of all your income. For example, if you receive $100 in income each week, you would put $10 in your savings drawer, and then you live off the $90 you have left. Eventually, your savings drawer will begin to get full. Imagine at the end of a year (52 weeks) you will have $520, 2 years $1,040 plus the interest that money is earning.

The odd thing, which I myself do not really understand, is that I continued to manage all my bills just as well with $90. When you first start saving 10%, it may seem difficult, and you might think you need that money for other things. However, in reality, you won't even miss it, and you'll still be able to handle your bills and expenses just fine. The great thing is, as time goes on, you'll notice your savings drawer filling up, which will make you happy, confident, and empowered.

It depends on you and what you desire the most. Do you desire instant gratification each day, such as; jewelry, clothes, more food, things that are quickly gone and forgotten, or do you have your sights on something more substantial, land or investments that provide income? The goal is to save enough money in order to put that money to work for you.

The concept described is known as the "Pay Yourself First" principle, and it's a powerful strategy for wealth accumulation. By setting aside a portion of your income (in this case, 10%) before spending on your expenses, you prioritize saving and building wealth. Do you think the money you earn is yours to keep? If you have a house or apartment, don't you have to pay for rent, food, and utilities?

The key is to prioritize yourself and your financial future by setting aside money first. By living on a little less and saving consistently, you'll start building wealth even if you get a weekly allowance. This approach teaches you how to manage your money wisely and make choices that bring long-term benefits and security. So, consider saving 10% of your income to unlock a brighter financial future for yourself.

Let's say you have been saving for 12 weeks now, and you just got paid your thirteenth payment of $100; you put $90 in your spending jar and $10 into your savings jar, which now has $130. Now you want to buy that new video game that costs $50. You still take the $50 from your spending jar, which leaves you $40 for other things. Meanwhile, your savings jar is still growing. Your good habits and discipline are evident.

By saving 10% consistently, you develop discipline and patience and learn to manage your money wisely. You'll find that you can still take care of your bills, buy things you need, and enjoy activities with your friends, with some sacrifices, all while building up your savings. It's like having the best of both worlds—enjoying the present and securing your future.

Remember, it's about making choices that align with what matters most to you. While it might be tempting to spend all your money on immediate wants, setting aside 10% helps you prioritize your long-term dreams and aspirations.

So, start small by saving a portion of your income each time you receive income. As your savings grow, you'll feel more confident and empowered about your financial future, knowing that you're taking steps toward building wealth.

Types of Savings Accounts and Investments

When you are getting into saving and investing, you will have tons of options. This might seem very overwhelming because you don't know which one to choose. This is why we are going to go through the different types of savings and investment accounts. There are many different types, and they suit different people. You definitely don't have to have all of them, but it's always good to do your research to make sure you're choosing the right one.

Traditional Savings Account

The first account is the most basic, and it's a traditional savings account. This is a great starting point if you haven't saved or invested before. It will help you to build up the habit and allow you to save for short-term goals. You will be able to open up a savings account with your bank, and this will be an account that is separate from your credit or checking account.

With a savings account, you will be able to earn some interest. This interest is usually not a high amount, so you shouldn't expect massive returns. You are usually allowed to make withdrawals from your savings account, but this might be limited, so check with your bank. A traditional savings account is a great way to save your money, but you also have access to it when you need it. When you need more money, transfer it from your savings to your checking account.

High-Yield Savings

A high-yield savings account basically works the same as a traditional savings account, but the interest you will be earning is higher. This means that your money will grow faster in this type of account. Because it is almost the same as a traditional savings account, you will not need a huge deposit in order to open the account. This means almost anyone can have a high-yield savings account, but not all banks offer this, so make sure you check before signing up.

MMA

This stands for Money Market Account. This may not be good for beginners because you need to have a specific amount of funds in order to put your money here. People who have large amounts of money that they want to keep safe can choose this account because it is insured for up to $250,000. This makes it a lot safer to save large sums of money and will give the investor some peace of mind. Not only that, but there is a higher interest rate with this type of account.

CDs

I'm not talking about how people in the early 2000s listened to music! A CD stands for Certificate of Deposit. If you have a very specific goal that you're trying to reach and you have a specific date you want to reach by, this is a great option. These types of accounts will pay you back with a higher interest rate because you are committing to leaving your money in the account for a specific amount of time. It is a great option if you have a financial goal in mind and you want to reach it in a few years. Just keep in mind whatever money you place in a CD, you will not have access to it for the length of its life. Most people use CDs for money they know they are not going to need. For example, you inherit $1,000 when you're in 6th grade; you don't need the money until you start college. You can put the money in an MMA or in a CD, depending on which one will give you the most interest.

Stocks

I've already mentioned stocks a bit earlier in the book, but let's dive into a bit more detail. When you buy an individual stock, you are buying a piece of a company. This makes you a partial owner, but because it is such a small piece, you do not have control over what happens in the company. There are large shareholders who do have control over the decisions made in the company, and these people will sit on the board. A company can choose to put its stock on the market so they are able to raise more funds to continue growing the business.

We call it the stock market because you can buy and sell your stocks in order to make a profit or to get what you want. The goal is to buy a stock at a cheaper price and then wait for the company to grow so you are able to sell your stock at a higher price. So, you buy it for less money and sell it for more. This is the most common way to make money from an individual stock. It is important to do your research when it comes to investing in stocks so you know whether or not it is a good company to put your money in. This is why stocks can be very risky, and you could lose all your money if you pick a losing company.

There is always going to be a risk when you are investing in the stock market because it can be difficult to predict how it's going to go. There are many different factors that come into play when discussing the price of stocks. Even if a company is really successful, the price of the stock could go down because the industry the company falls under is doing badly. Other reasons a stock might decrease in price is an economic issue or even if there is a change in the leadership of the company. As soon as people feel it's not safe to invest in a specific company, they will start pulling out their money, and this will cause the price of the stock to go down.

The stock market is a pretty volatile market, and this means the prices go up and down all the time. Throughout the day, the price of a specific stock could fluctuate hundreds of times. This is why many investors say it is best to purchase stocks and hold them. This means that you wait out any downturns and low prices because, eventually, the stock will increase in price again. In general, the stock market has always shown increases 70% of the time, and this is why it's a good investment, as long as you do your research. The stock market is like gambling, but unlike gambling, you are able to research the company you want to invest in to make a good decision.

Another way people can make money through the stock market is by investing in a stock that gives out dividends. When you invest in this type of stock, the owners will pay you a portion of the profit they make every few months. The amount you will get is usually reflected in the amount you invested in the company. Not all companies will give dividends for their stocks, so you should do your research and make sure you are investing in companies that you are comfortable with.

The great thing about the stock market is that you don't have to have a ton of money in order to start investing. There are stocks that are going for super cheap, so you can always start with what you have. Since stocks tend to increase in price over the years, the longer you hold out, the more money you will probably be making. However, it is important to diversify your portfolio. This means you have many different types of investments and stocks in your investment portfolio. This way, if one of the stocks were to take a dive, you would have many other investments that are making money for you. This is a very safe way to invest and definitely, one of the best if you know what you're doing.

Bonds

While the stock market can be quite volatile, and this does make it a risky investment, bonds tend to be a lot safer. When you take out a bond, you are essentially lending money to a company or government. They might need this money for a whole lot of reasons, and in return for the loan, they will pay you back interest on the loan. You have to agree to lock in the bond for a certain amount of time. This means you do not have access to the money you have invested until the time elapses. When the time is up, it is called the maturity date, and that's when you get back the original amount you invested, as well as all the interest you earned.

Even though bonds are safer than stocks, the interest rate is going to be smaller. One thing you do have to keep in mind when it comes to investments is that the more risk you are willing to take, the more potential rewards you will get from it. This doesn't mean you always have to make risky choices with your money, but many of the risky investments do give back a higher interest rate. There are strategies you can put in place to lower the amount of risk you will be facing. This includes diversifying your portfolio with both stocks and bonds. Since stocks are riskier and give you back more money, while bonds are safer, but the interest rate is lower, you can balance out your portfolio with both of these.

Investment Funds

Investing can be a tricky business, and sometimes people don't want to put all the time and effort into managing their investment portfolios. Investing in some sort of fund is a great way to invest and make sure you're getting the most out of your money. When you invest in a fund, you are essentially giving your money to someone else to manage for you. There will be a fund manager who chooses the investments based on your goals and the criteria you have given to them. They will then choose which investments are going to be best suited to you, and you just have to commit to paying the fee as well as the specific amount you want to be invested each month.

In most cases, a fund will give you back a good amount of money because there is a larger amount for the fund manager to play with. It's not just your money that's being invested, but a whole lot of other investors' as well. The fund manager will pool all of the money collected and make investment choices. There are many different funds out there, and they all have their benefits. It is always important to research what funds are available through your bank or other service providers. This way, you have a good idea of how much it's going to cost you and what's going to be best suited for you.

The most common types of funds are mutual funds, index funds, and exchange-traded funds. With a mutual fund, the fund manager will invest in a combination of stocks and bonds. They will diversify your portfolio based on your needs, age, and goals. An index fund works in a similar way, but it's not managed by a fund manager. This means that the fees you pay are going to be less because the fund is basically tracking a specific Index instead of investing individually. An exchange-traded fund or ETF also tracks popular indexes and tries to match the performance. These funds are sold on the stock market. This impacts the fees that you will be paying, and you can choose the amount you are willing to purchase them for. You basically make a profit from how well the overall market grows.

Retirement Plans

Retirement accounts are a great way to save for retirement. Most teenagers aren't really thinking about retirement, but the earlier you think about it and start investing, the more money you will have when you retire. The two most common retirement accounts are IRAs and 401(k)s.

An IRA stands for Individual Retirement Account. There are two types of IRAs, and these are traditional IRAs and Roth IRAs. The difference between both comes down to taxes. With a Roth IRA, you contribute funds on which you've already paid income taxes, commonly referred to as post-tax income. With a traditional IRA, you contribute money that has not yet been taxed, called pre-tax income, which can lower your taxable income level; the IRS gives tax deductions for contributions. Money then grows tax deferred until you take it out at age 59, and the tax will be higher.

A 401(k) is a great retirement account that can only be offered by an employer. This means that you won't be able to open up this type of account on your own. Your employer opens it for you and will also deposit money into this account for you. Some employers choose to match your contributions to the account. So, if you want to invest $200 into your 401(k), your employer will match this, and you won't end up investing $400 into your account each month. This means you can double your investment. Not all employees offer this, so make sure you read your contract to see if it is an option. If your employer does offer matching, you should try your best to max this out. Most employers will contribute up to a certain amount, and if you know what the limit is, you can essentially get as much of this "free money" as possible.

Real Estate

Investing in real estate means that you are investing in property. There are actually two ways to do this. The first one is traditional property investment, where you purchase a physical property, and the other one is called a Real Estate Investment Trust (REIT). We will dive more into this in a later chapter.

Tips and Tricks to Invest Wisely

Investing can be daunting because you are putting your money into a resource or assets and hoping that you'll get a good return on it. Investing with knowledge reduces the risk of losing or decreasing your capital. However, the rewards are worth it. Investing is mostly about forming good habits. By following these tips and tricks, you'll definitely see positive results.

Start With a Savings Account

Before you start investing in the stock market or anything fancy, you should start with a savings account. A savings account is going to really help you build the habit of putting money away for the future. It is also important that you have a good amount of money in your savings account before you start investing. Building an emergency fund should be one of your first financial goals.

Investing is a Long-Term Game

Most people want to invest so they can get rich quickly. I can't tell you how many people have tried to do this and ended up losing all the money. When you try to play games with investing, most of the time, you will lose out. Investing is a long-term thing. This means you will be putting money away in your investments and not doing anything with it until many years later. This is usually the best investment strategy because it takes the emotion out of it. If you see the stock market taking a dive and your investments are worth a lot less than you wanted, you might be tempted to pull out all your investments. In a few weeks, the stock market may pick up again, and your investments will be worth a lot more than what they are worth now. Because emotion took over, you have now lost out. This is why having a long-term mindset when it comes to investing is always the best way to go.

Always Do Your Research

Before you make any kind of investment, it is always a good idea to do your research. Understand the type of investment you are making as well as the companies you will be investing in. This is going to help you make smart choices. There are always going to be new investments that pop up, and you might want to give them a go. Taking some time to do some research can help you to think about things logically, and you can invest in something that you truly believe in.

Ask Your Parents to Help Open a Custodial Account

If you think you are ready to start investing in a retirement account, then why not ask your parents to open up a custodial IRA for you? You can open one even if you just have a short-time job because anyone who has an income can open one. This means you can start investing in your retirement from a very young age and will probably have a good amount of money when the time comes for you to retire. It is also a great way to get used to investing and seeing how your money grows over time.

In Real Life

Luke started getting interested in investing when he was about 13 years old. He was in a math class at school, and his teacher assigned a project to each one of them. Each student had to pick a specific stock on the stock market and write a report on how it performed over time. Most of the students picked very well-known brands, such as Starbucks and Apple, but not Luke. He decided he was going to pick a company that was founded in his hometown. He already knew a little bit about it and thought that it would grow over time.

He started becoming incredibly interested in investing. Even though this was just a project, he started watching how stocks performed in real life. By the time he was 17 years old, he had started trading fake stocks on a website online. This helps many investors to practice investing before they start using real money to invest. These websites just mimic the stock market, so you can play around and get used to investing in stocks. He actually got incredibly good at it, and his parents gave him some money to start investing for real. After about two years, he was able to triple the amount he had initially invested.

Many people believe that you cannot start investing until you are much older, but Luke is proof that you can. He now teaches other teenagers and even adults how to invest in the stock market. He practiced for so long, so he was fully prepared when he had real money to start investing. Even if you don't have any physical money to invest, why not open up a fake investing account online? These accounts allow you to pretend to invest and see how much you can profit from it. This way, when you get older and can invest with your own money, you already know how things work. You can already form a strategy from now and can hit the ground running as soon as possible.

You should never let your age be a barrier to what you can do. Teenagers who start early and think about their future tend to become a lot more successful. You have more time now to try things and see what works for you and what doesn't. This also applies to entrepreneurship and starting your own business. If this is something that you're interested in, you can start working on it starting now. You don't have to wait until you are an adult. That's exactly what we will be diving into in the next chapter.

4. Strategy 3—Exploring Entrepreneurship

Are you the type of person that dreams of doing something they are absolutely passionate about when they're older? Perhaps the thing you are passionate about or that you really want to do isn't even invented yet. Maybe you still want to follow your passions but know it's not going to be a high-paying job. Unless you are choosing a field that is high paying and in demand, you will always have a limit on how much money you can make. Building your own business is one of the best solutions for this.

Being an entrepreneur and starting up your own business is definitely not for everyone. It is a lot harder than working for a company, but the rewards are also greater if you can get it off the ground. If you are passionate about being your own boss and making your own decisions, then this could be a great path for you. This chapter is designed to help you understand what entrepreneurship is and to start thinking about whether it is the right fit for you or not.

What Exactly Is Entrepreneurship?

At the most basic level, entrepreneurship is being able to build and start up your own business. As the business grows and you put more work into it, it will start to make a profit for you and any partners you have. Some people decide to start a business all on their own, and others work as a group to get it off the ground. Depending on the type of business you want to start and who you have around will dictate whether or not you have partners at the beginning. You might find that other people want to join you in your business as it grows. This means you can start off solo but end up having partners along the way.

Becoming an entrepreneur is definitely a risk. You have to make sure your idea is something that other people want to buy into. Even if you think your idea is the best one ever, other people need to think the same otherwise, you're not going to make a profit. Successful entrepreneurs are people who find a problem and develop a solution for that problem. This could be a product or a service that helps people in a certain way. It doesn't have to be a brand-new innovation, but it does need to offer something that is not currently being offered. If you notice a problem in society, you can be the one that has the solution.

Being an entrepreneur also means a lot of work. Most small businesses end up failing because it takes a lot to get started. You have to remain committed, even when it is hard. The thing is that you never know when you're going to hit your lucky break. Most small business owners tend to bail a lot sooner than they should. This is why it's so important to be resilient when you are a business owner. This will help you persevere through any bad times so you can get the water at the end of it.

There are tons of positives that come with owning your own business. For one, you will be the one in charge, and that means you have a ton of flexibility. You can work whenever you want as long as you are able to do what is necessary for your business. This allows you to have full control over your life and your income. If you are able to run a successful business, you will be able to create more profit and income than if you worked a traditional job. Basically, your earning potential is going to be unlimited. Most people complain about their bosses or the culture of the company, and when you run your own business, you are the boss. You get to set the standard and can run it the way you want to.

With all of these positives, there are also some negative aspects that are important to take into consideration. Starting your own business isn't going to be free. You will need to put in some money in order to get it started. This is why a lot of business owners only start building up their businesses a little later in life. If you are planning to be an entrepreneur, it is a good idea to start planning now. You might need to get a traditional job for a few years so you can save up enough money to build your business. Another thing to take into consideration is that even though you have a lot of flexibility, you also will have to work a lot of hours. This is especially true at the beginning when you are just getting started. You might have to work through the night in order to get things ready and to plan.

When it's your own business, the responsibility is on you to make sure it is successful. If you have employees, they rely on you for their income. This means that you have to do your best for yourself and for the people that work for you. Businesses are always going through ups and downs when it comes to finances. Some months will bring in a whole lot of money, and others will be completely dry. It is your responsibility to make sure there are always finances in the business to pay for what is necessary. This kind of income fluctuation can stress out a lot of people, so it is important to make sure you can handle your finances properly before you start a business.

There are a lot of aspects coming into play when you want to start your own business. You need to be able to think about it clearly. It might be a good idea to talk to somebody who already runs their own business. Ask them questions about how they got to where they are now and tell them to give you a realistic idea of the work they put in. This is not to scare you but prepare you. When the time comes for you to start your own business, you want to have a clear vision of what it's going to take. This way you can actually create a plan that will work.

What Does a Successful Entrepreneur Look Like?

Being an entrepreneur is not a one size fits all thing. People of all shapes, sizes, and all backgrounds have been able to start successful businesses. It's not about how much money you have right now or how old you are. It is more about your character and the traits that you possess. Even though entrepreneurs look different, there are certain things that they all possess to help them become successful in any field.

If you don't have these skills right now, you don't have to panic. You can build them into yourself. Be honest and see whether or not these are skills you think you have or skills you can improve on. This will really help you when you start working toward your own business.

A Strong Leader

An entrepreneur is a leader. You will be providing a product or service to other people, and you will have other people working for you. Possessing good leadership skills is essential. When people think of a leader, a lot of people just think of someone who is bossy. Being bossy and being a leader are two completely different things.

A leader is somebody who builds up people and guides them to meet their goals and become successful. A true leader is somebody who cares about other people and wants them to be the best version of themselves. It's also somebody who's not afraid of making decisions and calling the shots. If you find other people always come to you to ask your opinion or for your help, then this is a good indication that you are a natural leader.

Self-Motivated

I think we all know somebody who will never do anything unless they are absolutely forced to. Sure, there's nothing wrong with a bit of encouragement every now and then, but an entrepreneur needs to be self-motivated. There isn't going to be somebody who is motivating you the whole way through. Sometimes it's going to be hard, and you need to tell yourself to do the work even when you don't want to. You need to be motivated by your goals and your passion for your future.

Not Afraid of Failure

You might not want to hear this, but being an entrepreneur means failure. I have not heard of a single business owner or entrepreneur that hasn't failed in their life. In fact, I haven't heard of a single adult who hasn't failed. Failure is a part of life, and it's an even bigger part of owning your own business. This can be very scary for people because nobody really enjoys failing. Can you imagine signing up for a race and expecting to come last? That sounds horrible, and you might think, "Why would you even sign up in the first place?" It is very counterintuitive for us as humans to do things when we know we're going to fail.

When you start a business, you shouldn't expect to fail, but you should be okay with it. Failure is not actually failure unless we give up. It's just a chance for you to learn something new and learn what not to do. The thing with failure is it can make us so scared to even try. This means we don't even give ourselves a chance. You never know what's going to work or what's not going to work unless you try. You will have to try quite a bit of different things when you have your own business. Some things will work, and others won't. What is most important is you get up and try again.

Innovation

Once you're able to start your own business, the work doesn't stop there. You are going to need to be a person who is always thinking of the next step. Think of huge companies like Microsoft and Apple. We know these companies because they are always innovating. This means they are always creating something new for their customers. Constant improvement in new products that are exciting makes everybody want to know what's going to happen next. They also improve the way they run the companies so they are more efficient. When you are innovative, you always think of new ideas and new ways to do things. This makes your business better and helps you to stay in front of your competition.

Being Okay With Not Knowing

For those of us that don't like asking for help, this is not going to be our favorite thing to hear. With anything in life, we are never going to know everything. This means we need to have other people around us who can help. These are people who we can ask hard questions and get advice from. It's okay to not know something if you are willing to go and ask for help when you need it. Ask for feedback and be willing to listen to what other people have to say. There might be something going on that you haven't even noticed yet. This is why it's so important to have the right people around you because it's going to help you see the bigger picture. Don't be afraid to start those hard discussions.

Good at Networking

This follows on from the previous point. You will find it very difficult to find an entrepreneur that has made it completely on their own. Everybody needs other people around them who will help them and support them. As your business grows, you will need connections, suppliers, people willing to fund you, and business partners. Have you noticed that businesspeople tend to go out on a lot of business lunches and dinners? It might seem very silly and like a waste of time, but during these lunches, they connect with other people and build relationships. This helps them in their businesses because when they need something, they have somebody to call.

Building up a network is essential even if you are an employee at a company. You can get advice and different perspectives from other people. Or you might just need support because you're going through a tough time with your business. Making sure you have the right network around you is essential.

Finding Your Passion

Finding your passion is a very important part of building the future you want. I'm sure you want to do something that gets you excited when you wake up in the morning. There are a few things that you can do to help you to find your passion, so let's talk about them.

Perspective

The first thing you need to do is believe that you can find something you're passionate about. There are so many different options out there in the world, and chances are you might be passionate about more than one thing. You might also find that you're passionate about something you've never thought of before. This is why it is important to have the perspective that there is good in the world and you will find your passion. If you walk into life with an open mind and optimistic attitude, it will be a lot easier.

What Do You Enjoy?

A passion is something that you actually enjoy doing and something that you care about. One of the easiest ways to find your passion is to look at the things you enjoy. Maybe you have a few hobbies or tasks that you really like to do. Perhaps there's a subject at school that you are really good at and look forward to. Looking at these things that bring you joy and excitement helps you in finding your passion.

Hobby vs. Passion

Even though there might be tons of things you really enjoy doing, not everything can be a job. For example, I love playing with puppies, but there isn't a huge market for a professional puppy petter. Going to the animal shelter and playing with puppies is a hobby because it's something I enjoy doing. However, I can't really turn that into a job that will bring in profit. I might be able to think of other ways to make a profit and still spend time with animals, or I could think of a way to work flexibly so that I can have more time to spend with animals. This way, it's not just a hobby, but I can turn it into a profitable passion. Make sure you draw a clear line between your passions and your hobbies.

It's actually a really good thing to have hobbies because it takes your mind off of work. It allows you to have fun and destress when needed. Every person needs a few hobbies in their life. If you are looking to turn a hobby into a full-time job, you might need to add a few skills to your arsenal to help you. For example, you might be an incredible artist who loves to paint and draw. It can be very difficult to become a world-renowned artist and get your art out there. There is no guarantee that it will be picked up and you can make a profit from it. However, there are plenty of ways to make money through art. For example, there are tons of people who have blogs and websites that need things designed for them. If you become a digital designer or illustrator, you can still be an artist and earn a good amount of money from it. You will just need to learn how to make art digitally and have some tech skills. This way, you can turn a hobby into a job and a business.

Break Down Your Fears

Even if you are incredibly passionate about something, there might always be a little voice at the back of your head that makes you want to back down. We all have this little voice that makes us second-guess ourselves and think that we may not be realistic. If you look at the stories of very famous entrepreneurs, you usually find that they went through their own seasons of doubt. People didn't believe they could be successful with the ideas they had, and if they let this drag them down, then we wouldn't have half the technology and products we have now.

If you ever feel scared to do something, it's actually a good thing. When you are scared or have a little bit of fear, it means that you are going to be doing something important and you are moving forward. It's just the uncertainty that is making the fear pop up and not the fact that you cannot do it. Take some time to think about where the fear comes from and whether or not it is actually legit. In most cases, it's not going to be something you should let hold you back.

Take the First Step

One of my best friends always loved to be prepared, and she loved to plan. When it came time to study for an exam or do a class project, she would have a list of everything she needed to do before she actually sat down and studied. If you walked into a room a few days before an exam, you would notice that it is completely clean and neat. Her desk was spotless, and all her study materials were laid out and filed incredibly neatly. She always said that she needed to plan before she got started. The problem was this was actually just a distraction. She didn't need to clean her entire room and make sure that everything was laid out perfectly. She was just procrastinating, so she didn't have to sit down and actually study.

We do that a lot in life. Instead of actually taking the action needed, we get stuck in the planning and preparing phase. If you want to start a business or make a job out of a hobby, you will need to take the first step. The first step is always going to be the hardest, but it is something you need to do. In all your planning, make sure you know what action you need to take and then do it. One of the best things you can do is set a deadline for yourself to take the first step. This makes it a commitment, and you are more likely to follow through.

Starting Your Own Business

Okay, so now we've gotten all of that out of the way, and you are looking to start up your own business. You don't have to wait until you are older to start a business. There are so many teenagers that have started businesses out of their homes, and this has set them up to be businesspeople when they are older. You can start a small business using a skill that you have already, so you know what it's like to handle money and run the operations of a business. You may not be doing this exact same thing when you graduate, but at least you have an idea of what it takes to run a business.

Write Down Your Ideas

The first thing you need to do is write down all your business ideas. You might be someone who has a ton of ideas. However, if you have way too many, it can be difficult to narrow it down. Having a list right in front of you will help you to weigh out the pros and cons so you can pick one to start with.

Think about what's going to be the easiest for you to start and what you think you will enjoy the most. Then you can choose that idea. If it doesn't work out, you can always go back to the list and pick another one.

Do Your Research

Once you have narrowed down your idea, it is time to start researching. See if there are any other businesses in your area that are doing something similar to you. Perhaps you want to start a dog walking business, then you would need to go online and find out if there aren't any dog walking businesses in your area. If there are none, this could either be a really good thing or a bad thing. Ask yourself why there are no dog-walking businesses in the area. Perhaps there aren't enough people who need someone to walk the dogs. If this is the case, then you are probably not going to be that successful. However, if there is a need but someone just hasn't started it up yet, then you might have hit a business gold mine.

Doing your research also helps you to understand your competition. It's not a bad thing to have competition, and you can actually learn from them. Look at how they market themselves on social media and on their websites. You can also look at the types of products and services they have so you can replicate this. It is usually easier to start a business when there is already a market for the product or service. Just make sure you can offer something slightly different that will make you stand out from the crowd.

Start Planning

Now, you will need to start planning. Your plan needs to include financial planning, as well as starting up the actual business. You might need some finances in order to get started, so you need to know how much. Think about how much you will need for marketing and for supplies. Try and be as realistic as possible with this. Once you know how much your product or service is going to cost you, you can then set the price you will be charging the customers. Make sure you are charging a competitive rate so you do not charge too little or way too much. You will also need to decide how long your product or service will take to make or develop. This way, when people order from you, you can give them an accurate waiting time.

Planning also includes looking at different suppliers so you can get the right prices. You will also need to do some research on your potential customers and see what they need. All of this should be written down on your business plan so you can easily find it. If you need to ask your parents or another adult for some money to help start up your business, you should know exactly how much you need and be able to tell them what your business is all about. This will make them a lot more likely to invest in your business.

Take Action

After all the planning is done, make sure you are willing to take action. Don't stay too long in the planning phase because then you might get stuck there. It is always best to take action as soon as possible so you can gain momentum.

In Real Life

Juliette was a 16-year-old girl, and she just wanted to hang out with other girls who were her age. She saw that there wasn't really a safe place online for girls around her age to just have fun and connect with each other. This is when she got the idea to start up a business called Miss O and Friends. She needed some help to finance the website since she was still in school and didn't really have any money. She asked her parents to help her out, and they were happy to fund the website.

She designed it and made sure that it was a good place for teen girls to connect with each other. The girls could talk about issues that were specific to the age group and get advice if they needed to. It is a great place to find new friends and to have some fun safely online. Her website launched in 2012 and just continued to grow. At one point, it had 10 million monthly visitors, which is absolutely crazy. The website and her business are valued at over $15 million. It's crazy to see how an idea can turn into a real business that benefits her and many other young girls.

Juliette decided she was not going to wait until she was older in order to make a difference and start a business. What was just an idea because she noticed there was a gap in the market became a multi-million dollar business. If you are willing to put in the work and try something new, then you could have a story similar to this. There are also many other ways you can make money. One of these ways is through real estate investing. We did touch on that a little bit in a previous chapter, but now we're going to dive in a bit deeper in the next chapter.

5. Strategy 4—Building Wealth through Real Estate Investing

 "90% of all millionaires become so through owning real estate."

— Andrew Carnegie

R eal estate is probably one of the most solid investment decisions anyone could make. However, as a teenager, you probably don't have enough money to invest in real estate right now. Don't worry, your time will come, and you will be able to invest in real estate at some point. In the meantime, it is a good idea to know what this type of investment looks like so you can be prepared for it. Since it is something that costs quite a bit of money, it is always a good idea to plan and prepare for it as early as possible. This way when you are older, you will be able to purchase a property and start investing as soon as possible.

Real Estate Investing and the Benefits

Real estate investing is when you purchase a property, or you invest in a property indirectly. Essentially real estate is all about physical property. This is one of the best investments out there because the price of housing and property tend to continuously grow over time. There are definitely some exceptions to the rule, but if you are able to do your research properly and purchase the right property, then you will set yourself up well.

The other great thing about investing in real estate is that you can do it in many different ways. You can make a passive income through real estate, or you can use it as a business. Even if you don't do anything with your property, you could likely make money from it. One of the most important things that you should consider is the location of the property. The location is what will determine the price at the end of the day. Some people only look at the physical property, but that is definitely a mistake. If you look at the price of property in a city, you'll see that it is usually a lot more expensive to live closer to the hustle and bustle than if you were to live on the outskirts. This is because the location in a city tends to be more in demand because it's easier to get around and there is a different lifestyle. There are even cases where you can get a house in one area and a one-bedroom apartment in another area for the same price. This is why research is key.

When you invest in real estate, you shouldn't expect the same returns as you would get if you invested in the stock market. The growth is definitely slower, but it is also more stable. The other thing that is important to understand about real estate is that it doesn't fluctuate the same way the stock market does. It is a lot steadier, and you will see a steady growth in your investment with very little chance of decline.

Another great thing about real estate is that you can leverage it. This is a fancy way of saying you can purchase an investment without actually using your own money. When you are buying a property, you will most likely need to get a loan or a mortgage in order to pay for it. You will need a sizable down payment, but depending on the type of property and your mortgage broker, you can get one as low as a 3% down payment. This means you only have to pay 3% of the total price of the property upfront. The rest of the money will be paid through the mortgage. If you want to rent out the property, then your tenants will be paying for the mortgage. You will charge the tenant a specific amount of money to stay in the property and can use that money to pay toward the mortgage. This means that you are not using any of your own money for the investment but will benefit from having a solid investment and a property. There are also some tax benefits to owning a property which is also a huge plus.

When the mortgage is completely paid off, you now have a property that you can use as a form of passive income. Some people decide to rent out their property long-term, which means the tenants will be living there for years on end. If someone is living in your property for multiple years, you'll be getting paid for that, and you really don't have to do anything. You will be a landlord, so you will need to take care of the property within reason. However, most long-term tenants will handle things on their own. You just need to make sure you have a solid contract in place so everyone knows what their responsibilities are when it comes to the property.

The Different Types

Understanding the different types of property and real estate investments you can make is essential. Not everything is going to work for every person. You don't want to get caught up in an investment that is unsustainable for you and that is simply not going to work. When it comes to real estate, it's always important that you do your research as much as possible. Since this is quite a big investment, you can't just wing it.

REIT

A real estate investment trust is a great way to start investing in property without having to actually buy a property. It is quite similar to a mutual fund since many investors will pool all the money together, and this money will be used to invest in real estate. This means you can get involved in real estate investing at a much lower price, but your return on the investment will probably be smaller. The other benefit of doing this is that you don't actually have to take care of or manage a property which can be a lot of work.

Crowdfunding

Another way to invest in property without actually owning the property is through crowdfunding platforms. These can work similarly to REITs. The difference is that these are not bought and sold on the stock exchange markets. Essentially a property will be put up on the platform, and anyone who is willing to invest will invest a certain amount of money. This will allow an individual to purchase the property, and the profits through rental income or any other kind of property activity will be shared amongst everyone who invested.

Residential Real Estate

Residential real estate just means that it is a property where people live. Your house or apartment is a residential property. An investor can make money through residential property by buying it and renting it out to tenants or house flipping. House flipping is when someone purchases a property, usually at a lower price, and then renovates it to sell it at a higher price. This type of real estate investment makes money quite quickly, but it is essential to do your research prior since you need to make sure people will be willing to buy a property in that area for the price you are looking to sell it for. You can also make money through residential real estate by simply buying the property and waiting a few years to sell it for a profit. If you live in a house or an apartment, this is typically what people do.

Commercial Real Estate

Property that is used by businesses is called commercial real estate. This can be anything from an office building to a mall. The owner of commercial real estate will rent out rooms, areas, or the entire building to a business, and this is how they would make money. Other examples of commercial real estate are warehouses, restaurants, or factories. These are quite expensive to start investing in since the properties are much larger, but the profit is also larger because business owners will pay more for rent. Businesses also tend to stay much longer, so it is a steady form of income.

Land

It is also possible to buy raw land that doesn't have anything built on it. This isn't a good investment opportunity for a beginner because there is a ton of research that needs to go into it to make sure the land is good to build on and the location is something that will possibly be in demand in the future. An investor looking to invest in land needs to know the ins and outs of the regulations and building codes as well as the environmental impact that will go into building. This can get very technical, so if it is your first investment, it is probably not a good idea to dip your toe into raw land. This might be a future goal when you are more solid in your knowledge of real estate investment.

A Few Tips and Tricks

There are a few small things you can do when it comes to real estate investing that will make a huge difference. If you do these things, you will be able to make smarter decisions when it comes to real estate, and you will probably be able to make a lot more profit.

Look Into Location

One of the most important things you can look out for when you are investing in real estate is the location. This is actually more important than the actual property you are buying. You will need to understand the location you are purchasing a property so that you can be sure it is a good buy.

But what makes a good location? It is going to take a lot of research to be sure that the neighborhood you want to purchase in will be profitable. Firstly, you will need to look at what is available in that neighborhood. A neighborhood that has a high population density, which means there are lots of people living in the area, is a good place to start. Areas that are quite desolate and don't have a lot of people typically won't have high property values. Another thing to look out for is whether or not the neighborhood is developing. If there is new construction taking place in and around town, you know there are people investing in it. Look out for amenities such as shopping centers, hospitals, and other things that will take care of people's needs.

The next thing you can look into are things such as the crime rate. Areas with a high crime rate will be cheaper because it is more dangerous to live there. Easy access to public transportation and being able to walk around easily and safely are also good things to keep an eye out for. A family-friendly area that has good school options as well as parks and other leisure activities also increase the price of a property in the area.

Buy at Low Prices

There are going to be times when property is priced lower than normal. When you are buying property for profit and not just to live in, it is important to look out for these moments. There are many reasons property might be selling for less. This includes when the economy is taking a dip. Times like these lead people to sell their properties because they want to downsize. For example, in a recession, people naturally have less money. They might not be able to afford a larger house, so they decide they want to sell it for something cheaper. Since they know they are in a recession and they want to sell their property quickly, they will put the house up for sale at a cheaper rate. You can end up saving a ton of money by looking for opportunities like this. The lower you are able to buy, the more profit you will make from your property.

Know All the Costs

The price of a property is not just the amount you will be paying when you first buy it. There are lots of other costs that come into play. A property needs to be maintained, and this costs money. You will need to consider paying things like utilities and property tax. Utilities include things like electricity, trash, pick up, and water. If your property is part of a homeowners association, you would need to pay a fee to them as well. A homeowners association takes care of things in the neighborhood and makes sure the neighborhood runs smoothly, and everybody is playing their part.

Increase the Value

There are tons of things you can do to increase the value of your property without spending a whole bunch of money. Many people make the mistake of selling it as is, and then they miss out on a large chunk of profit. For example, simply giving the house a fresh coat of paint can do wonders for it. It will look brand new, and you can probably sell it or rent it out for more because of this.

It is always a good idea to be on the lookout for what people want in a place to stay. This will help you to add value to your property easily. Perhaps you could add a cleaning service or even a security guard or concierge to your property. This works if you have multiple properties. You could always charge a little bit more on your rental fees because you're adding value through these services. It makes your property look a lot more attractive, and people are willing to pay more for these small conveniences.

Understand the Rules

Every area, country, and state has its own rules and regulations in place when it comes to real estate. If you are not aware of them, then you could be at risk of making a huge mistake down the line. Rather than putting yourself in this horrible situation, you should do your research to make sure you are aware of all the rules and regulations in your area.

Be aware of things like zoning laws because this can stop you from building an additional room on your property or a second-story floor. You might think it's a good idea to place vending machines around your property or even provide meals to your guests or tenants. However, there are some places that prohibit food services or are very strict when it comes to this. You could end up getting sued or taken to court because you didn't follow the food service rules. You might be allowed to do these things if you get a permit, but there is work and costs involved with getting a permit. Understand all of these little facts before you get started in renovating or adding value to your property.

Quick Facts

REITs can help you get involved with real estate with very little money. It is a great first step!	Leveraging real estate means buying real estate with someone else's money. You can do this by renting out a bought property and using the rent to pay off the mortgage.
You can find the type of real estate investing that works for you at different stages of your life.	Small things can increase the value of a house by a large amount.
Always think of location first.	The rules and laws surrounding property are different based on area and location. Always do your research before buying.

6. Strategy 5—Developing a Positive Money Mindset

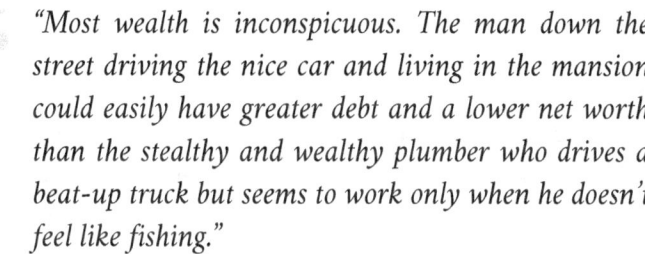

"Most wealth is inconspicuous. The man down the street driving the nice car and living in the mansion could easily have greater debt and a lower net worth than the stealthy and wealthy plumber who drives a beat-up truck but seems to work only when he doesn't feel like fishing."

— Loral Langemeier

The Importance of the Money Mindset

Mindset is one of the most important things when it comes to money. This may sound really strange because it seems like actual money should be the most important thing when it comes to... well, money. The thing with money is that it is just a tool that we use to get what we really want. If money did not buy anything, then we would not care about it. It would just be random pieces of paper with old guys' faces on it!

Let's look at it this way. Do you have a dad or uncle who has a toolbox or tool shed? There are probably hammers, scissors, nails, screwdrivers, and a few more things in there. Do you think those adults would still have those things if these things didn't serve a purpose or if they didn't help them with stuff around the house? Probably not. Even the coolest tool would have no value if it wasn't useful. People like to have these tools because they need them for the end goal. It is important for someone to hang up a photo frame with precious memories in it. In order to do that, they need a hammer and nails. It is important to install a bookshelf for your favorite books, so you would need a drill, screws, and a screwdriver. The importance of the tool is in how you use it and not in the tool itself.

When you start looking at money in this way, you don't have to be so obsessed with getting more money because it is not the most important thing. The important thing is what the money can do for you and how you can use it in your life. This is a healthier way to look at money. This is a good start for a money mindset, but it is not the end. You also have to think of things positively and abundantly. This means throwing out any belief that is limiting you. If you get hung up on money and don't believe there is anything you can do to increase your wealth, then that is what is going to be true for you. People usually follow in the footsteps of their thoughts. The more positive you are, the more opportunities you will find in your life.

When you feel like what you have will never be enough, it leads to some bad money habits. You might want to hoard all your money and never spend it because you are scared to waste it. Or you might go to the other end of the spectrum where you spend all your money when you get it because you just want to enjoy it while you can. Both are bad ways to handle money, and there needs to be a better balance.

Don't Let the Myths Get To You

When there are negative money mindsets; there are also myths that pop up. These are things that can really hold you back. If you are able to identify the myth, then you can avoid it. The first and biggest myth that surrounds money is that you are simply not enough unless you have enough. Money can quickly become an identity, and people can only see their worth based on how much they have in the bank. This actually plays on something called a scarcity mindset, where you think you don't have enough and you urgently need to take action to make it. This leads to making so many bad decisions because you don't allow yourself the time to think about it, and you can actually get caught up in scams that promote getting rich quickly.

The next myth is, "Everything is exactly how it seems." Now that we live in a social media world, it can be easy to get distracted by what is happening online. We see people living the good life. Just because these people look like they're living the dream and appear wealthy does not mean they are. There isn't a lot of transparency when it comes to social media, so you could be comparing yourself to something that is completely false or unrealistic. Don't get in the habit of envying what other people have.

Another big myth that surrounds money is that things can change in a matter of weeks or months. Everybody wants their life to change with the snap of a finger, but the truth is this hardly ever happens. If you want your money and your finances to change, it's going to take planning and time in order to start seeing results. If anyone tells you that you can make a whole lot of money in a few weeks, then they are probably lying to you. Look, I'm not saying that it's impossible to make large amounts of money in a short amount of time, but this is highly unlikely. It is better to live with realistic standards, so you don't feel like you've been cheated if it doesn't work out the way you thought.

Don't Let Your Money Beliefs Limit You

What you believe about money can come from so many different places. Some people see how their parents or other adults in their life handle the money, and this filters down to them. Someone who has parents who are very frugal and don't spend money will probably be similar to that. However, this is not always the case because it can go in the opposite direction. If your parents are very strict with money and don't spend it on any luxuries, you might feel like you want a different life when you're older. This might cause you to overspend and just buy luxuries without thinking about it. It is important to understand where your beliefs about money come from so you can get to the root of the problem if there's one.

With a little bit of planning and thinking about things clearly, you can change the way you think about money. If you start framing things in a more positive light, you'll see more opportunities, and it will be easier to look at money from a healthier perspective. For example, a lot of people believe that the only way they can make a lot of money and be financially secure is to get a corporate desk job. This could definitely be true for some people, but it is not the overarching rule. Having this kind of mindset can stop you from pursuing your dreams and maybe even stop you from starting your own business.

At the end of the day, your money mindset should be flexible. There are tons of ways you can make money and reach your dreams. If you're able to look at things realistically but also positively, that is going to be key. You are able to do something you love and make money if you have a plan in place for it. People do it all the time. You just need to know how. I would go so far as to say that people who love what they do tend to make more money because they don't have to force themselves to do something they do not like.

Another huge mindset problem I've seen recently is that people believe that money is evil. Money is not evil, and it's not good either. It is just a neutral thing. It is how you use it and how you think about it that makes it either good or bad. Thinking that money is something bad or evil can lead you to completely avoid it. And while money can't actually buy happiness, it can bring happiness into your life. You are able to use money for good and for things that will improve your life. Money might not be the be all and end all but it definitely has some value. If you grew up believing that money is the root of all evil and look down on people who do have money, it is a good idea to start changing this belief. This is something that's really going to limit you as you grow up because it's training you to run away from money instead of training you how to use money for your own benefit.

Another limiting mindset is that where you are is where you will always be. If you grew up in a family that isn't rich or you don't have a lot of money to start off with, it can be so easy to believe that this is just how your life played out. Some of the richest people in life are ones that are self-made. This means that they didn't need their parents' money in order to become wealthy and increase their standard of living. They decided to do it on their own, and you can too. You don't necessarily need money in order to make more money. If you have an idea and are willing to put in the work, then you can go very far. Where you are now, it's just the starting point, and as you take steps in order to build wealth and become a more successful person, you will see the money rolling in afterward.

Every person deserves to have enough money to live the life that they want. The good news is that this is possible for all of us. If you remember that money is just a tool, you will look for ways to use it in a way that's going to be beneficial for you. It's not something that's scary; it's not something that's going to hold you back or make you into an evil person. Money is just a thing, and you can choose how you want to use it.

Creating a Positive Mindset About Money

Now that we have talked about a negative money mindset and what it can do, we also want to dive into creating a more positive money mindset. This is so important, and it's something that you are probably going to need to do throughout your life. Negative mindsets and thoughts can always creep in, so it is important to check yourself every now and then.

Move Forward From the Past

At this point in your life, you might not have made too many financial mistakes, but as you grow up, you'll probably make at least a few. Mistakes are how we learn, and in most cases, it is pretty much inevitable. We end up doing things based on emotion or because we got some bad information. Even if you have made a few bad choices with your money, it is time to forgive yourself. If you are resentful about the decisions you have made in the past, it's going to make it very difficult to trust yourself to make better choices in the future. Rather than being mad about the mistakes you've made, be thankful that you have learned from them. Now you are a better person and can avoid those mistakes in the future.

Have a Plan

Having a plan for your money is essential to being able to use it effectively. We usually call this plan financial goals and a budget. You first set your financial goals so you know what is important to you, and then you work it into your budget so you have a step-by-step plan to get there. This will help you to see yourself progressing, so even if you aren't reaching your goals as fast as you would like, you can see that there is progress happening. Simply moving toward a goal can make you a lot happier, and you'll feel a lot more secure in your finances.

Make Room In Your Budget For Enjoyment

It is all well and good to have a budget that is filled with important life goals, but you also have to have some enjoyment in your life too. A lot of financial gurus tell people they have to cut out everything unnecessary from their life so they can save for things that are important to them. It is important to think about your financial goals and what is important to you, but it's also important for you to be happy right now. If you are only thinking about the future, then you are going to have a miserable time in the present. You will never be able to go back and live this day again, so you need to make sure that you are balancing your future and your present.

There are some things in your life that other people might think are unnecessary but that actually bring enjoyment to you. For some people having a gym membership is not worth it because they don't use it and prefer to take a jog outside. However, you might be the type of person that loves going to the gym, and it really adds something to your life. Even though you have to pay for a gym membership, if it makes you happy, then do it. This is something important to you, and it is benefiting you as well. Maybe you are someone who really enjoys going out to a fancy dinner every once in a while. Sure, cooking at home definitely will save you some money, but it's probably not going to fulfill you in the same way. Instead of cutting out the fancy dinners completely, you can commit to doing it once a month and set a specific budget for how much you are willing to spend. This way, you have the thing that you enjoy doing, and you don't have to cut it out completely. This will actually make it a lot easier to reach other financial goals because you're not going to feel like you're always in some sort of lack.

Always Be Thankful

Gratitude is one of the most important things that we can all implement in our life. I remember social media went through a huge moment when everybody was talking about gratitude and writing gratitude journals. This is when people would write out things they are grateful for every morning and evening. It seems like this practice has fallen out of popularity, but it doesn't mean that it isn't something good to follow. There are tons of benefits to practicing gratitude.

When you are grateful for the things you have now, you don't feel like you have to keep getting more or have to pretend. At the end of the day, where you are now is based on the decisions you made in the past. While you might've made some mistakes, you have also grown and become a better person. Being grateful for the things you have now allows you to look at your life from a more positive perspective. You won't feel like you always need the next best thing because you know that your life is already amazing.

If you struggle with staying grateful, why not pick up the habit of a gratitude journal? It's usually better to do this in the morning because you can set your mind to gratitude from the beginning of the day. All you have to do is write out two or three things that you are grateful for that day. You will quickly realize that there are a lot more positive things in your life than you might have thought.

Take It Step By Step

Now is the time when you can create a plan for yourself to create a more positive money mindset. Below is a checklist of things that you can do. However, you can feel free to change it up however you want, based on your own personality and needs.

- Identify any money myths you have believed.
- Think about how your parents view money and how that has impacted you.
- Write out a counter statement for all the myths and beliefs you had in the past. Make sure it is positive.

- Forgive any money mistakes you have made in the past.
- Track your financial goals so you can see how far you have come.
- Allow yourself to enjoy your money every now and then.
- Be grateful for where you are and what you have.

7. Strategy 6—Navigating Financial Challenges and Pitfalls

W hen I was younger, there was this video game where the character was in a jungle. The goal was to get to the finish line by avoiding pitfalls or holes in the ground. There were also some jungle animals that used to chase you, so you had to be quick. The first few levels were pretty easy, as you just had to jump over the holes that were clearly visible. As you got onto the harder levels, you had to be a lot quicker, and the holes were larger. Not only that but some of them were hidden. This meant that I could never finish the higher levels in one go. I had to keep starting back from certain checkpoints and trying again. After some planning and practice, I would move on to the next level until I eventually won the game.

This is actually pretty similar to the pitfalls we have when it comes to money. Some of the traps or holes that we can fall into are very easily avoidable. We can see them from a distance because they are so small. It's easier for us to hop over them and completely avoid them. Then there are others that are much bigger and well hidden. It makes it a lot harder for us to avoid these things, and sometimes we get caught. Even if we have the best financial plan set out in front of us, we can still make a few mistakes. This might sound very discouraging, but the truth is that mistakes help us to learn. It is a good idea to avoid as many mistakes and pitfalls as possible, but if you do land up in one, it's okay. Just make sure you have a plan to move forward, and that you have taken the time to learn from this mistake.

In this chapter, we are going to go through a few financial mistakes that teenagers typically make. We will also talk about how you can avoid them if possible. This is going to set you up for your future and allow you to be in a good financial position when you are managing your own money and handling your own finances.

Teenage Financial Challenges

As a teenager, you probably have a lot of adults in your life thinking that you don't have any financial challenges. Anyone of any age can have a financial struggle or financial challenge that they have to overcome. This is very normal, and even though it might not be as stressful as what an adult would go through, this is still your story and your challenge. Understanding what challenges you go through financially can actually help you when you are an adult. You'll be able to deal with your financial problems a lot better because you've learned how to deal with smaller issues already.

Never Having Enough Money!

Ugh, feeling like you never have enough money is the worst! There might be tons of things that you want to buy, but you just don't have enough money. This can make you feel like you are an outsider because everyone else around you is going to all these fancy places and buying all these cool things. It can make you feel like you are just not in with the popular crowd or that you are worth less than them. Let's add social media into it, and this can make it even worse.

It is important to realize that just because other people have more money and they are able to do more doesn't mean that you are less than them. Let me tell you something about life. There are going to be points in life when people have more money and others when they have less. There is probably going to be a point in your life when you have more money or more opportunities than the people you are looking at right now.

Spending More Than You Have

When you are a teenager, it is so easy to spend more money than what you are actually making. This is because you can always go to your parents and many parents are willing to give you a little extra if you need it. This can be a really bad habit because you are teaching yourself not to follow a budget or plan. Instead, whenever you need something, you are getting money from somewhere else, and when you are older, it's not going to be your parents. This is teaching you how to be in debt. If you notice you are doing this, it is time to create a budget and only spend the amount that you are actually making.

Trying To Keep Up With Friends

Have you ever watched the TV show *Keeping Up With the Kardashians*? It is an incredibly popular show, and most people have heard about this family. The reason the show has this name is that the Kardashians are incredibly wealthy, and they live the lifestyle that many people want to live. They have tons of houses and are always going on these expensive vacations and wearing the most expensive clothes. It makes people want to live the exact same lifestyle or aspire to it at some point in their life.

We can also do this when it comes to our friends and the people that are around us. We can look at all the things they have in the types of lifestyles they are living and want that as well. This makes us compare our lives to the lives of other people, and then we are unhappy. The thing is that most of these things are just trends. You can ask your parents or any other adults, and they will tell you the things that they used to do and, like when they were younger, they don't really do or have anymore. As the trends change, so do they. It's just something temporary, so trying to live your life up to a certain standard isn't really beneficial to you. If you want to buy all the coolest clothes and technology in a few months or years, it's not going to mean anything. This means there's no point in trying to compare yourself now to what your friends have or what they are doing. It's not really going to have any long-term benefit for you, and you'll be a lot happier if you just lived your life within your means now.

Not Wanting to Work

Learning the value of money is incredibly important when you are younger. If you don't work for your money, it can be easy to think that money really does grow on trees. You won't be motivated to budget properly and create financial goals if there is no value being placed on money. If you can quickly run to your parents and get money whenever you want, you aren't really learning how to manage it properly.

This isn't completely your fault, but you do have the power to change it. If you have an honest conversation with your parents and let them know that you want to learn how to be more responsible with money, they might be willing to change the way they handle money with you. This might be a big change for you, but it's definitely going to help you in the long run. Let them know that you want to learn how to budget and manage your money properly and that you want to know the value of what you get. Some parents love to spoil their children, and it comes from a good place. This is definitely not a bad thing but work with your parents so you can be set up for success when you are ready to handle your own finances. This means setting boundaries on how much your parents give you and when they give you money.

Other People Always Paying For You or Vice Versa

Peer pressure is a normal thing that most teenagers go through. If you are around the age of 14 or 15, this is when it peaks. By the time you are a little bit older, usually after high school, you won't feel it as bad. However, during this peer pressure stage of your life, money can cause problems for you. If you look at the things that your friends have, you might also want those things. Your friends might be going out all the time, and you also want to join them. If you don't have the money, then your friends might offer to pay for you all the time. Or perhaps you have some friends that don't have money, and you are the one paying for them all the time.

If this happens once in a while, it might not be a big deal, but if it's a pattern, then it's something you need to watch out for. Being on the receiving end of this can lead you down a debt or credit cycle when you are older. You are not learning how to use your own money, and even though other people are being generous toward you, it's difficult for you to learn financial responsibility this way. On the other hand, you might be the one with a lot of money and want to pay for other people. This is definitely fine once in a while, but if you are always doing it, then you become the provider for these other people. It's easy for people to take advantage of those who are generous. This is why it is important to manage your money properly so that you are not taken advantage of in any way.

Parents' Money Problems

It is so common for teenagers to be worried about their parents' financial situations. If your parents aren't the wealthiest, you can start getting nervous about whether or not you can afford certain things. You might notice that your parents are being a little more frugal with how they spend their money, or that they aren't buying the types of things they used to. In this case, it is always a good idea to have an honest conversation with your parents.

Parents don't like to burden their children with financial issues, and that might be the case here. Even though your parents are trying to protect you, if you are feeling stressed out by the financial changes that are happening, then it's not doing you any good. Showing your parents that you are old enough and mature enough to understand finances and what they are going through is going to help them be more honest with you. This will also help you to navigate the financial situation a bit better. You will be a lot more understanding if your parents cannot afford certain things, and you might look for ways to save and make more money to help out. This helps you to be a lot more responsible, and it might also take a bit of pressure off your parents.

Credit and Debt

As you get closer to the point in life where you are going to be more financially independent, it is important to understand credit and debt. Now we have touched briefly on these two topics, but it is important to dive slightly deeper, so you have a better understanding of what it is. Sometimes people think they have to avoid these two things completely. Otherwise, their finances are going to be ruined. However, this is not actually the case. Just like money, these two things can be tools and can be used in a positive way. Most people just don't know how to use it and end up getting themselves into trouble.

Let's first talk about how credit actually works. When we talk about credit, it's not just about your credit card. If you think about the word credit, it is used in many other contexts. Like when we say, give credit where credit is due. This saying means that we need to acknowledge the good that someone else has done. A credit statement or credit report can do the same thing. It shows lenders that you are able to take out a loan or borrow money and are good for it. When people look at your credit report, they are looking to see whether or not you are responsible with your money and can handle borrowing more.

Debt and credit are different because the definitions and what they can do for you are not the same. Credit gives you the ability to purchase something you don't have the money for right now. You can think of this as future purchasing power. You can choose whether you are going to use it or not. When you have a credit card, you will be given a specific limit on the credit card, and it's up to you to decide whether you want to use it or just leave it as is. If you do use your credit card, then it will form part of the debt. Debt is when you owe someone money. You would have agreed to pay back a certain amount at a certain interest rate and will need to make sure you are in good standing. Otherwise, this can impact your credit score and other aspects of your finances.

In life, you're probably not going to be able to afford everything in cash. If you plan on purchasing a property or another large investment or item, you might need to take out a loan or use a credit card. In order to do this, you need to receive a loan from someone who trusts that you can pay it back. This is why having a good credit score is so important. There are lots of things that are used to create a credit report. In order to check out your credit score, you will need to have an account that offers credit. This will need to be up and running for around six months, and then your credit score will be calculated. This is also known as the FICO score. You will get a number between 300 and 850. There are some calculators at work that are slightly different, but this is the standard. The higher your credit score, the better for you. It means that you will be more likely to be offered financial assistance, loans, and higher credit.

It is so important to start building your credit as young as possible so there are no hiccups when you are older and want to purchase something. Your credit score is worked out in terms of how well you've handled your debt, the types of debt you have, the length of time you've had it, and how long you have been building your credit. You might be wondering how you can start building your credit at such a young age because you don't have access to a credit card. This confuses many teenagers, and I totally understand that. The good news is there are things you can do to help build your credit even at a younger age. One of these things is to be added as an authorized user on an adult's credit card. Your parents can do this for you, so make sure to have an open and honest conversation with them. When you choose someone, make sure that this person has good credit; otherwise, it could affect you negatively.

Avoid the Pitfalls

While there are definitely situations where you will need to use credit or take out a loan, this shouldn't be all the time. If you decide to use your credit card and spend all over the place, then you'll end up in a financial pitfall. Most people don't even see it coming, and that's how they land up in a big problem. Debt can creep up on you, so it is important to make sure you're making good financial decisions as often as possible.

Know Your Due Dates

When you get older, you'll have to pay bills. These are what you owe specific companies because you are using their services. For example, you might have to pay for Wi-Fi or a cell phone contract. Your rent, electricity, other utilities, contracts, and subscriptions will all fall under this. Most of them will have a specific due date, and you will need to pay it before or on the due date. If you miss the due date, then your service will be suspended until you are able to pay. This could also impact your credit score because now you are in debt.

To avoid this, you need to know exactly when your due dates are and make it obvious. Putting it on your calendar app on your phone is very helpful. When the due date is closing in, you will get a reminder, and you can make payment. Another great option is to call all your service providers and ask if you can change the due date to a specific one. You can choose the day after you get paid so you can pay all of your bills at one time. This will make it a lot easier for you. Another option is to set up automatic payments so the money goes out of your account without you having to do anything. You just have to make sure there is enough money in your bank account for the automatic payment to clear.

Have Your Credit in Your Budget

We've already discussed how it is important to use credit but you do have to use it wisely. This means it's always best to plan for using your credit. The main goal for your month-to-month spending should be to use credit only to build up your credit score. You should not be using it to actually purchase unnecessary items. Remember, when we were talking about budgeting, you have to only spend the amount of money you make.

A good way to use credit is to have a look at your monthly spending. You'll probably have a specific amount allocated to things like your groceries or your gas. You can use your credit card to pay for these things and set aside that amount in your budget. At the end of the month, you will pay back the money you spent, so you do not have to go into debt. This way, you are still using your credit card, but you aren't putting yourself in a bad financial position.

When you do have a credit card, it is so easy to just swipe when you want something. It doesn't have any repercussions right now, so it's easy to just not think about it. However, you can get yourself into a huge amount of financial stress if you do not keep track of your credit card and spending. If you know that you cannot control your spending when it comes to your credit card, it might be best to just leave it at home. This way you can just use your debit card for your regular spending and you know there's going to be a limit to it. You can take your credit card out when you want to purchase something specific.

Save First

Saving for the things you want is so important. Instead of quickly swiping and putting things on your credit card, take some time to save for the item. This can be easily put into your budget so you can prioritize it. This will also allow you time to think about whether you actually want the item or not. Sometimes we can impulse buy items that look cool, but we don't actually need them.

Avoid Overextending Yourself

If you can't do something or can't afford something; it is totally fine to say so. Speak up and let your friends and family know that whatever is happening is something that you cannot afford. I know it can be so difficult to say no to people, especially when you actually want to do that thing or spend your money. It's just not going to be good for your finances right now.

Learning how to say no to other people is very important when you are working on your financial health. If you have already spent your entertainment budget for the month and your friends say they want to go watch a movie, you know that you don't have the money for it. Sometimes it's not a case of saying absolutely no. You can make another suggestion. Suggest doing something cheaper so that you can afford to hang out with your friends or you can ask if they can move the movie date to the next month. This way you are still able to do things but you are working within your budget.

Whoops, I Messed Up! Now What?

Even somebody who is amazing at managing their finances will probably make a mistake once or twice. Unfortunately, this is just something that we all get ourselves into, but the first step is always acknowledging that there was a mistake made. If you are aware that you overspent or you got yourself into debt that you didn't mean to, then at least you can start working on a plan. If you're in denial, it's going to be very difficult to get out of the mistake, and you'll probably end up worse off.

Once you know that you have made a mistake, it's time to assess the damage. This is going to look different, depending on the type of mistake you made. If it is overspending on your credit card, then have a look at how much you owe in total. At this point, you can feel very disheartened but don't allow yourself to get too stressed out about it. Almost any situation can be fixed if you have the right plan. Accept the situation that you are in for now, and then start looking at different options to get out of the problem.

In the example of overspending on your credit card, you can start thinking about paying it back. You will need to pay back more than what you would regularly pay back so you can finish paying off the debt completely. This means that you will have to look at your budget and see where you can cut back so you can put more money into paying off the credit card. Depending on how much you spend, this could be a long-term thing or something that can be fixed in a few months.

Regardless of the type of mistake you have made, it is so important to make clear goals for yourself. Know exactly how much money you need to put into your goals every month and put measures in place so you can actually reach them. This will help you to prioritize the things that are most important so you can recover as soon as possible.

In some cases, you might not be able to do it on your own, and you might need to talk to somebody about it. It is usually best to talk to somebody who is good with their finances or maybe you need to get in touch with a professional. This way, you can find a solution quicker, and you will have someone to be accountable to. In some cases, you might have to completely freeze your spending and stop buying things that are unnecessary. Certain mistakes take drastic measures, like saying no to something you really want but is not a necessity. Remember to add everything to your budget so you can look at your finances from a broader perspective.

It's also important to understand that not all mistakes can be fixed in a matter of weeks. Sometimes you will have to spend a few months or even years working on it. That is okay as long as you are tracking your progress; you will eventually get there. Thinking that you can solve the problem as soon as possible can actually leave you feeling very disheartened if you can't. This is why it's important to be as realistic as you can when it comes to your finances.

In Real Life

After Cory had graduated from college, he started working at a good and stable company. He enjoyed his job, but he wasn't really earning as much as he would've liked. His friends were always going to fun events and living a lifestyle that he also wanted. This is what prompted him to take out a credit card. When he first got the credit card, he didn't want to use it all the time. It was just for emergencies and the occasional nice thing. He thought that it should be okay because, in a few years, he would get a promotion and earn more money, so he could pay it back if he owed something on the credit card.

Five years down the line and he ended up in tons of debt. In fact, he had to pay back $50,000 worth of debt, and it kept growing. Over the years, it wasn't just his credit card that he was using, but he was taking out loans for other items. He had started living a lifestyle that he couldn't afford, and he just kept spiraling down the rabbit hole. It's not where he wanted to be, but that's where his choices left him.

Unfortunately, he did not earn as much as he thought he would at this point in his life. There were some economic issues that caused the company not to give the increases they would've liked. This meant that Cory's plan to pay it off when he was earning more money was not working out for him. At this point, he felt his debt was so much that he simply could not get out of it. He knew that he needed some professional help, so he contacted a debt counselor. Honestly, she was a godsend because she went through everything to help develop a plan for him to pay off the debt. Sure, Cory had to pay a fee for her services, but it was well worth it because now he had a plan. She advised him that whenever he had a little extra money, it should always go toward paying off the debt, even if it was just $20 or $50. Every small amount counts. Since she was keeping him accountable, it was a huge motivation for him to keep going and just stay on track.

Over the next four years, he was able to pay off the debt completely. Once the credit card was paid off, he decided that he was going to cancel his credit card for the time being. He wanted a completely fresh start and didn't want to be tempted to get back into this situation again. He learned how to create a budget and prioritize his savings and spending goals. Managing his money was a lot easier now, and he wanted to see if you could do it without a credit card. After about a year, he decided he was going to get another credit card, but he was going to be a lot more responsible with it. He left it at home every time he went out and didn't use it for online purchases. This way, he was able to control his spending, and ever since then, he did not get into large amounts of debt again. He was able to learn his lesson and make better financial decisions for his future.

Cory needed some extra help to develop some good financial habits. These financial habits helped him get out of debt and stay out of debt. There are tons of financial habits that someone can have, and it is important to develop them as soon as possible. In the next chapter, we are diving into the money habits that will allow you to build success in your life for the long term.

8. Strategy 7—Developing Effective Money Habits for Long-Term Success

"It is tempting to try to get rich quickly, but the process of getting rich slowly and steadily via saving and long-term investing is tested and reliable."

— Nimi Akinkugbe

We live in a world where everything can happen at the snap of a finger. We all want things to happen super quickly, so we can get the benefits of it now. It's not surprising that we are always looking for quick fixes since that is what we are basically trained to do. These days all you have to do is click a few buttons, and you can get your groceries, clothes, technology, or basically anything else delivered to your door the next day. You don't even have to leave your house to get a delicious meal from your favorite restaurant. Since everything is so easy and we live in this world where we get what we want when we want it, it can be very difficult to move out of that mindset.

The truth is that most good and sustainable things do take time. You won't be able to build a successful business in a matter of weeks. You can't get a degree in a few days. You definitely can't build sustainable wealth in a short time. All of these things take years to put into place and to grow. This means that you need to have good habits to help you. Habits are things that you do every day that lead you to success. These are small things that can change your entire life. The great thing about habits is that once you have put them in place, you will do them without thinking about them. It's like how most people just brush their teeth in the morning; It becomes a habit. This is a good habit, and it's probably the reason why your teeth are not rotting and falling out (thanks Mom and Dad!). You probably have quite a few good habits that you haven't even thought of. Imagine what habits could do if you were intentional in developing the right ones.

Developing Habits That Stick

If you are struggling with setting up habits for your life, then the section is really going to help you. The advice here is not just for financial habits but can be applied to every other habit in your life. It will help you make habits that stick for the long term so you can make better choices and live a much more successful life.

Start With a Routine

A routine and a habit are two different things, but creating a routine can help you create a habit. A routine is a collection of small things that you do repeatedly. Then a habit can be birthed out of this. Sometimes we need something to trigger our brains into performing a habit, and that's why a routine works. So, if you want to build the habit of sitting down and creating a budget each month, you will need to think of a routine that will work with this.

The first place you can look is at what you are already doing. Look at your schedule and see how you can fit budgeting into it. Let's say on a Sunday, you do a full self-care Sunday routine. This is where you take care of your mental and physical health. You might do a skincare routine and get your week sorted out. This is the perfect time to slip into budgeting. You can say that after you are done with your skincare and have tidied up your room, you will sit down and budget. Since you already have an established routine, it's easy to just add something to it. Eventually, budgeting will just form part of the routine, and it will be an easy habit to continue with.

Once you have built the habit, you might not need the routine to continue doing it. It's something that you are already used to doing, so if you have to move it to a different time or place in your week or your month, it will still work for you.

Know What You Are Doing

When you are trying to create a habit, you need to know exactly what that habit is. You won't be able to create a habit if you are too vague about how or what it actually is. For example, you can't say you want to be better with money and expect a habit to come from that. Dig a little deeper and specifically tell yourself what habit you are trying to build. Being better with money could be learning how to budget, tracking your spending, saving a certain amount each month, or writing down financial goals.

Expect a Few Setbacks

Even the most perfect person is going to have a little trouble when it comes to setting and sticking to habits. If it truly was easy, then everybody would have these awesome habits already instilled in them, but this is not the case. Because good habits are naturally more difficult to build than the bad ones, you are probably going to hit a few setbacks.

One of the biggest misconceptions is that you have to do something for 21 days in order for a habit to stick. This seems like a great guideline, but when people fail to keep the habit up for 21 days, they think they have to start all the way from the beginning. This becomes incredibly demotivating, and then they don't want to do it anymore. The truth is that a habit can take shorter or longer than 21 days to stick. It depends on the individual person and the type of habit you are trying to make work for you.

If you miss one or two days of your habit, it's not going to be the end of the world. You can just pick up where you left off and continue. Consistency is not about perfection. It's about trying to do your best over and over again.

Notice What Is Stopping You

We all have certain things in our life that block us from doing our best. If you keep failing at setting up your habits, it might be because you have one of these blockers in your life. It is a good idea to stop and think about what is actually causing you to fail. Perhaps you have set a savings goal for yourself for the month, but each month, you never have enough money to save. This means it's very difficult for you to set this habit as something concrete in your life.

Instead of just giving up and thinking that it's too difficult to implement this habit, you can take a step back and look at what is stopping you. When you set your budget at the beginning of the month, it may look like you have enough money to save, but when you want to put the money away, you realize you don't. This is very strange, so you decide that you are going to start tracking your spending to see where your money is going. It turns out that you end up spending some money on random items at the mall when you go out with your friends. This means that your money is not going toward saving because it is being spent somewhere else. Now that you know this, you can be more conscious of the amount you spend when you go out. You can also decide to start saving before you allow yourself to spend on other items so you can make sure you are hitting your savings goals.

Include a Reward

Have you ever noticed that when you compete in a competition or do really well in something, there's always a reward at the end? When you have to run a race at school or maybe participate in a sport, there is usually a prize for the winner. Kids that get the highest marks in class will get recognition. Even when adults go to work, there are prizes for the top performers or for reaching goals and targets. The reason this happens is that rewards are a great incentive to motivate people. This is especially true when we have to do things that we don't really want to do and that are quite difficult.

You can use this to your advantage by creating rewards at the end of doing something difficult. Creating rewards for your habits will help you stick to them because you want to get the prize at the end. A reward can be anything that motivates you. You don't have to spend a lot of money on the reward. Even something small can still be a huge motivating factor when it comes to building a habit.

Let's say one of the habits you want to get into is to start saving your money first. This is the pay-yourself-first principle that we learned earlier on in the book. If you are used to spending all your money on yourself immediately, then it might be quite difficult to start practicing this habit. Think about something you really enjoy and would be a good prize. Maybe your favorite candy bar or watching your favorite movie on Netflix. You can tell yourself that as soon as you put a specified amount of money into your savings account, you can get the prize. Even though you are doing something difficult, there is something for you to look forward to. You get to enjoy your favorite candy bar or watch your favorite movie. Your brain will start associating the hard thing with something good, and it will become a lot easier for you to do.

Getting Help and Support

Even the most disciplined person needs a little bit of help when it comes to meeting their goals. I know that I've had so many good ideas, but I've never done anything to make them work. This is not because I'm not motivated or I'm lazy, but simply because there needs to be a little extra push for me to get going. You've probably experienced this every now and then. Perhaps at school, you are given an assignment or a project to do, but you end up doing it at the last minute because there are more interesting things that pop-up. I mean, somebody has to tell Netflix to stop adding new shows to the lineup!

But let's say you were doing a group project. The group needs you to pull your weight to get it done in time, so they can complete their side of the project. This is a lot more motivating because other people are relying on you, and they are holding you accountable. They will be checking up on you, and that means you will do the work a lot quicker and probably a lot better because you don't want to let someone else down or seem stupid in front of them.

It's amazing how simply being accountable to another person can unlock motivation like nothing else. I guess this is also why many schools ask parents to sign notes to confirm they have received letters or notices. Kids and teenagers would be a lot more motivated to get things done if they knew their parents were aware of them. Not only that but parents can now motivate their kids and make sure they have everything they need to get the work done.

It is pretty unlikely that you will actually reach your goals. If all you do is think about the goal in your head. In fact, you are probably going to forget about the goal and never think about it again. It's not concrete in your mind, and you haven't put it out into the world, so the chances of you reaching it is quite small. I don't mean to sound discouraging when I say this because this is not just about you but about every human. We all need something solid in order to start reaching our goals. Simply having a goal is not enough. You are only 10% likely to reach a goal when you just have the idea in your mind, and you are 95% likely to reach a goal when you have someone you are accountable to and meet with them on a regular basis (Newland, 2018). Now that's a huge leap.

This statistic shows us that we are almost 100% more likely to reach our goals when we just tell someone about it and we make sure we are accountable to them. It's such a small change, but it's going to make a huge difference. This doesn't just apply to financial goals but, basically, any other goal you have in your life. At this point, you might be wondering how to be accountable when it comes to finances. This is a great question, and it's not as difficult as you might think.

The first thing you need to do is identify somebody you can be accountable to. This person needs to be someone you trust and someone you know will give you good advice when it comes to finances. This means your best friend, who spends all his money on video games and McDonald's, is not going to be a good choice. It might be better to choose an adult or somebody older than you who is responsible for their money. They can help you think of ways you can cut down on your spending and save more. They will also be able to give you advice from what they have learned throughout their life. It doesn't have to be one of your parents. Just as long as it is somebody you trust and know is good with money.

Once you have your person in mind, you have to go to them and ask them whether they would like to be your accountability partner when it comes to handling your finances. If you explain that you have specific financial goals that you really want to reach, they will probably be happy to help you with them. Next, you'll need to set an appointment with them. These appointments are not going to be something you do once and forget about. Depending on your goals, you might need to set an appointment with them every week or every month. Just make sure they are consistent so that the person has a good idea of where you are in your financial goals. You don't have to meet face-to-face with them all the time; a phone call or video call will be good enough.

Once you have done all that, you will need to be completely transparent with your financial goals and what you hope to achieve. They will probably have some questions for you, so make sure you have the answers ready. You should know how much money you are making and exactly what your financial goals are. The other person can help you find better ways to spend your money and give you ideas on what you should be doing. Even if they don't have any groundbreaking ideas on how you can make more money or save more, just being accountable to them for your goals is so important. You can ask them to check in on you every so often so they can keep track of how well you are doing.

Simply knowing that you have to be accountable to another person is going to be life-changing. If there is a particularly difficult situation that you are going to be facing, you can let them know about it. Perhaps you know that you are going on holiday with a few of your friends and you have a weakness for overspending in this situation. You can show your accountability partner your holiday budget, and they can check in on you to make sure you are not blowing it unnecessarily.

Having somebody you are accountable to is also good for celebration and enjoying the process. You have somebody to share your wins with and to celebrate when you reach your goals. They will probably be really proud of you when you are able to get to where you want to be with your finances. Plus, it's really fun to have somebody who is walking alongside you as you reach your goals.

Quick Facts

A routine can help you create a long-lasting habit.	The 21-day habit rule is not always true. Forming a habit can take longer or shorter than that.
Writing down your habits and being specific will allow you to create habits that stick.	Rewarding yourself is the fun part of creating financial habits. Don't skip it!
Having an accountability partner can almost guarantee you reach your goals and stick to your habits.	Creating a habit is all about progress and not perfection.

Conclusion

Yay! We made it to the end of the book. There has truly been a lot of information you have learned and you're probably quite excited to start implementing it. As much as having all the information is a great first step, you're not going to see much change unless you actually start doing something with that information. It is so easy to learn something and forget about it. This is why the sooner you start taking action, the better it's going to be for you.

Take some time to think about what your next step is going to be. This will be different for every person because we all start from different places. If you are starting from complete scratch, I would suggest that you write out a budget first. This way, you will know how much money is coming in and what you are spending it on. From here, you can look at creating some financial goals. Start off with one or two goals, as you don't want to overwhelm yourself right from the start. Once you start getting the hang of managing your finances, you can look into other financial goals and other habits you can implement.

Another important part of finances and becoming financially successful is to continue learning. While you have already learned so much from this book, there is so much more for you to learn. The world of finances is typically always changing, and there are always new tips and tricks coming out. Especially when it comes to investing, you want to keep your finger on the pulse so you know what's going on. One of the best things you can do is subscribe to a newspaper or magazine. Many newspapers and magazines have online content that is easy to access and read. A few suggestions are The Wall Street Journal, The Economist, and Baron's. You can access a few free articles from the sources, but you will need to subscribe in order to get all the content.

Another way to get some up-to-date information is to subscribe to a podcast. Podcasts are usually free to listen to, so you can get insider information without having to pay anything. It also helps you to be productive because you can switch on a podcast and listen while you are doing something else, like cleaning your room or doing household chores. Some podcasts you can look into are *Money Girl*, *Planet Money*, and *Everyone's Talkin' Money*.

Building wealth and accessing financial freedom is a journey, so it's not going to happen with a snap of a finger. It can feel incredibly overwhelming. When you see how far you have to go and what you have to do to get there, just take it one step at a time. Think about what you have to do in the week or in the month to reach your goals. This will make things a lot more manageable, and you will feel a lot less overwhelmed.

Don't worry; everyone started somewhere, and the fact that you are starting young is putting you ahead of the crowd. If you keep going along this money journey and are willing to learn and implement what you are learning, you will go far. Don't wait until it's too late to start building wealth. Start taking action toward a financially successful future with the simple steps and strategies that you found in this book!

If you found the information in this book helpful, please consider leaving a review so other people can find it. I wish you great luck and success on your financial journey! Remember, "A budget is telling your money where to go instead of wondering where it went." –Dave Ramsey

References

Adams, R. (2023, March 13). *Goal setting strategies to help teenagers - investing money*. Young and the Invested. https://youngandtheinvested.com/goals-for-teenagers/

Affinity Credit Union. (n.d.). *5 good habits of successful investors*. Affinity Credit Union. https://www.affinitycu.ca/investing/tools-and-resources/advice/5-good-habits-of-successful-investors

Alvarez, S. (2023, March 2). *Common finance terms every newbie needs to know*. Investopedia. https://www.investopedia.com/articles/investing/061313/10-common-financial-terms-every-newbie-needs-know.asp

Annesley, J. (2015, October 27). *Top 20 inspirational quotes to develop your money mindset*. Mindset2Millions. https://www.mindset2millions.com/top-20-inspirational-quotes-money-mindset/

Atkinson, J. (2020, October 14). *The power of compound interest*. Penn Student Registration & Financial Services. https://srfs.upenn.edu/financial-wellness/blog/power-compound-interest#:~:text=When%20you%20invest%2C%20your%20account

Benson, A. (2022, November 16). *Types of real estate investments*. NerdWallet. https://www.nerdwallet.com/article/investing/types-of-real-estate-investments

BFI. (2022, September 23). *Financial risk is: Definition, types, and tips for good management*. BFI. https://www.bfi.co.id/en/blog/risiko-finansial-adalah-definisi-jenis-dan-tips-manajemen-yang-baik#:~:text=This%20is%20included%20in%20the

Bieber, C. (2022, June 16). *15 tips for recovering from a financial mistake*. The Motley Fool. https://www.fool.com/slideshow/15-tips-for-recovering-from-a-financial-mistake/

Brian Tracy's Self Improvement & Professional Development Blog. (2020, November 13). *How to develop a positive money mindset | brian tracy*. Brian Tracy's Self Improvement & Professional Development Blog. https://www.briantracy.com/blog/financial-success/how-to-develop-a-positive-money-mindset/

BuyProperly. (2022, January 19). *Why invest in real estate: 7 key benefits to know.* BuyProperly. https://buyproperly.ca/resource-center/posts/why-invest-in-real-estate

CFA Institute. (n.d.). *Real estate investments.* CFA Institute. https://www.cfainstitute.org/en/membership/professional-development/refresher-readings/real-estate-investments

Consumer Financial Protection Bureau. (n.d.-a). *Adult financial education tools and resources.* Consumer Financial Protection Bureau. https://www.consumerfinance.gov/consumer-tools/educator-tools/adult-financial-education/tools-and-resources/

Consumer Financial Protection Bureau. (n.d.-b). *Financial habits and norms.* Consumer Financial Protection Bureau. https://www.consumerfinance.gov/consumer-tools/educator-tools/youth-financial-education/learn/financial-habits-norms/

Copper. (n.d.). *Ultimate guide: Copper's guide to budgeting (for teens).* Copper. https://www.getcopper.com/guide/budgeting

Credit Counselling Society. (n.d.-a). *How to identify income & expenses for your budget.* Credit Counselling Society. https://nomoredebts.org/budgeting/build-household-budget/separate-income-from-expenses-step-2

Credit Counselling Society. (n.d.-b). *Money management tips for teens.* Credit Counselling Society. https://nomoredebts.org/budgeting/budgeting-for-teens

Debt.org. (n.d.). *Credit explained: What is it and why is it important?* Debt.org. https://www.debt.org/credit/#:~:text=The%20main%20difference%20between%20credit

DePaul, K. (2021, February 2). *What does it really take to build a new habit?* Harvard Business Review. https://hbr.org/2021/02/what-does-it-really-take-to-build-a-new-habit

Doghudje, K. (2016, January 24). *20 inspirational money quotes to set you on the path to wealth.* Businessday NG. https://businessday.ng/uncategorized/article/20-inspirational-money-quotes-to-set-you-on-the-path-to-wealth/#:~:text=Money%20is%20meant%20to%20serve

Elkaslassy, L. (2018, April 25). *How to understand and overcome your limiting beliefs around money.* Laura Elkaslassy & Co. Coaching. https://www.lauraelkaslassy.com/limiting-money-beliefs/

EU Business School. (2022, August 16). *How to identify business opportunities in any market.* EU Business School. https://www.euruni.edu/blog/how-to-identify-business-opportunities-in-any-market/

Financial Samurai. (2021, January 3). *What percent of americans own stocks?* Financial Samurai. https://www.financialsamurai.com/what-percent-of-americans-own-stocks/#:~:text=As%20of%202021%2C%20the%20top

Garrate, C. (2022, June 25). *The impact of artificial intelligence on kids and teens.* Aimagazine.com. https://aimagazine.com/machine-learning/the-impact-of-artificial-intelligence-on-kids-and-teens

Gillespie, P. (2015, April 28). *Meet the 17-year-old investor who tripled his money.* CNNMoney. https://money.cnn.com/2015/04/28/investing/millennial-investor-17-year-old-brandon-fleisher/

Go Henry. (2022, October 10). *Common financial problems for teens and how to resolve them.* Go Henry. https://www.gohenry.com/uk/blog/financial-education/common-financial-problems-for-teens-and-how-to-resolve-them

Gobler, E. (2022, June 20). *Investing guide for teens (and parents).* The Balance. https://www.thebalancemoney.com/investing-guide-for-teens-and-parents-4588018#:~:text=Some%20of%20the%20best%20investments

Gordon-Barnes, C. (2014, October 12). *6 fresh ways to find your passion.* The Muse; The Muse. https://www.themuse.com/advice/6-fresh-ways-to-find-your-passion

Grossman, A. (2021, December 27). *11 common (and surprising) teenage financial problems.* Money Prodigy. https://www.moneyprodigy.com/teenage-financial-problems/

Hakeenah, N. (2022, March 9). *Why personal accountability is the key to financial success.* Money254. https://www.money254.co.ke/post/why-personal-accountability-is-the-key-to-financial-success-money-management

Harbour, S. (2021, October 22). *4 savings accounts for investors.* Investopedia. https://www.investopedia.com/articles/personal-finance/090314/4-savings-accounts-investors.asp

Hathaway, J. (2022, November 13). *Everything you need to know about cultivating a "wealth mindset."* Real Simple. https://www.realsimple.com/work-life/money/wealth-mindset

Huang, E. (n.d.). *10 money management tips for teens.* Echo Wealth Management. https://www.echowealthmanagement.com/blog/10-money-management-tips-teens

Indeed. (2022, November 22). *14 characteristics of an entrepreneur.* Indeed. https://ca.indeed.com/career-advice/career-development/entrepreneur-characteristics?aceid=&gclid=Cj0KCQjw3a2iBhCFARIs

AD4jQB3YS_vMZjR4JuuxyABlJR-5su_-WTAdWk18LSdzcjbsEXH ERnktEdAaAlUGEALw_wcB&gclsrc=aw.ds

Insurance Information Institute. (n.d.). *How to build and maintain a good credit history*. Insurance Information Institute. https://www.iii.org/arti cle/how-can-i-build-and-maintain-good-credit-history#:~:text=Your% 20proven%20ability%20to%20manage

Investopedia. (n.d.). *Credit & debt: Managing both wisely*. Investopedia. https://www.investopedia.com/credit-and-debt-4689724

Irby, L. (2022, March 31). *7 best ways to build good credit*. The Balance. https://www.thebalancemoney.com/ways-to-build-good-credit-960109

Island Savings. (n.d.). *11 ways to stick to your budget*. Island Savings. https:// www.islandsavings.ca/simple-advice/money/ways-to-stick-to-your-budget

Kagan, J. (2019). *Compound interest definition*. Investopedia. https://www. investopedia.com/terms/c/compoundinterest.asp

Karr, A. (2023, May 3). *Why it's important to save money at an early age*. Mydoh. https://www.mydoh.ca/learn/money-101/why-kids-and-teens-should-start-saving-money-early/

Knueven, L. (2022, December 9). *How to save money as a teenager so you can get yourself a car, pay for college, or take a trip*. Business Insider. https://www.busi nessinsider.com/personal-finance/how-to-save-money-as-a-teenager

Kurt, D. (2023, March 23). *Best resources for improving financial literacy*. Investopedia. https://www.investopedia.com/best-resources-for-improving-financial-literacy-5091689

Lake, R. (2022, March 16). *6 types of savings accounts*. Forbes Advisor. https://www.forbes.com/advisor/banking/savings/types-of-savings-accounts/

Marquit, M. (2023, March 3). *Financial goals for students: How and why to set them*. Investopedia. https://www.investopedia.com/financial-goals-for-students-7151682#:~:text=Financial%20Goals%20Early%3F-

MBDA. (2010, July 20). *8 traits of successful entrepreneurs--Do you have what it takes?* Minority Business Development Agency. https://archive.mbda. gov/news/blog/2010/07/8-traits-successful-entrepreneurs-do-you-have-what-it-takes.html

Milliken, M. (2022, August 26). *12 easy ways to cut expenses at home*. Debt.org. https://www.debt.org/advice/how-to-cut-expenses/

Mint. (2020, August 25). *6 Ways to Instill a Positive Money Mindset*. MintLife

Blog. https://mint.intuit.com/blog/personal-finance/6-ways-to-instill-a-positive-money-mindset/

Mint. (2022, January 18). *23 better money habits you need to start doing in 2022.* MintLife Blog. https://mint.intuit.com/blog/planning/better-money-habits/

Money for the Mamas. (2021, January 10). *50+ budgeting quotes to motivate you (and your bottom line).* Money for the Mamas. https://www.money forthemamas.com/budgeting-quotes/#:~:text=%E2%80%9CA%20bud get%20tells%20us%20what

Money Mentors. (n.d.-a). *How chris paid off $47,000 of consumer debt.* Money Mentors. https://moneymentors.ca/resources/stories/how-chris-paid-off-47000-of-consumer-debt/

Money Mentors. (n.d.-b). *How to move forward after a financial mistake.* Money Mentors. https://moneymentors.ca/money-tips/how-to-love-yourself-after-a-financial-mistake/

Morris, G. (2021, November 18). *12 ways to cut your expenses & save money.* InCharge Debt Solutions. https://www.incharge.org/financial-literacy/budgeting-saving/how-to-cut-your-expenses/

Muller, C. (2022, September 5). *Best investments for teens - 9 ways to get your teens to invest.* Dough Roller. https://www.doughroller.net/investing/best-investments-for-teens/

Newland, S. (2018). *The power of accountability.* AFCPE. https://www.afcpe.org/news-and-publications/the-standard/2018-3/the-power-of-accountability/

Nolo. (n.d.). *Avoiding financial trouble: Ten tips.* Nolo. https://www.nolo.com/legal-encyclopedia/avoiding-financial-trouble-ten-tips-29485.html

Norada Real Estate Investments. (2021, September 7). *10 tips to be successful in real estate investing.* Norada Real Estate Investments. https://www.noradarealestate.com/blog/10-ways-successful-real-estate-investment/

O'neill, B. (2009, February). *The benefits of saving money (rutgers NJAES).* Njaes.rutgers.edu. https://njaes.rutgers.edu/sshw/message/message.php?p=Finance&m=122#:~:text=Saving%20provides%20a%20finan cial%20%E2%80%9Cbackstop

O'Shea, A. (2021, March 12). *How to invest in real estate: 5 ways to get started.* NerdWallet. https://www.nerdwallet.com/article/investing/5-ways-to-invest-in-real-estate

O'Shea, B., & Schwahn, L. (2021, January 13). *Budgeting 101: How to budget money*. NerdWallet. https://www.nerdwallet.com/article/finance/how-to-budget

Oak, R. (2022, August 3). *Top 7 reasons why 90% of US millionaires invest in real estate & why you should follow the lead*. Red Oak Development Group. https://redoakvc.com/top-7-reasons-why-90-of-us-millionaires-invest-in-real-estate-why-you-should-follow-the-lead/#:~:text=%E2%80%9C90%25%20of%20all%20millionaires%20become

Paris, D. (2023, May 3). *8 reasons why financial literacy is important*. Mydoh. https://www.mydoh.ca/learn/money-101/8-reasons-to-teach-financial-literacy-to-kids-teens/#:~:text=By%20teaching%20kids%20about%20money

Practical Money Skills. (n.d.). *Evaluating your finances*. Practical Money Skills. https://www.practicalmoneyskills.com/learn/budgeting/evaluating_your_finances

Ramsey Solutions. (n.d.). *How to stick to your budget*. Ramsey Solutions. https://www.ramseysolutions.com/budgeting/steps-to-help-you-stick-to-your-budget

RBC Wealth Management. (n.d.). *Why financial literacy is an important life skill for youths*. RBC Wealth Management. https://www.rbcwealthmanagement.com/en-ca/insights/why-financial-literacy-is-an-important-life-skill-for-youths

Ronis, H. (2023, January 31). *How to start a business as a teenager*. WikiHow. https://www.wikihow.com/Start-a-Business-As-a-Teenager

Rose, S. (2022, November 28). *Financial literacy quotes*. OppLoans. https://www.opploans.com/oppu/articles/quotes-financial-literacy/#:~:text=%E2%80%9CFinancial%20literacy%20is%20the%20ability

Royale, O. (2020, October 20). *14 teen entrepreneurs and how they succeeded*. Oxford Royale Academy. https://www.oxford-royale.com/articles/14-teen-entrepreneurs/

Rule 1 Investing. (n.d.). *Types of investments*. Rule 1 Investing. https://www.ruleoneinvesting.com/investing-guide/types-of-investments/?network=g&utm1=&gc_id=19978600309&h_ad_id=654987284305&utm_source=google&utm_medium=cpc&utm_campaign=&utm_content=&utm_term=&hsa_acc=8939821212&hsa_cam=19978600309&hsa_grp=148438539015&hsa_ad=654987284305&hsa_src=g&hsa_tgt=aud-1961450892464:dsa-1122117810636&hsa_kw=&hsa_mt=&hsa_net=adwords&hsa_ver=3&gad=1&gclid=Cj0KCQjw3a2iBhCFARIsAD4jQB1zNDGQIcIqYFGJPLAJAMv8fVxcS5QX8BcumtMhlMLxT7zyvQK5sEIaAoq3EALw_wcB

Shopify. (2022, August 4). *What is entrepreneurship? Definition and guide for 2022.* Shopify. https://www.shopify.com/ca/blog/what-is-entrepreneurship

Shubel, M. (2022, September 1). *How to overcome your limiting beliefs about money.* Clever Girl Finance. https://www.clevergirlfinance.com/build ing-wealth/financial-empowerment/money-mindset/limiting-beliefs-about-money/

Stanford Online. (n.d.). *What is entrepreneurship?* Stanford Online. https://online.stanford.edu/what-is-entrepreneurship

Stowers, J. (2019). *A step by step guide to starting a business.* Business News Daily. https://www.businessnewsdaily.com/4686-how-to-start-a-business.html

StudySmarter UK. (n.d.). *Basic financial terms: Definitions & statements.* StudySmarter UK. https://www.studysmarter.co.uk/explanations/busi ness-studies/introduction-to-business/basic-financial-terms/#:~:text=Revenue%2C%20costs%2C%20profit%20and%20loss

The Investopedia Team. (2020). *A real estate investing guide.* Investopedia. https://www.investopedia.com/mortgage/real-estate-investing-guide/

The Jed Foundation. (n.d.). *How to deal with financial stress .* The Jed Foundation. https://jedfoundation.org/resource/how-to-deal-with-financial-stress/

ThinkImpact. (2022, July 20). *47+ entrepreneur statistics (full list 2023) ++ charts.* ThinkImpact. https://www.thinkimpact.com/entrepreneur-statistics/#:~:text=Within%20their%20first%2010%20years

Velocity Club. (2023, February). *The importance of your mindset in building wealth.* Velocity Club. https://www.velocityclub.co.za/blog/2023/2/the-importance-of-your-mindset-in-building-wealth

WallStreetMojo. (2022, April 1). *Real estate investing.* WallStreetMojo. https://www.wallstreetmojo.com/real-estate-investing/

White, J. (2023, February 2). *The majority of teens feel unprepared to finance their future.* Savingforcollege. https://www.savingforcollege.com/arti cle/majority-of-teens-feel-unprepared-to-finance-their-future#:~:text=February%202%2C%202023-

Wong, R. (2021, January 14). *9 inspiring financial stories.* YNAB. https://www.ynab.com/9-inspiring-financial-stories/

Image References

Barbhuiya, T. (2021, October 21). A man holding a jar with a savings label on it [Image]. Unsplash. https://unsplash.com/photos/0ITvgXAU5Oo

ErikaWittlieb. (2017, July 8). Summer lemonade stand [Image]. Pexels. https://pixabay.com/photos/lemonade-stand-lemonade-summer-2483297/

Evans, A. (2020, May 18). A person holding credit cards against a white background wall [Image]. Unsplashed. https://unsplash.com/photos/RJQE64NmC_o

Grabowska, K. (2020, May 7). Crop anonymous financier planning budget writing numbers in notebook [Image]. Pexels. https://www.pexels.com/photo/crop-anonymous-financier-planning-budget-writing-numbers-in-notebook-4386339/

Li, K. (2021, October 20). Symbolic house made from one hundred dollars isolated on white background [Image]. Unsplashed. https://unsplash.com/photos/1sCXwVoqKAw

Nekrashevich, A. (2021, February 4). Businessman with stock market on laptop [Iimage]. Pexels. https://www.pexels.com/photo/marketing-businessman-person-hands-6801647/

Wilcox, K. (2017, September 16). Four Men Sitting on Platform [Image]. Pexels. https://www.pexels.com/photo/four-men-sitting-on-platform-923657/

The Teenage Healthypreneur

8 Simple Strategies on How Teens Can Learn
Entrepreneurial Skills and Live Healthy

E. T. Mulloney

Introduction

You're scrolling through your Instagram feed, mindlessly double-tapping cute puppy videos and pics of delicious-looking food. Then a story catches your eye about an average teenager turned healthypreneur.

So, what's a healthypreneur, you ask? Well, it's not your typical teenage part-time job of flipping burgers or babysitting. It's a whole new ball game, where both hustle and health are involved, and success takes on a new meaning.

Let's take a look at the life of this healthypreneur. Just like you, Thomas had a regular life filled with school, sports, online gaming, and valuable time spent with his friends. But then he discovered the world of healthypreneurship—a fusion of being an entrepreneur while also maintaining a healthy, feel-good lifestyle.

Thomas had discovered his passion in life. He was no longer content with just cramming for exams and amusing himself with regular teenage pastimes during his free time. He found he had a passion for fitness, nutrition, and well-being.

He promoted his passion by starting to post-workout routines, meal prep hacks, and motivational quotes on social media. He was surprised when people actually started following him like crazy. In a very short time period, he managed to get a tribe of motivated teens rallying behind him, all eager to jump on the healthypreneur train.

Thomas decided that he also wanted to empower his friends to improve their lives. So, he further boosted his social media presence by organizing virtual fitness challenges, and he even launched his own line of sustainable workout gear.

Thomas got all this done by preaching balance. He certainly wasn't the type to burn the midnight oil and sacrifice sleep for success. He was smart enough to realize that real achievement comes from a blend of ambition and self-care. There's simply no point in working until you burn out, as you wouldn't be able to achieve anything else.

You see, healthypreneurship isn't just a trend. It can help you become the boss of your own life. You need to understand that success isn't worthwhile if you burn out and destroy your health in the process.

As a teenager, you're probably wondering how you can work toward a financially secure and fulfilling future. When you're young, you have big dreams of making money, but also of doing something you really enjoy, and that adds meaning to your life.

School doesn't really prepare one for becoming an entrepreneur, and this book will help you a great deal with your preparation.

In today's world, there are many opportunities, but it can be difficult to find the right guidance. We will help you develop much-needed entrepreneurial skills, while you also maintain a healthy lifestyle.

So, why should you read this book? What exactly is in it for you? Let's summarize its main benefits.

Firstly, this book will accompany you on a journey of empowerment. It's here to provide you with practical strategies, actionable insights, and a roadmap to becoming a healthypreneur—someone who not only excels in entrepreneurship but also prioritizes their health and well-being.

You're probably wondering what is the point of all this. In today's ever-changing and fast-evolving world, it's not just about making money; it's about making a meaningful impact on your life and those around you. You want to achieve financial stability, but without sacrificing your health and your relationships with others.

You could be wondering how this book is different from the books already out there. The answer is that it recognizes that as a teenager, you have unique needs, aspirations, and challenges, and it provides you with relatable practical advice.

The book will equip you with the knowledge, skills, and confidence to create your own unique path. You can seize your destiny and live life on your own terms.

But before we dive into the strategies that will help you become a healthypreneur, let's explore the main points and challenges that encourage you to buy this book.

You likely don't know that much about entrepreneurial education and healthy living. This book will help you understand entrepreneurship and healthy living. It will provide you with tips on how to choose a startup business wisely and how to manage your finances, all while maintaining a healthy lifestyle at the same time.

We will also look at the psychological and social aspects of financial decision-making. It will help you understand how important it is to make financially responsible decisions while also helping you deal with peer pressure and expectations. You'll be able to make smart financial choices without succumbing to overspending and peer pressure.

Fear of failure is one of the most important things you will have to overcome as an entrepreneur. We will guide you on how to embrace your failures as a valuable learning experience.

Strategy 1
Unleashing Your Inner Healthypreneur and Thinking like a Boss!

"It's easy to be fooled by everyone's highlight reel or Instagram feed—business can look easy and flexible, but it's a really, really hard sport. Get ready for one of the hardest things you'll ever do but as someone who actually started a business at 14, it's totally worth it."

— Taj Pabari, ASE Group Chief Executive

Joe was a determined high school student who had an entrepreneurial vision and that set him aside from his peers. He had always wanted to work for himself and do something significant with his life, so at the age of 16 he decided to become a healthypreneur.

During his freshman year of high school, he noticed that his classmates were often stressed, sleep-deprived and struggling with their academic workload. He also felt the pressure to excel, but he refused to let it take over his life and decided to take matters into his own hands.

Joe invited his friends to his house one day after school, and they sat around, telling each other about how they were struggling with stress and staying focused in school. That gave him the idea to create a space where teenagers could find support and balance.

Joe started his journey to becoming a healthypreneur by doing research on stress management, mindfulness techniques, and the benefits of exercise for teenagers. Armed with all the knowledge he gathered, he created an after-school program.

His program focused on teaching his peers how to cope with stress and pressure in healthy ways. He organized weekly yoga and meditation sessions in the local park where he encouraged his friends and everyone else who joined to embrace mindfulness as a tool for personal growth. Eventually, he also organized workshops where he invited nutritionists and mental health experts to speak and provide insight to teenagers about holistic well-being.

He convinced his sister Melody to go into business with him, and he branched out his business to make and sell natural stress relief bath products. Melody was very enthusiastic about their business together, as she believed that self-care was an important part of well-being and she wanted her friends to also experience the benefits.

The word spread about Joe and Melody's business, and their turnover increased rapidly. They sold more and more products, and children from different schools started to attend their meetings and workshops. They were soon surrounded by a thriving community of like-minded individuals. Joe started to understand that they weren't only helping their peers but that they were also making connections and creating positive change.

Joe's journey wasn't without challenges. He had to balance his schoolwork and the demands of his growing business. At times he wondered if he had taken on too much, but his commitment to his vision kept him going. He understood how important it was to have balance in his life, and made sure he had time for self-care.

His hard work eventually paid off, and he received recognition from his school and the local community, his business even started receiving attention from regional media.

Like Joe, you too can be a successful healthypreneur, and we're going to look at some ways in which you can get started.

Why Healthypreneurship Matters For Teens

Healthypreneurship might sound like a fancy word, but it's really a simple term to describe a unique form of success that is much needed in today's busy world since it is so focused on achievement. It's all about being smart, healthy, and ready for what's coming.

Starting and managing a business is an exciting journey, but it can also be demanding and stressful. You can easily find yourself caught up in non-stop workdays and sleepless nights. However, if you work this way for a long time, you can experience burnout both in your professional and private life. There are things you can do to maintain a balance between success and your overall well-being. We'll take a look at the essential habits shared by successful entrepreneurs who are able to maintain their momentum without sacrificing their health.

The Importance of Healthypreneurship at a Young Age

So, why is healthypreneurship so important for teenagers?

It teaches you to think outside the box and how to be a creative problem solver. You'll learn to think in new ways and come up with unique solutions to everyday problems. These skills will not only help you in your business, but also your everyday life. Critical thinking skills are often not taught in schools and we have to find ways to develop them on our own.

It helps get you into the right mindset to prepare for your future. It might feel to you like retirement is light years away, but it's really much closer than you think. You need to build a strong base to provide you with income in your golden years while you're still young and healthy enough to do so.

Healthypreneurship can help you understand money and how to make it work for you. It's like planting a tree now so that you can enjoy the fruits when you're older. Becoming a young entrepreneur will help you learn early on that making money isn't only about working hard for it, but also knowing about how to make money work for you. You'll learn the language of budgeting, investment, and building wealth.

You'll get a head start when it comes to managing your time and money, and before you know it, you'll be adulting before all your friends. You'll be the responsible one who can make all your own decisions.

It's also a way of future-proofing your life. The world is changing fast, and healthypreneurship will help you stay ahead of the rest. You'll learn how to adapt, bounce back from setbacks, and be strong when challenges come your way.

Stories of Successful Teenage Entrepreneurs Who Overcame Challenges

Young entrepreneurs have always been good at identifying opportunities and transforming them into successful businesses. Just consider Steve Jobs, who founded Apple and revolutionized technology in the twentieth century.

Let's take a look at a few more of these success stories.

The remarkable Kamaria Warren started her business when she was just seven years old. Kamaria and her mother, Shaunice Sasser, set out to find birthday invitations for Kamaria's upcoming party when they realized there were no products that represented Brown and Black girls (Lodge, 2019).

They got the idea to create Brown Girls Stationery. Kamaria, who is from McDonough, Georgia, began her mission to design party and school supplies, stationery, vegan purses, and accessories specifically tailored to girls like her. Her creations feature cheerful illustrations of Black and Brown girls, and she even started selling dolls.

At only 13 years old, Kamaria oversees a thriving business with five employees and five volunteers. She sells her products through various channels, including Shopify, Faire Marketplace, wholesale partnerships, and also at local events.

On average, her business sells an impressive 10,000 notebooks, 2,500 notepads, and 1,500 backpacks yearly. Kamaria also develops and expands her offerings. She has introduced 1,000 packs of party supplies and 1,000 new lip glosses and also releases a purse with an uplifting message every month.

Kamaria is motivated by the idea of seeing other girls wearing her creations and embracing their true selves. Her motto encapsulates her spirit: "Dear Brown girl, you have the ability to change the world."

Ryan Hickman, who is from Orange County, California, started his entrepreneurship journey when he was only three years old. He had always hated seeing bottles and other rubbish strewn on the ground, even when he was a small child, and he eventually decided that he wanted to do something about it.

Ryan started collecting items that could be recycled, and his dad took him to the local recycling center, where he received $5 for his efforts. This made him even more excited about recycling.

At only seven years old, he started his own business, named Ryan's Recycling Company. Ryan started receiving widespread attention. He received recognition from news organizations, including CNN Kid Wonder in 2017, and he also appeared on national TV shows like "Ellen" and "Today," where he shared his inspiring mission with the world.

Ryan sells t-shirts on his website that have messages like "Make the Sea Trash Free." He also supports the Pacific Marine Mammal Center with the proceeds of his sales and the income from his recycling efforts.

Not stopping there, Ryan also launched a nonprofit called Project 3R. The mission of this organization is to educate people of all ages worldwide about the importance of recycling and to coordinate community clean-up efforts. Ryan's message is that if a kid like him can contribute to changing the environmental situation, we can all do our part.

Moziah Bridges, from Memphis, is a stylish young entrepreneur. When he was nine years old, he struggled to find a bowtie to match his outfit. He decided to do something about this and started the popular business, Mo's Bows.

He started his business journey by learning how to sow. He made bowties from leftover fabric from his grandmother's sewing projects. As time progressed, he expanded his operations. He employed skilled tailors to handle the manufacturing while he focused on the creative and business aspects of Mo's Bows.

By the age of 20, Moziah Bridges had already achieved remarkable success and he specialized in meticulously crafted men's ties and accessories. He had the honor to present former President Barack Obama with a custom-made "Obama Blue" tie. His creations are also being sold by retailers like Cole Haan, Bloomingdale's, and Neiman Marcus.

Moziah also established the Go Mo Summer Camp Scholarship Fund, which sends underprivileged children from Memphis to summer camp. This also shows Moziah's commitment to making a positive impact beyond the world of fashion.

In the next chapter, we'll look at how effective time management can help you reach your goals.

How To Start Your First Business With Limited Financial Resources

Sarah was determined to start her own business, but she had only limited financial resources to help her do so. Her dream started to look impossible when she realized she would have to start her business with as little money as possible.

She knew she would have to be resourceful and come up with creative solutions that cost as little as possible. She couldn't rely on her parents to help her with money or bail out her business, as she knew they were also struggling financially.

We'll explore the practical steps and strategies that can help you kickstart your business on a shoestring budget. It's entirely possible to do it without breaking the bank. The path to entrepreneurial success begins with frugality, innovation, and unwavering determination.

Starting your first business with as little money as possible is a common goal for many young entrepreneurs. The following can help you get started on a limited budget.

Keeping Your Costs Down

Make sure you choose a business idea that doesn't require a substantial upfront investment. An online or service-based business will have lower startup costs than businesses that rely on physical products being sold. For example, if you don't have cash to develop products, but you're good at helping others and you have specialist knowledge on a certain subject such as math, it might be easier for you to advertise your services as an online tutor.

Creating a lean business plan can also help you keep your expenses in check. Develop a simplified business plan that outlines your business concept, target market, revenue model, and budget. Your plan should be focused and flexible.

Use your existing skills and resources. This could include using your own laptop, smartphone, or tools related to your business. If you have a laptop and internet connection, you may already have all the resources you require to start your online business.

Look for ways you can reduce your overhead costs. If you're working from home on your laptop, you shouldn't have that many overheads.

If you need someone to help you with something, such as creating content for your business website, consider outsourcing the work. It will save you money in the long term if you don't have to hire someone permanently to do the work for you. Who knows, maybe you'll even get the time and the motivation to learn the skills that will make it easier for you to do this type of work yourself in the future.

When it comes to marketing your services, it's possible to learn and implement basic marketing strategies yourself. You can also use free or low-cost online marketing tools, social media, and content marketing to reach your target audience.

Start small and grow your business gradually. Begin with a minimal viable product (MVP) to test the market. As your business gains support and starts making money, reinvest the profits to expand and improve your offerings.

If your business does provide products, negotiate with suppliers and service providers for discounts or better terms. You can also consider looking for crowdfunding platforms or small business grants that align with your business idea. This can give you additional funding without having to take loans.

Build a network of like-minded entrepreneurs who can provide advice and support, and potentially collaborate on projects, reducing costs and risks.

Be careful with your money. Prioritize spending on activities and resources that directly contribute to increasing your business number and growth. You should also keep on learning about affordable business practices.

Starting a business with little money requires creativity and resourcefulness. While it may be challenging, it's entirely possible to build a successful business if you plan carefully around your finances.

Checklist of Skills For Young Entrepreneurs

To be a successful young entrepreneur, you need a combination of skills and abilities:

- You should be able to think outside the box, come up with innovative ideas, and solve problems creatively.
- Entrepreneurship often involves setbacks and failures. You need resilience, which involves the ability to bounce back from these and keep going.
- Effective communication is vital for pitching ideas, networking, and working with a team.
- As an entrepreneur, you'll likely be leading a team or project. Leadership skills will help you inspire and guide others.
- The business world is constantly changing, and you need to be able to adapt to this.
- Understanding budgets, cash flow, and financial planning is necessary for running a successful business.
- Good time management helps you prioritize tasks and be productive.

- Building relationships and networks can open doors and opportunities for your business.
- You need to be able to promote your product or service effectively.
- Entrepreneurs take risks, but they should be calculated risks. It's important to be able to understand risk and reward.
- In the digital age, having a basic understanding of technology and online tools is essential.
- You should focus on meeting the needs of your customers.
- You'll need to make important decisions quickly and effectively.
- Setting clear goals and working toward them is one of an entrepreneur's most important skills.
- Negotiating with partners, investors, or clients is a common part of entrepreneurship.
- You'll encounter many challenges, and problem-solving skills are critical.
- Understanding and managing your emotions, as well as those of others, is valuable in business relationships.
- Basic knowledge of business laws, contracts, and regulations is important.
- Understanding your target market and industry trends will help you make informed decisions.
- You can take acceptable risks, and you should always have a backup plan.

Entrepreneurship is also an ongoing learning experience. You can improve your abilities and skills as you gain experience and learn more in your field.

Developing Entrepreneurial Abilities Worksheet

This worksheet is designed to help you explore and develop your entrepreneurial abilities. Answering these questions can give you a better idea of the skills you already have and where you would still need to work on yourself. You can use the spaces provided below to answer them but if you need more space feel free to write in a notebook or use one of your digital devices.

Identify Your Passions

- List three things you are passionate about.

_____

_____

_____

- Could you turn your passions into potential business ideas?

_____

Innovative Thinking

- Think of a common problem in your community or school.

_____

_____

- Brainstorm three solutions to this problem.

_____

_____

_____

Problem-Solving

- Recall a time when you faced a significant challenge.

_____

_____

_____

- Describe the challenge and how you overcame it.

_____

_____

_____

Identify Your Strengths and Weaknesses

- List three strengths you possess that would benefit an entrepreneur.

_____

_____

_____

- List three weaknesses on which you would want to improve.

_____

_____

_____

Business Ideas

- Create a list of ten business ideas that interest you. These can be creative ideas that would still need some work to refine them.

_____

_____

_____

- Highlight one idea that particularly appeals to you, and which your gut feeling tells you would be the right one for you.

_____

_____

_____

Market Research

- For the highlighted business idea, conduct basic market research.

_____

_____

_____

- Who is your target audience? Is there a demand for your product or service?

_____

_____

_____

Networking

- Connect with someone who has experience as an entrepreneur or business leader. List your potential meetings below.

_____

_____

_____

- Ask them about their journey and any advice they can offer.

_____

_____

_____

Decision-Making

- Imagine you have to make a difficult decision regarding your business idea.

_____

_____

_____

- Write down your thought process for making this decision.

_____

_____

_____

Financial Awareness

- Calculate the startup costs for your business idea.

_____

_____

_____

- Create a simple budget for the first year of your business.

_____

_____

_____

_____

_____

_____

Presentation Skills

- Prepare a 2-minute pitch for your business idea. Write it below and then practice delivering it with enthusiasm.

_____

_____

_____

Continuous Learning

- Research a successful entrepreneur you admire. Summarize your research below.

_____

_____

_____

- What qualities or strategies have contributed to their success?

_____

_____

_____

Resilience

- Recall a setback you've faced in the past.

_____

- Describe how you overcame it and what you learned from the experience.

_____

_____

_____

Vision and Goals

- Define your long-term entrepreneurial vision.

_____

_____

_____

- Set three specific, achievable goals to work towards this vision.

_____

_____

_____

Action Plan

- Create an action plan outlining the steps you need to take to pursue your highlighted business idea.

_____

_____

_____

_____

_____

_____

Reflection

Write about what you've learned about yourself and your entrepreneurial abilities by completing this worksheet.

_____

_____

_____

_____

_____

_____

Entrepreneurship is an ongoing journey, and your abilities will continue to develop as you gain more experience and knowledge. Keep this worksheet and revisit it to keep track of your progress.

Key Takeaways

- Healthypreneurship combines success with well-being.
- It teaches creative problem-solving and innovative thinking.
- It can prepare you for the future and the importance of managing money.
- It will empower you with early financial knowledge.

- It will help you develop your time and money management skills.
- Healthypreneurship can help you stay ahead in a fast-changing world.
- It will teach you adaptability, resilience, and strength in the face of challenges.

Strategy 2
Crush Your Goals, Rule Your Time

> *"Your complaints, your drama, your victim mentality, your whining, your blaming, and all of your excuses have NEVER gotten you even a single step closer to your goals or dreams. Let go of your nonsense. Let go of the delusion that you DESERVE better and go EARN it! Today is a new day!"*
>
> — Steve Maraboli

As the quote says, every day is full of endless opportunities that you need to get out there and earn. You've got big dreams, and there are lots of possibilities out there waiting for you. But there's one catch—you need a plan, a roadmap to turn those dreams into reality. Perhaps you've heard about goal setting, but you've never really tried it, because it just sounds like something that will bore you to death, so you've been winging it. This won't work In the long-term though, and you need to plan for success.

Don't worry, goal setting isn't about dull routines or boring to-do lists; it's your key to creating a successful and exciting life. It can actually be exciting to sculpt your dreams into achievable milestones.

We'll also introduce you to the SMART way of setting goals —Specific, Measurable, Achievable, Relevant, and Time-bound.

We'll also help you nurture your growth mindset. You can change challenges into opportunities to overcome your setbacks. They're all just stepping stones on your path to success.

Goal Setting

Imagine goal setting as a way of unlocking your talents. Without goals, we tend to go through life aimlessly, and we might never reach our full potential.

Tailored Techniques

You can choose from various goal-setting techniques that suit your style the best. Maybe you're someone who wants to visualize your goals or break them down into smaller steps. Let's take a look at some of these goal-setting techniques.

SMART Goals

This is one of the most popular and easiest techniques to use.

Specific: Be clear about what you want to achieve. For example, if you decide you want to be healthier, you need to set out specific ways in which you're going to achieve this such as deciding that you will follow a specific healthy diet plan and exercise for 30 minutes every day.

Measurable: You should be able to track your progress toward achieving your goals, for example, I will walk for 20 minutes every day.

Achievable: The goals you set for yourself should be achievable and realistic. For example, it's unrealistic to want to learn a new language in a week, but you could learn some basic phrases in a month.

Relevant: Your goals should align with your interests and values. If you love writing, a goal related to painting or drawing might be more relevant than something unrelated.

Time-bound: You need to set a deadline for your goals. The sense of urgency this creates will help you stay focused on achieving your goals. For example, this could be a specific date by which you're going to finish a school project.

Chunking Goals

This means breaking your big goals into smaller, manageable chunks. If you want to improve your grades, instead of aiming for an overall average increase right away, focus on getting better scores in one subject at a time.

Journaling

Record your goals and progress in a journal. Writing down your goals can make them feel more concrete, and it can motivate you to keep track of your progress.

Vision Boards and Mind Maps

Create a vision board with images and quotes that represent your goals and dreams. Place it where you can see it daily to stay motivated.

Creating a mind map is also a visual way to represent your goals, and it's useful for brainstorming and planning.

So, how do you create a mind map? Below is a simple sketch, but you can use different colors and pictures to make ideas stand out on your map.

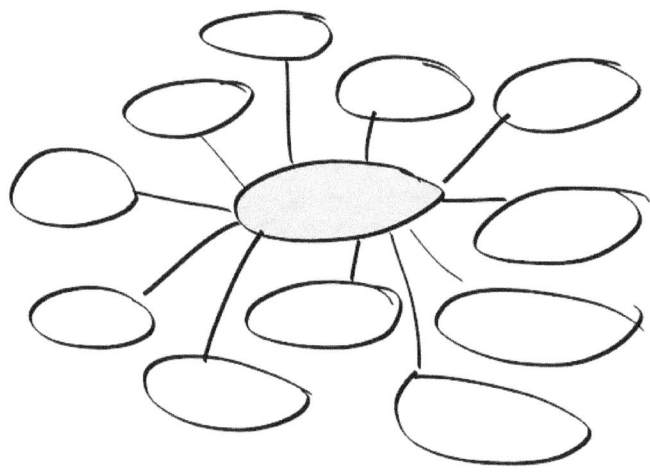

The basic idea of the mind map is as follows:

- Start your mind map with a central idea or topic in the center of the page.

- Draw main branches from the central idea to represent key categories or concepts related to the topic.
- Add subtopics as smaller branches extending from the main branches, that give specific details or ideas.
- Use keywords, short phrases, or simple images to represent ideas instead of long sentences.
- Connect related ideas with lines and arrows to show relationships and the flow of information.
- Organize the mind map hierarchically, placing the most important ideas at the top or center.
- Use colors, icons, or symbols to differentiate categories and highlight key points.
- Avoid clutter by focusing on capturing the main ideas and their connections.
- Review and refine the mind map to make sure it's logical and accurate.
- You can also do your mind mapping digitally on your computer or any of your digital devices.

Gamification

You can make it fun by turning your goals into a game with rewards and challenges. For each goal you achieve, treat yourself to something you enjoy.

Accountability Partner

Team up with a friend who has similar goals. You can motivate and support each other, and this can make the whole process more enjoyable.

Finally, you need to be flexible and willing to adjust your goals if needed. Your priorities can change, as life is often unpredictable.

Short-Term vs. Long-Term Goals

Short-term goals are like mini-missions. If you're an online game player, you'll know about the challenges your favorite character faces throughout the game.

Completing these mini-goals will also give you a sense of achievement and bring you closer to achieving your main goal.

You can see your long-term goals almost like the longer quests in your games, where you have to save your world from a villain. These are the big dreams you want to achieve, and they require time and dedication.

So, why both short-term and long-term goals? It's like having a game with different levels. You can't jump straight to the final level, you need to pass the earlier stages first. Short-term goals prepare you for the epic battles ahead!

Effective Time Management

Effective time management is a valuable skill that can benefit you in various aspects of your life, from your schoolwork to extracurricular activities and personal goals. You should implement the following practical tips:

Set Reminders For Your Tasks

As a teenager, your life can get pretty hectic with school, sports, social activities, and more. You could find that you easily forget about important tasks or deadlines. If you have a smartphone or a digital planner, use it to set reminders for your homework assignments, project due dates, and even your chores like doing the dishes, or taking out the laundry. This way, you won't miss out on anything important, and you'll feel more in control of your responsibilities.

Create a Daily Planner

A daily planner, whether it's a physical notebook or a digital app, can help you solve the puzzle of your daily life, and keep your wits together. It's only too easy to become overwhelmed when you have many things going at once. Write down everything you need to do, including schoolwork, practice sessions, and even your times for relaxation and socialization. Plan your day the night before or in the morning to give you a clear roadmap, and to make sure that you do everything that's important.

Set Time Limits For Tasks

Avoid spending too much time on your assignments or becoming distracted by assigning specific time limits to your tasks. For instance, if you have an English assignment, tell yourself you'll work on it for 30 minutes, take a short break, and then work on it for another 30 minutes. This will make your tasks more manageable and will prevent you from procrastinating.

Block Out Distractions

You may find it challenging to stay focused, especially with social media, games, and other digital temptations. Set "focus" times where you turn off notifications or use apps that block distracting websites. This will help you concentrate on your tasks and complete them more efficiently.

Establish a Routine

Developing a daily routine can change your life. It not only helps you manage your time better but also creates a sense of stability. Set aside specific times for studying, exercising, socializing, and relaxation. Over time, your routine will become a habit, and it will help you manage your time more effectively.

Prioritize Your Tasks

You need to prioritize your tasks. Some will always be more important than others, and you should focus on the urgent ones first. You will also have to learn to say no and to prioritize and find a balance between your commitments. If you say yes to everything, you'll just become overwhelmed. Being selective about the activities and responsibilities you take on ensures you have enough time for your priorities.

Effective time management is a skill that takes practice. It's okay to make adjustments along the way as you figure out what works best for you. Implementing these tips and staying committed to managing your time wisely will help you excel in your studies, pursue your passions, and maintain balance in your life.

Exercises and Activities to Help You Adopt a Growth Mindset

Developing a growth mindset as a teenager can help you when it comes to your personal and academic development.

So, what is the difference between a growth and a fixed mindset?

If you have a fixed mindset, you believe that your abilities, talents, and intelligence are things that you were born with and that they can't change. You might think that if you're not good at something, you'll never be good at it. For example, if you're struggling with a certain subject at school, you don't believe that you'll ever be able to improve at this subject.

If you have a fixed mindset, you'll probably avoid challenges because you'll be afraid of making mistakes. You might give up easily when things get tough because you believe you can't improve.

In a growth mindset, you believe that your abilities, talents, and intelligence are not fixed and that you can develop them with time and effort. For example, you enjoy drawing and art, but you realize and accept that you will have to put a lot of work into it if you want to pursue this as a career on a professional level.

The following activities and exercises can help you develop a growth mindset.

Think About Your Mindset

Consider the difference between a fixed and a growth mindset. Ask yourself questions about your abilities and intelligence:

- Have you ever thought that you're not good at something and that you'll never be?
- Do you think you can learn and improve at something if you put in the effort?
- Which mindset do you think you have?

Embrace Mistakes and Failures

If you want to develop a growth mindset, you have to be able to accept your failures and mistakes.

- Think about a recent mistake or failure you experienced, whether at school or in your personal life.
- What did you learn from the experience? Did it help you improve?
- Share your story with your friends to normalize that making mistakes is a normal part of learning and growing up.

Look For Challenges

Developing a growth mindset involves looking for challenges and new experiences that will help you grow as a person.

- Start taking part in an activity you've never tried before, like coding, a new sport, or a different style of art.
- Step out of your comfort zone and persevere, even in situations where you're experiencing difficulties.
- Write in a journal to keep track of your progress and the skills you acquire along the way.

Visualize Your Growth

Visualization can help you develop a growth mindset.

- Imagine a skill or subject you struggle with, like math or perhaps playing a certain sport.
- Visualize yourself gradually getting better at it. Imagine all the small steps you take to get better.

- Create a vision board or journal where you document your progress over the weeks or months.

Learn From Your Role Models

It can be inspiring to learn from role models who have a growth mindset.

- You should do research and choose a role model—whether it's a famous person, a teacher, or a family member—who has overcome challenges through their growth mindset.
- Study how they overcome obstacles and challenges.
- Let their experiences motivate you when you're facing your own challenges.

Encourage Positive Self-Talk

Positive self-talk can help you develop a growth mindset, in the following ways:

- You should pay attention to your self-talk, and challenge negative self-talk.
- Replace negative self-talk with positive affirmations such as a belief that you can learn and improve.
- Create a list of positive statements, and read them whenever you need a boost. Put them up somewhere in your home where it will be easy for you to see them.

Set Growth-Oriented Goals

As you know by now, goal setting is an important part of your personal growth.

- You need to set specific, achievable goals for yourself, whether they are related to academics, hobbies, or personal development.
- Break your goals down into smaller, more manageable goals.
- Celebrate your progress along the way, as you get closer to achieving your goal.

Embrace Feedback

Constructive feedback is important for your growth. Listen to the feedback you receive from your teachers, coaches, or peers on your work or performance. See it as an opportunity to learn and improve, rather than as criticism.

Sarah's SMART Success Journey

Sarah was a determined and ambitious teenager with a passion for fashion. At sixteen, she had a vision of creating her own sustainable fashion brand. However, she knew that turning her dream into a reality would require more than just ambition and that she would need to set some goals. She decided to use the SMART strategy to do so.

S - Specific

Her first goal was to be specific about her business idea. She wanted her fashion brand to focus on eco-friendly, handmade clothing. She aimed to promote sustainability and ethical fashion practices. Sarah spent hours researching sustainable materials, production processes, and suppliers. She ensured that all the details aligned with her vision.

M - Measurable

Sarah knew she needed a way to measure her progress, as she would likely be successful sooner if she followed this process. She set targets for herself, such as designing and creating her first line of products within six months. Sarah also tracked the number of garments she produced and the materials she used. This helped her to assess her progress and adjust her goals accordingly.

A - Achievable

Sarah also decided to break her main goal down into smaller, achievable steps. She started by learning the basics of sewing and design, attending workshops, and connecting with local artisans who shared her passion. She was determined to make her brand unique, which meant learning about sustainable production techniques and marketing strategies. All these steps took her closer to achieving her ultimate goal.

R - Relevant

Sarah ensured that her goals were relevant to her vision. She constantly asked herself if her actions were contributing to the success of her sustainable fashion brand. This helped her stay focused on what truly mattered, and she didn't get distracted by anything that could derail her.

T - Time-Bound

Time was of the utmost importance to Sarah. She knew that setting deadlines was crucial. Her SMART goals included launching her brand's website within a year, gaining her first 100 customers within 18 months, and turning a profit by the end of her second year in business. She kept working towards these deadlines and kept adjusting her goals as needed.

This wasn't easy. There were moments of doubt, late nights, and inevitable setbacks. But Sarah's SMART goals kept her on track and motivated.

Two years later, Sarah's sustainable fashion brand was flourishing. Her brand was not only a financial success but a symbol of hope for a more sustainable and ethical fashion industry.

Self-Guided Activity To Set Smart Goals

This activity will help you set SMART goals independently. You can use the spaces provided below to answer them but if you need more space feel free to write in a notebook or use one of your digital devices.

Begin by writing notes on the importance of setting SMART goals for personal development, academic success, and future planning.

Definition of SMART goals. Before you begin setting your SMART goals, you need to understand the definitions:

- **Specific:** Goals should be clear and well-defined.
- **Measurable:** Goals should include criteria to track progress.
- **Achievable:** Goals should be realistic and within reach.
- **Relevant:** Goals should align with their interests and values.
- **Time-bound:** Goals should have a set deadline for completion.

Jot down at least three goals for yourself. These can be related to education, personal development, hobbies, or any aspect of life that is important to you.

Choose one of your goals and analyze it using the SMART criteria. Use the following questions to guide you:

- **Specific:** What is your goal? Can you make it more specific?

_____

_____

_____

- **Measurable:** How will you measure your progress? What criteria will you use?

_____

_____

_____

- **Achievable:** Is this goal realistic given your current resources and constraints?

_____

_____

_____

- **Relevant:** Why is this goal important to you? How does it align with your values?

_____

_____

_____

- **Time-bound:** When do you want to achieve this goal?

_____

_____

_____

If you choose to use a notebook (whether physical or digital) find a fresh page where you can write your selected goal and create a table with the headings: Specific, Measurable, Achievable, Relevant, and Time-bound. Fill in each column with the answers you would have received from your analysis. You can do the same for the questions below.

Visualize Success: Visualize yourself successfully achieving your goal. What does it look and feel like?

_____

_____

_____

Action Plan: Create a basic action plan for your goal. What steps will you take to work toward it? Can you overcome potential obstacles?

_____

_____

_____

Reflection: Reflect on how setting SMART goals makes you feel.

_____

_____

_____

Regular Review: Regularly review and adjust your goals as needed and track your progress in your notebook or the space provided below.

_____

_____

_____

_____

_____

_____

Key Takeaways

- Goals are essential for turning your dreams into reality.
- Goal setting is exciting and not just about dull routines.
- SMART goals (Specific, Measurable, Achievable, Relevant, Time-bound) are a very effective way of setting your goals.
- Tailored techniques for goal setting include visualization, chunking, journaling, vision boards, and mind maps.
- Be flexible and adapt your goals to your changing priorities in life.
- Short-term goals are like mini-missions, leading to a sense of achievement.
- Long-term goals are like longer, epic quests, and you need to be dedicated to achieve them.
- Short-term goals prepare you for long-term success.
- Use reminders for your tasks and create a daily planner.
- Set time limits for tasks to prevent procrastination. If we don't have deadlines or time limits, it will usually take us much longer to complete certain tasks.
- Block out distractions and establish a daily routine.
- Prioritize tasks and learn to say no when necessary.
- Effective time management is a skill that you can improve with practice. It will set you ahead of the rest if you learn these skills at a young age.

- If you have a fixed mindset, you believe you were born with your skills and talents, and you can't do anything to change them. If you have a growth mindset, you believe you can keep on learning and improve your skills throughout your life.
- You should regard mistakes and failures as opportunities for learning. Don't get depressed by them, just keep on going.
- Seek out challenges and new experiences.
- Make sure you surround yourself with role models with a growth mindset. You can learn a lot from these positive people.
- Encourage positive self-talk and replace negative thoughts. As soon as you realize you're starting to think in a negative way, work on changing your thoughts.
- Set growth-oriented goals, break them into smaller steps, and celebrate your progress.
- Embrace constructive feedback as a tool for improvement.

In the next chapter, we look at how you can energize your body and supercharge your brain.

Strategy 3

Energize Your Body and Supercharge Your Brain

> *"The human body, like the human mind, is best at versatility and adaptability. This is our greatest skill and our greatest chance to unlock natural potential. What that means in terms of physical movement is that a fairly equal amount of time and effort should be allocated to the widest possible range of activity. That includes strength, flexibility, precision, and endurance, but it certainly doesn't stop there."*
>
> — Darrell Calkins

As the quote says, your body and your mind are versatile and adaptable. It's not just a tool for lifting stuff or running around; it's a finely tuned machine that can do so much more. That's your secret weapon, and in this chapter, we're going to unleash its full potential.

You see, it's not just about being strong or flexible. It's about being an all-rounder, a dynamic force to be reckoned with.

So, what's the deal? It's not just about pumping iron or mastering yoga poses. It's about exploring the wide world of physical movement. You're going to discover strength, flexibility, precision, and endurance, but guess what? We're not stopping there. We're delving into the vast spectrum of what your body can achieve. Get ready to unlock your full physical potential and become a true champion of versatility.

Discovering The Mind-Body Connection

There's a strong connection between your physical and mental health. If you feel better, you'll think better too. So, you can say a healthy body is your secret weapon to developing superthinking powers.

Your mind and body are two sides of the same coin. What happens on one side will influence the other one. When you're physically fit, your mind will be sharper and you'll be better equipped to tackle challenges.

Stress is a part of life, and in your case, it's probably the result of schoolwork, exams, and social pressures. But here's the twist—when your body is in good shape, you'll also be able to handle stress more efficiently. Exercise, a healthy diet, and enough sleep act will bust your stress and help your mind stay cool under pressure.

Exercise isn't just for muscles; it's for your brain too. Physical activity increases blood flow to the brain, which makes your brain work better. It's almost like giving it a power boost.

Exercise triggers the release of "feel-good hormones" endorphins, which can lift your mood. A healthy body can help you deal with your teenage years with more resilience.

Your mind and body both benefit from a healthy diet. A balanced diet, rich in essential nutrients, supports optimal brain function. Quality sleep also helps you concentrate and learn better.

A healthy mind also supports your physical well-being. When you're mentally strong, you'll also be more likely to make choices that are better for your body.

Diet, Exercise, and Sleep

Sleep might not be the first thing on your mind, but it's important for a successful and healthy life. Your teenage years are a whirlwind of changes and experiences, and getting the right amount of quality sleep can make a massive difference.

Diet and Sleep

Think of your body as a car that needs the right fuel to run smoothly. A balanced diet with plenty of fruits, veggies, whole grains, and lean proteins is like premium gasoline for your system. Spicy and sugary foods should be avoided close to bedtime, as they can give you indigestion and disrupt your sleep.

While it's important to stay hydrated, you should monitor your fluid intake in the evening to prevent nighttime trips to the bathroom. You need to find the right balance as dehydration can also disturb your sleep.

Love your caffeine and sugary snacks? They can be your buddies during the day, but late afternoon or evening caffeine and sugar can linger in your system and keep you tossing and turning at night. Avoid these treats before you go to bed.

Try to establish a regular eating schedule and stick to it as much as possible. Regularity helps regulate your internal body clock, making it easier to fall asleep and wake up.

Exercise and Sleep

Exercise doesn't only help you keep your weight down, it will also help you sleep better. Physical activity during the day can help you fall asleep faster and also sleep deeper. So, get out there and start moving around. Exercise doesn't have to be a punishment, it can be something you enjoy, such as dancing.

Exercise boosts your adrenaline and energy, so don't do too much right before you go to bed. Complete your workout at least a few hours before sleep to give your body a chance to wind down.

A consistent exercise routine can help you improve your sleep quality. Find an activity you love and stick with it by making it a part of your regular routine.

Sunlight plays an important role in regulating your body's internal clock. Outdoor activities, especially in the morning, can help synchronize your circadian rhythms and promote better sleep.

It's not about making drastic changes overnight. Small adjustments can improve your sleep quality, which will make sure you have more energy and a brighter outlook on life.

Your teenage years are about self-discovery and growth, and you need quality sleep and energy to get the most from your energy. So, eat well, move often, and sleep tight.

Good Ways to Recharge

You can give your body the TLC it deserves in the following ways.

Spend Time in Nature

Try to spend as much time as possible in nature, as this can also be your escape from a stressful life. Take a break, go for a hike, sit by a lake, or take a walk in the park. The fresh air and greenery can clear your mind and lift your spirits.

Keep a Gratitude Journal

Keep a journal and write about the things for which you're grateful in your life. Write down the good stuff—a friendly chat with great friends, a tasty meal, or even just a sunny day. It can boost your mood and remind you of all the positive things in your life.

Expand Your Consciousness

Feed your curiosity. Read, and watch documentaries, or podcasts on topics that interest you. Expand your horizons and explore the world beyond your immediate surroundings. This is especially important for your personal growth and development throughout your life.

Meditate

Meditation isn't just for monks; it's for anyone who wants a clear mind. Take a few minutes to sit quietly, breathe deeply, and let go of stress. Your brain will feel refreshed.

Express Yourself Creatively

It doesn't have to be perfect, it's just about finding a way to express yourself. Whether it's painting, short story writing, or playing music, get creative. It will be a helpful outlet for your emotions and thoughts.

Treat Your Body Like a Temple

Your body needs to last for your entire lifetime, so treat it as well as you possibly can. Eat a balanced diet, get enough sleep, and drink plenty of water. Your future self will thank you for these healthy habits.

Start a Mindful Morning Routine

Mornings will set the tone for the rest of your day. Start with a healthy breakfast where you allow yourself a chance to quietly think about your intentions for the rest of the day. It can help you feel grounded and ready to take on challenges.

Regularly Learn Something New

Your learning doesn't have to be limited to the classroom. Learning keeps your mind agile and can open the doors to exciting opportunities. The new skills you learn can even lead to business opportunities.

Volunteer

Helping others can be a powerful way to recharge if you give your time to something you're passionate about. The satisfaction of making a difference can boost your self-esteem and well-being.

Living the Healthy Life: Alex's story

Alex was a high school student and aspiring entrepreneur with big dreams. He was passionate about technology, and he had recently launched his own startup, which designs innovative apps to make people's lives easier.

Alex's days were filled with excitement, challenges, and countless new ideas. His journey was a whirlwind of online meetings, brainstorming sessions, and coding marathons. On top of that, he still needed to do his schoolwork. It seemed like there was never enough time in the day to tackle everything on his to-do list.

He often didn't get enough sleep, as he felt this was the only way he could get more hours into his hectic, busy days. His startup's success was his top priority, and he believed that sacrificing a few hours of sleep each night was a small price to pay for his dreams. However, his friends and family were worried. They knew that something had to change.

One evening, Alex's best friend, Sarah, invited him to a local park for a chat. They sat down on a bench and she told him about her concerns. She told him that she admired his dedication, but that he also needed to take care of his health by sleeping more. Sarah said that he was starting to appear worn out and anxious.

Alex told her that he had so much to do that he simply couldn't afford to sleep a full 8 hours every night.

Sarah told him that he could start by making small changes and that a well-rested mind is more creative and efficient.

Alex decided to take Sarah's advice seriously, as he had also started to get worn out and had recently noticed that he was getting more sick than ever before. He began to prioritize his sleep by establishing a bedtime routine. He turned off his phone and computer an hour before bedtime, opting for a relaxing book instead. He started going to bed and waking up at the same time every day, ensuring he got at least 7 hours of sleep. It took a while, but he finally started seeing the positive effects of his changed routine.

As Alex started sleeping better, he noticed a remarkable change in his work. His mind was sharper, and he could think more clearly. His coding became more efficient, and he came up with innovative solutions faster than ever before. He even found more time for exercise, which gave him the energy to tackle each day's challenges.

With improved sleep habits, Alex's startup began to thrive. Investors were impressed by his creativity and energy, and the quality of his work improved. Alex realized that Sarah was right all along—sleep was a game-changer for his business journey.

His story also encouraged his friends with entrepreneurial ambitions to prioritize their sleep. They learned that quality sleep wasn't a hindrance but could actually help them achieve their dreams earlier.

Worksheet: Discover Your Mind-Body Connection

Complete the following exercises to discover your mind-body connection. Find a quiet, comfortable space to focus and reflect.

Start your journey by keeping a Mind-Body journal. Create a two-column table in your journal or on a blank piece of paper. Label the first column "Mental" and the second column "Physical."

In the "Mental" column, jot down any thoughts, emotions, or stressors you've experienced recently. For example, you might write that you feel stressed about exams, or anxious when you have to do a presentation in class.

In the "Physical" column, write down how you have experienced these factors in your body. Are there any physical sensations associated with these thoughts or emotions? For example, you could have stomach pains or a tight chest when you feel stressed.

Breathing Exercise

Practice deep breathing to feel the connection between your breath and your state of mind. Close your eyes, sit up straight, and take a deep breath in through your nose for a count of four. Hold for a count of two, and then exhale through your mouth for a count of six. Pay attention to how your body and mind feel before and after this exercise.

Body Scan Meditation

Sit or lie down somewhere it's quiet. Close your eyes and focus your attention on different parts of your body, starting from your toes and moving up to your head. As you focus on each body part, notice any tension, discomfort, or sensations. Be aware of how your mental state may be affecting your body.

Emotion Check-In

Reflect on your most common emotions throughout the day. Are you frequently stressed, anxious, happy, or relaxed? Write your emotions down. Try to identify patterns in your emotional states and see if they agree with specific physical symptoms.

Physical Activity

Engage in a physical activity of your choice, like a short workout, yoga, or a walk. While doing this, pay attention to how your physical activity affects your mood. How do you feel after exercising compared to before?

Gratitude Journal

Write down three things you're grateful for today. Reflect on how this exercise makes you feel both mentally and physically. Do you notice any changes in your body when you focus on gratitude?

_____

_____

_____

_____

_____

Reflection

- How do your thoughts and emotions impact your physical well-being?

_____

_____

_____

- How does your physical health affect your mental state?

_____

_____

_____

- Can you identify any patterns in the mind-body connection through this exercise?

_____

_____

_____

- Are there any actions you can take to improve this connection for your overall well-being?

_____

_____

_____

Action Plan

Based on your reflections, write down a simple action plan. What steps can you take to strengthen your mind-body connection and promote better health? This will include stress management techniques, regular exercise, mindfulness practices, or seeking support when needed.

_____

_____

_____

_____

_____

_____

Regular Check-Ins

Check in regularly with your mind and body connection. Make a point of regularly reviewing your journal entries.

A Lifelong Learning Mentality

If you have a lifelong learning mentality, also known as a growth mindset, you follow a psychological and intellectual approach to life where you focus on gaining knowledge and skills throughout your life. A lifelong learning mentality has certain key characteristics.

People who have a lifelong learning mentality are naturally curious and eager to explore new ideas, concepts, and experiences. They're always interested in learning new things, and will even learn new skills from watching programs on YouTube.

They can also embrace change and view challenges as opportunities to learn and grow, rather than as setbacks. If you overreact to every challenge in your life, you run the risk of getting caught up in a victim mentality, and you could start believing that you're not capable of doing anything.

You need to be open to different perspectives and willing to consider new viewpoints, even if they conflict with your existing beliefs. You recognize your strengths and weaknesses, and this helps you recognize areas in your life where you still need to make improvements. You're committed to becoming a better version of yourself.

You're open to receiving feedback and you seek guidance from mentors or experts in your field.

A lifelong learning mentality also consists of informal learning, skill acquisition, personal development, and a mindset that encourages growth and self-discovery throughout one's life.

Cassandra's Lifelong Journey to Success

Cassandra, a dynamic and driven entrepreneur, understood that the key to achieving success in the ever-evolving world of business was a lifelong commitment to learning. From a young age, she believed in continuous education and self-improvement, which helped her build a successful business.

Cassandra's entrepreneurial journey began when she launched her tech startup at the age of 16. She was passionate about creating innovative software solutions, but she also knew that the technology landscape was constantly changing. She had a vision for her company, but she also recognized that it was essential to stay ahead of the curve.

Embracing Change

Cassandra knew that technology was a field where change was the only constant. She not only embraced change but actively sought it out. She stayed updated with the latest industry trends, attended conferences, and read research papers. This allowed her to pivot her business when necessary and adapt to new technologies and methodologies.

Networking

Cassandra understood the value of networking. She built a strong professional network by attending industry events and engaging with experts in her field. These connections provided her with insights, mentorship, and collaborative opportunities that were instrumental in her business growth.

Formal Education

Cassandra didn't stop with her initial degree. She pursued additional formal education through online courses, workshops, and certifications. She even encouraged her team to do the same. Her business benefited from the collective knowledge and expertise of her educated workforce.

Experimentation and Innovation

Cassandra fostered a culture of experimentation and innovation within her company. She encouraged her team to try new ideas and technologies, allowing them to learn from their mistakes and successes. This culture of innovation helped her business stay competitive and ahead of the curve.

Feedback and Adaptation

Cassandra actively sought feedback from her clients, team, and mentors. She used this feedback to refine her business strategies and improve her products. This commitment to ongoing improvement was a driving force behind her company's success.

Resilience

Despite the inevitable challenges and setbacks in business, Cassandra remained resilient. She saw failures as opportunities for learning and growth, and she shared these experiences with her team to inspire a culture of resilience and adaptability.

Over the years, Cassandra's company grew into a renowned tech firm, known for its innovative solutions and adaptable approach. Her commitment to lifelong learning created a dynamic and agile business that thrived in a rapidly changing landscape. She also became a mentor to other aspiring entrepreneurs, sharing her wisdom and emphasizing the importance of continual education and growth.

Cassandra's story serves as a powerful reminder that a lifelong learning mentality is not just a personal philosophy; it's a powerful strategy for success in today's dynamic business world. Her journey highlights the transformative impact of staying curious, open to new ideas, and committed to personal and professional growth.

Key Takeaways

- Your body and mind are versatile and adaptable.
- Focus on being an all-rounder in terms of physical movement.
- You should explore strength, flexibility, precision, endurance, and more to unleash your full potential.
- Your physical and mental health are interconnected.
- Physical fitness sharpens your mind and helps you tackle challenges.
- If you have a healthy body, you'll be better able to manage stress, it will boost your mood and support better decision-making.
- Quality sleep is important during your teenage years, as you're still developing physically and emotionally.
- A balanced diet with regular eating patterns will fuel your body.
- You should avoid caffeine and sugary snacks should be avoided near bedtime.
- Exercise helps you sleep better and should be a regular part of your routine.

- Sunlight and outdoor activities will help regulate your body's internal clock.
- Spending time in nature can reduce your stress levels.
- Maintaining a gratitude journal can boost your mood.
- Expand your consciousness through reading and exploration.
- Practice meditation for a clear mind.
- Expressing yourself creatively can help you with emotional regulation.
- Prioritize self-care and healthy habits.
- Continue learning beyond the classroom. People with a lifelong learning mentality often have the most meaningful lives.
- Volunteering can also give you a sense of fulfillment and well-being.

In the next chapter, we will look at entrepreneurship and how you can create your own unique healthypreneurial path with confidence and purpose.

Strategy 4
The Teen Entrepreneur's Toolbox

"If you've got an idea, start today. There's no better time than now to get going. That doesn't mean quit your job and jump into your idea 100% from day one, but there's always small progress that can be made to start the movement."

— Kevin Systrom, Instagram

So, what exactly is this "entrepreneurship" thing, and why should you, as a teenager, care about it? A good way to think of it is as the ultimate adventure in creativity, innovation, and problem-solving. You identify a problem, find a solution, and then take the initiative to make it happen. You may think this journey is only for adults, but you can also be an entrepreneur.

Let's take a more in-depth look at what it means to be an entrepreneur.

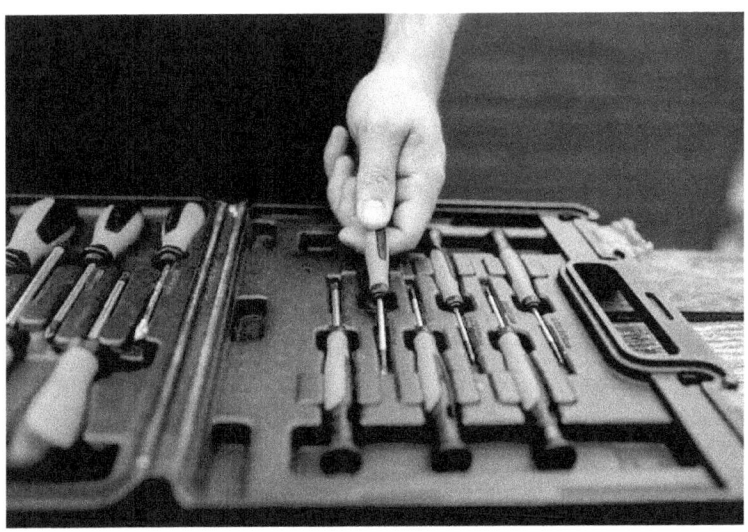

Entrepreneurship: What It's All About

Entrepreneurs are problem solvers. They spot issues, both big and small, and come up with smart and innovative ways to fix them. Business owners need to be able to think outside the box, so their imaginations are often their most important tool. They need to be able to dream big and bring fresh ideas to the table.

It's a huge responsibility because as a business owner you need to work out your own way in which you will achieve success. The answers aren't always in books, and you can't always rely on adults to provide you with the answers you're looking for. You need to step up and take charge of making your dreams a reality.

Keep looking for better ways to do things, and make sure you stay up to date with the latest ways of doing things. Push the boundaries. To be a successful entrepreneur, you need to be able to adapt and evolve.

Entrepreneurs are usually hands-on. It's not only about being book smart. You learn by doing, taking calculated risks, and even embracing failure as a stepping stone to success. Your mistakes are simply learning opportunities.

Being an entrepreneur isn't limited to a specific age group. It's a mindset that will empower you to shape your future and make a mark on the world.

Why Teenagers Should Become Entrepreneurs

So, why should you start as a teenager?

You're bursting with creativity, and you likely have lots of fresh ideas. Even though you don't have all the knowledge you need yet, you have tons of energy and you want to do things differently. You also don't have as many responsibilities as older entrepreneurs who may have to balance their work and family life and can focus most of your attention on your business, except for your school work.

Entrepreneurship gives you the practical life experience you need, as you learn by doing. It's an opportunity to learn practically, instead of just theory from textbooks and lectures. You can learn by taking action.

You don't have to wait until you're older and have completed your education to make a difference. As a teenpreneur, you can start making your mark on the world right now. Your ideas have the power to solve problems, inspire change, and leave a legacy. The challenges that come with being a young entrepreneur also help you build your resilience. After all, you can only survive as an entrepreneur if you're able to bounce back from challenges and face them head-on.

Entrepreneurship can also be a good fit for you if you want independence and freedom. You can be the boss and set your own goals, make your own decisions, and enjoy the freedom to work when and where you want. Just make sure that you're always open to learning from others when they offer you useful advice. Being the boss doesn't mean that you know everything and you should keep on learning to improve your business.

You could end up discovering your true passion in life through entrepreneurship. We often don't know what we want until we try different things. Entrepreneurship can be like a journey of self-discovery, as it helps you find out what you really care about.

Being a teenpreneur can give you the opportunity to connect to people who can help you get further in life. You'll build a network of mentors, peers, and supporters who can guide you along the way. These connections can be valuable for you throughout your life and can help you build your business.

The Advantages and Disadvantages of Being an Entrepreneur

Like with everything in life, there are advantages and disadvantages to being an entrepreneur. Let's go through them together so you can decide for yourself if you think the pros outweigh the cons.

+ *The Pros*

There are many pros to being an entrepreneur, and once you're on this journey, you won't want to look back.

Freedom and Independence

Entrepreneurs can set their own schedules and decide how and when they want to work. For example, if you love photography, you can start your own photography business and choose when and where to take photos. People can hire you to take photos at events, and you can structure your time in a way that suits you best.

Creative Expression

You can use entrepreneurship as a canvas for your creativity. For example, if you make a unique range of clothes, you can start your own online art store, and showcase and sell your unique creations to a global audience. You could do the same with any other artistic item and you have the creative freedom to express yourself through your work.

Learning From Your Mistakes

Every setback in your business is a valuable lesson. It might be difficult to see this at first, but every time something goes wrong there's an opportunity for you to learn more and not make the same mistake again. For example, you have a business where you make healthy food and deliver it to people. You have a small delivery vehicle, and you have to learn the ins and outs as you go. However, your mistakes in the kitchen become opportunities to improve your recipes and customer service.

Leaving Your Mark

Healthypreneurship gives you the chance to leave your mark on the world. For example, you start a company that provides clean drinking water to poor communities. Your business is changing lives and leaving a lasting legacy of positive change.

Flexibility

When you're an entrepreneur, you don't have to follow a nine-to-five schedule. You have the flexibility to work when and where you want. This is brilliant for teenagers who are still at school, as you can structure your business ventures around your learning time. Your office is basically wherever you connect to the internet. For example, you can share quick blog updates while waiting for your friends in a restaurant, or squeeze in some work between doing your homework.

Potential for Unlimited Earnings

Unlike a regular office job, there's no limit to what you can earn. For example, you could create a new app that becomes a massive hit and provides you with substantial income. The harder you work and the more value you can provide to people, the more money you will earn.

Pursuit of Passion

Entrepreneurship allows you to turn your passion into a profession. If you're an animal lover, you can start a pet-sitting or dog-walking business. If you love children, you could become a babysitter. You get to spend your time doing whatever it is you love, and making money from it.

Control and Decision-Making

You have complete control over your business and you can make decisions that align with your vision. For example, if you want to sell eco-friendly products, you can start a business dedicated to sustainable, environmentally conscious goods. Product development, marketing, and company values are all your decisions.

Networking Opportunities

As an entrepreneur, you have the chance to connect with people from various backgrounds. Let's say you're an aspiring fashion designer, with a passion for exercise gear and you want to promote good health. By starting your fashion brand, you can work with models, photographers, and content creators who can help you promote your range. In this way, you will expand your network and learn from different experts in the industry.

Leaving a Legacy

The business you build can be a legacy for your family. A successfully owned family business that can be passed down to your children, providing them with a secure future.

— *The Cons*

Before you set out on your journey to start your business, there are certain disadvantages you have to keep in mind.

Uncertain Income

This one won't apply so much to you if you're a teenager living with your parents who provide you with food and a roof over your head. However, we'll take a look at it anyway, so that you can get a comprehensive idea of all the risks involved.

Starting your own business can be financially uncertain, especially in the beginning. You might not have a regular paycheck for a while, and your income can be unpredictable. For example, if you launch an online store selling handmade crafts, some months may be better than others when it comes to sales. This is why entrepreneurs need to be able to budget.

Responsibility Overload

When you're the boss, you're responsible for every aspect of your business. From the big decisions like what products to offer or how to market them, to the small details like managing inventory and customer service. It can be overwhelming, especially if you still have school work and a social and family life.

No Safety Net

This one is also for the older entrepreneurs whose parents aren't providing for their basic needs, but it's good to know about it all the same. When you're an entrepreneur, there's no safety net like a traditional job. You're on your own, and it's very possible that you might fail. You need grit and resilience to keep going, even when things get tough and it looks like the business might not work out. If you face challenges, you have to be able to persevere and adapt.

Work-Life Balance

The line between work and personal life can blur when you're an entrepreneur. You might find yourself working around the clock to keep your business afloat. Balancing school, personal life, and your business can be a challenge. For example, if you're a young tech enthusiast who is creating a mobile app you could find it difficult to keep up with managing your school assignments and social activities while also developing and marketing your app.

Risk and Stress

The risks of entrepreneurship can be stressful. You're putting your time, money, and effort on the line, and that can be nerve-wracking. For example, you could start a small lawn care business and take risks by investing in equipment and marketing. If you have a period with few customers, it can be stressful as you've invested your savings into the venture.

The Traits of a Successful Entrepreneur

There are certain character traits that can help you be successful as an entrepreneur.

Strong Leadership Qualities

Strong leadership qualities will count in your favor, as you need to inspire and guide your business team to be successful. For example, think about starting a school club. You have to have a vision for the club and need to be able to motivate your peers to work together to make it a success.

Self-Motivated

As an entrepreneur, you need to be incredibly self-motivated. You need to have an inner drive to push yourself even when you're faced with challenges. For example, you might decide to start an online art store. Once you start, you need to motivate yourself to create new artwork, manage the online store, and promote your work without anyone supervising them. You basically need to keep going after you start, otherwise, your store won't be a success.

Strong Sense of Ethics and Integrity

Entrepreneurs make decisions that are not only good for their business but also for society. For example, if you decide to start a small clothing brand you should ensure your products are ethically produced, with fair labor practices and sustainable materials.

Willingness to Fail

You're able to accept failure as part of your entrepreneurial journey. For example, you might decide to start a YouTube channel. Your early videos might not get many views, but if you keep learning and improving and understanding that each video—even if it doesn't go viral—is a learning opportunity, you will eventually achieve success.

Serial Innovators

Successful entrepreneurs can keep coming up with new ideas and solutions to problems. For example, if you're passionate about environmental issues and you create a series of eco-friendly products, such as reusable shopping bags, upcycled fashion, and organic soaps.

Know What You Don't Know

Entrepreneurs recognize that they can't be experts in everything, and they try to learn from others. For example, if you have a tech startup idea and you reach out to mentors or join coding classes to gain the knowledge and skills you need.

Competitive Spirit

A competitive spirit will encourage you to continually improve as an entrepreneur. Imagine a teenager who enjoys creating digital art. They see others in online art communities gaining recognition and strive to enhance their skills and create even more impressive artwork.

Understand the Value of a Strong Peer Network

Successful entrepreneurs understand that they can't do everything alone. You will need to build a strong network of peers and mentors. For example, if you have a passion for photography you could join photography clubs or forums to connect with like-minded individuals and gain more knowledge.

Finding Your Passion And Identifying Business Opportunities

Before you can start your business, you need to discover your passion and identify business opportunities. Here's how you can go about doing this.

When you set out to start your business, you should think about what you already enjoy doing. Think back to times when you were super excited about what you were doing. Those moments hold the secret to your passions. What is particularly exciting is that your passion can be the foundation for a successful business. You could end up making money from your hobbies. For example, if you enjoy making healthy food and snacks, you can think of finding a way of marketing and distributing them to others.

Also, surround yourself with people who love what they do and talk to them about their experiences. They'll inspire you.

You should also look at tying the things you enjoy doing together. Try to find common threads among your interests. For example, if you enjoy painting, drawing, and creating art, and you're into technology and programming, you can look at offering both a graphic and web design service.

You should evaluate which of your interests has the potential to solve a problem or meet a need in the market. There needs to be a demand for what you want to do, not all of your hobbies would be profitable and should be monetized. It will save you time and money if you first do research about which of your hobbies would be worth turning into a business.

Fear of failure is something you'll need to overcome before you can make headway with your business. A business will always involve financial concerns and uncertainty. Acknowledge your fears, break them down into more manageable steps, and concentrate on overcoming them.

Begin small when you start out. First research your field, and then find mentors and online resources that can give you guidance. You'll probably have to take some risks, but these don't necessarily have to be scary. For example, enroll in classes that give you the skills you need.

Finally, your journey to finding your passion and dream job is all about blending what you love with what you do for a living. It can be an exciting phase of self-discovery and growth.

Starting Your Business

It's exciting and rewarding to start your own business. Before you can get started, you need to brainstorm and come up with a plan.

Brainstorming Ideas

Begin by brainstorming business ideas that align with your interests, skills, and passions. Consider what you're good at and what you love to do. It could be anything from starting a small online store to offering tutoring services in the school subjects that you're good at.

Conducting Research

You need to research your business idea thoroughly. Study your target audience, market trends, and competitors. For example, if you plan to sell handmade health food, explore the demand for your products, what the ingredients will cost you, and where you will be able to buy them.

Put Your Plan Into Action

Once you've done your planning and research, it's time to put your plan into action. Find out what resources you need and create a business plan. You also need to figure out how you will fund your business. This could be through your savings, family support, or even crowdfunding. If you're running an online business, set up a user-friendly website or online store.

Taking Your Business to the Next Level

As your business grows, look for opportunities to take it to the next level. You should always be working on developing and growing your business. This could mean expanding your product or service offerings, increasing your customer base, and looking at new ways of marketing it. Stay open to learning from your experiences and adapt your business according to what you've learned.

Teenagers Who Started Successful Businesses

Let's walk along with three teenagers who managed to start successful businesses.

Shubham Banerjee

The remarkable story of Shubham Banerjee's began when he was 13 years old and he introduced his own creation, a Braille printer, at his school's 7th-grade science fair. The typical cost of Braille printers was well over £1,500, but Banerjee's innovative design came in at just £250. When his idea became more popular, he decided to share the design and software freely with others.

Following his initial success, Banerjee went on to establish a company aimed at manufacturing Braigo v2.0, with the support of an investment from Intel. He got well-deserved recognition for his brilliant idea, and he's using this to advance his vision further.

Juliette Brindak

Juliette Brindak entered the online world as a teenager with a unique vision. At the age of 16, she created a social networking site specifically for tween and teenage girls. She got her idea from the belief that girls in this age group needed a safe and exclusive space where they could connect. Brindak also personalized the platform by adding cartoon characters she had drawn as a child.

The website's mission was clear: to offer girls a secure place to discuss their experiences, look for advice, and just have fun. With the support of her family, Brindak brought her vision to life. By 2012, the website was enjoying a remarkable success, with approximately 10 million monthly visitors and a value of about $15 million.

Benjamin Stern

At the young age of 14, Benjamin Stern got an idea while he was watching a documentary that shed light on the vast amount of unrecycled plastic waste, particularly in the form of shampoo bottles found in bathrooms. He decided to create single-use shampoo pods enclosed in biodegradable, plant-based packaging. He started fundraising to bring his idea to life. With the support of his family, he launched his company by the time he turned 16.

Stern's Nohbo shampoo balls remain solid until they come into contact with water, eliminating the risk of leaks in your bag. Environmental consciousness is at the core of this product, as Stern proudly highlights that the balls are plant-based and animal cruelty-free. They're also free from parabens and sulfates.

In the next chapter of the book, we're going to look at how you can overcome villains and bounce back from adversity in your life.

Business Opportunities

You should consider the following business types that also align with wellness and well-being. The following businesses shouldn't be too hard to manage along with your schoolwork.

You can offer online coaching or tutoring services in subjects you excel in, whether it's academics, sports, or music. This can mostly be done in the comfort of your own home unless it's very specific sports coaching.

If you're passionate about fitness and nutrition, you can become a fitness coach and offer workout plans, meal guidance, or online classes. In this way, you're also helping others by living healthier lifestyles.

Creating a blog or a YouTube channel about health, wellness, or personal development can be an excellent way to share knowledge, connect with your audience, and eventually monetize through ads or affiliate marketing. This is something that's easy to do while you're still at school, as you can just log on to your business once you've taken care of your other obligations.

You could even set up an online store that sells health and wellness products, focusing on drop shipping to minimize inventory costs. E-commerce can be done through platforms like Shopify or Etsy.

If you have coding skills, you can also use them to create health or fitness-related mobile apps. This can be done as a solo project or in collaboration with others.

Offering social media management services to small businesses, particularly those in the health and wellness sector, for example, a chiropractor's office could also be a viable business.

Teens with crafting skills can create and sell handmade wellness products like natural soaps, candles, or jewelry online or at local markets.

Writing articles or creating graphics for health and wellness blogs, magazines, or social media accounts can be a source of income for teens with writing or design skills. Even if these online jobs don't pay that well to begin with, it's also a way of building skills for your future career, and it could help you decide which field you want to study or undergo further training.

If you love animals, you can offer pet sitting, dog walking, or pet grooming services, which can be not only a profitable venture but can help you stay active.

If you have good organizational skills and a passion for wellness, you can plan and organize wellness events, retreats, or fitness workshops in your area.

When you're starting out, focus on businesses that match your skills, interests, and resources. Consider the legal requirements, such as permits or parental consent. Regardless of the chosen business, maintaining a balance between entrepreneurship and personal well-being is essential to their long-term success and happiness.

Worksheet: Identifying Business Opportunities

This worksheet will help you identify potential business opportunities within the health and wellness industry. It guides you through a series of questions and exercises to find areas where you can make a positive impact.

Work on these questions in a quiet and comfortable place. Be honest and creative in the way you answer them.

Self-Reflection

- What are your personal interests and passions when it comes to health and wellness?

- List your skills, such as research, cooking, fitness, or communication.

_____

_____

_____

- Think about health issues or challenges you or your family have faced. Are there any areas where you'd like to see improvements or solutions?

_____

_____

_____

Market Research

- Research the current health and wellness trends. What products or services are becoming more popular?

_____

_____

_____

- Investigate local or global health challenges and gaps in the market. Are there unmet needs or underserved communities?

_____

_____

_____

- Explore your community or school for health-related issues or concerns. Speak with peers, teachers, or parents to gather insights. Summarize your findings below.

_____

_____

_____

Identify Your Target Audience

- Define the specific group of people you want to help or serve (e.g., athletes, children, people with specific conditions).

_____

_____

_____

- Consider their demographics, interests, and needs. What are the problems they face regarding health and wellness?

Brainstorming

- Generate a list of health and wellness business ideas based on your interests, skills, and market research. Be creative and don't limit yourself.

- Think about products, services, or solutions that address the needs of your target audience.

Evaluating Ideas

- Review your list of ideas and choose one that you think will work for your target audience.

_____

_____

_____

- How feasible is your chosen idea? Is it something you can realistically pursue with the resources you have available?

_____

_____

_____

- Consider the potential impact and benefits your idea could bring to your target audience and the community.

_____

_____

_____

Unique Selling Proposition (USP)

- Define what makes your idea unique or better than existing solutions in the market.

_____

_____

_____

- How does your idea address the needs of your target audience in a way that sets you apart from the competition?

_____

_____

_____

Prototype or Concept

- Create a rough sketch or concept of your product or service. This could be a simple drawing, outline, or description.

_____

_____

_____

- Think about how your idea will work, what it will look like, and how it will benefit your target audience.

_____

_____

_____

- If it's a service, outline the steps and processes involved.

_____

_____

_____

Feedback and Refinement

- Share your concept with a trusted friend, family member, or mentor and gather feedback. Record the feedback below.

_____

_____

_____

- Use this feedback to refine your idea and make necessary adjustments. List those adjustments in the space provided.

_____

_____

_____

Next Steps and Action Plan

- Outline the steps you need to take to move forward with your healthypreneur idea.

_____

_____

_____

- Consider aspects like research, development, funding, and marketing.

_____

_____

_____

Ongoing Exploration

Commit to exploring new trends, attending relevant events, and continuously researching the health and wellness field.

Keep a notebook or digital journal to write down the ideas and insights that may lead to future opportunities.

Final Thoughts

- Reflect on how this exercise has helped you identify a healthypreneur opportunity.

_____

_____

_____

- Set a goal or timeframe for when you plan to take the first step toward making your idea a reality.

_____

_____

_____

The health and wellness industry is large and there are many different opportunities that you can explore.

Key Takeaways

- Entrepreneurship is the ultimate adventure in creativity, innovation, and problem-solving.
- As a teenager, you can identify problems, find solutions, and take the initiative to make things happen.
- Being an entrepreneur is about being a problem solver, thinking outside the box, and dreaming big.
- It's a responsibility that involves taking charge of making your dreams a reality, often without relying on adults for answers.
- Entrepreneurship provides practical life experience and the opportunity to learn by doing.
- Entrepreneurship offers you freedom and independence in setting schedules and work locations.
- It allows you to pursue your passion in life.
- One of the disadvantages of entrepreneurship is an uncertain income, especially in the initial stages of the business. You also don't have job security.
- As an entrepreneur, you need to be willing to accept failure as part of the journey.
- You need to have the ability to come up with new ideas and solutions, and also be willing to learn from others.
- You need the desire to continually improve.
- Offer online coaching or tutoring services in subjects you excel in, from academics to sports or music.

- Become a fitness coach and provide workout plans, meal guidance, or online classes to promote healthier lifestyles.
- Create a blog or YouTube channel about health, wellness, or personal development, which can be managed around school commitments.
- Set up an online store selling health and wellness products, focusing on drop shipping to minimize inventory costs.
- Use coding skills to create health or fitness-related mobile apps, either as a solo project or in collaboration with others.
- Offer social media management services to small businesses, especially those in the health and wellness sector.
- Craft and sell handmade wellness items like natural soaps, candles, or jewelry online or at local markets.
- Write articles or create graphics for health and wellness publications, building skills for your future career.
- Offer pet sitting, dog walking, or pet grooming services for pet lovers while staying active.
- Plan wellness events, retreats, or fitness workshops in your area, utilizing organizational skills and passion for wellness.

Strategy 5
Overcoming Villains and Bouncing Back

 "Winners are not afraid of losing. But losers are. Failure is part of the process of success. People who avoid failure also avoid success."

— Robert Kiyosaki

Mia was a teenager with big dreams, but she didn't realize she would face challenges that would test her resilience.

She has always been passionate about art, especially painting. Her dream was to become a well-known artist who would produce work that would touch people's hearts. However, in her sophomore year, she was diagnosed with a medical condition that affected her vision. She felt that the universe had conspired to rob her of her greatest passion.

The diagnosis was devastating, and she felt as if her world was falling apart. The thought of not being able to see the beautiful colors of her own creations was almost unbearable.

But Mia didn't give in to her despair and decided to fight back. She learned about techniques that worked well for other artists with visual impairment. She also met some of these artists and asked them for their guidance. Mia knew that the only thing she could do was to fight against this adversity that was threatening to kill her dreams.

Mia discovered the world of tactile art and learned how to use her other senses to create. The touch of the canvas, the smell of the paints, and the rhythm of her heartbeats guided her strokes. She learned how to use her hands to feel the texture of her artwork.

Her resilience and grit also inspired others, and she was able to determine her path.

Mia became a well-known name in the world of art. Her unique approach to painting, born out of adversity, touched people's hearts. She was invited to art exhibitions and interviewed by magazines. Her story was a testament to the superpower of resilience.

Mia's story demonstrates the superpowers of resilience and grit. We all have the superpowers of resilience and grit, even though they might not have been fully developed yet as teenagers. Imagine resilience as the shield that helps you stand strong against the villains in your life story—the setbacks, challenges, and adversities that make you feel as if you're facing an insurmountable foe.

What Is Resilience And Grit?

Life can be a roller-coaster with unexpected dips and turns. It's not always smooth sailing. Resilience is what helps you stay strong and positive even when you have to deal with setbacks and disappointments.

Most of us have learned to ride bikes as children. You've probably wobbled and fallen off a few times. Resilience is what keeps you going and getting back on that bike, even when you've got a scraped knee, and then trying until you can pedal without a hitch. Resilience is that inner voice that tells you that you can do something.

Resilience isn't about avoiding problems; it's about facing them head-on. You're like you're own superhero; ready to tackle the challenges you come across in your life. When you fail a test, have a disagreement with a friend, or face any tough situation, resilience helps you handle all setbacks with a positive attitude.

Resilience can be practiced and strengthened over time. Every time you overcome a challenge, your resilience grows a little stronger. It's a superpower that helps you keep going, learn from your experiences, and come out even more powerful and confident.

So what is grit and perseverance? Grit is like the engine that drives you toward your long-term goals. It's that inner fire that keeps you going, no matter how tough the journey becomes. It's the determination and passion that fuel your dreams.

Grit is all about hanging in there, even when the going gets tough. It's not giving up on your dreams when faced with challenges. When you have grit you keep moving forward, even if the path is steep.

Grit is fueled by your deep love and enthusiasm for what you're pursuing. It's that burning desire to reach your goals. Think of it as a flame that keeps you warm even during cold times.

Grit is the long-term effort you put into something, that you can compare to a marathon. You're prepared to put in the same amount of hard work day after day. Just like a long-distance runner, you keep going, step by step, until you finally get to where you want to be.

No matter how many times you stumble or face setbacks, grit encourages you to get back up and try again.

Strengthening Your Resilience

There are practical ways in which you can develop your resilience and become more confident.

- You need to develop self-awareness and this involves understanding your emotional responses to stress. Take a moment to recognize how you react when things get tough. Awareness is the first step to building resilience.
- Try to reframe your thoughts when you're stressed, instead of reacting in impulsive ways. You should approach situations with a balanced perspective and rethink your initial reaction to things, especially if it's overly negative.
- Don't get stuck in all-or-nothing thinking when facing problems. Focus on pinpointing the specific problem instead of generalizing and simply saying "Things just always go wrong."
- Keep track of your successes, even the small ones, and celebrate them. Maintaining a success journal can boost your motivation and positive emotions such as pride.
- Spread positivity wherever you go. Even simple gestures such as thanking someone when they do something for you can improve your relationship. Find a positive routine in your life, like sharing daily highlights with loved ones.
- Strengthen your social networks and share your connections with others. You should do your best to figure out what you have in common with your

colleagues, friends, and family, as this will help you build deeper connections with them.

- It's part of being human to feel regret and make mistakes. Don't worry too much about them, learn and move on from them instead. Share your missteps with loved ones, laugh about them, and decide how you can do better next time.

Coping With Failure

Setbacks are like the plot twists in the adventure of healthypreneurship, and they're as inevitable as rainy days during the winter. They're the villains in your story or the hurdles in your race. They show up when you least expect them, and they can be daunting.

Failure is simply part of the game of entrepreneurship. It's almost like the "Game Over" screen in your favorite video game. When you stumble or fall, it's simply time to get up and try again. After all, the point of failure is to turn it into your stepping stone for long-term success.

So how can you, as a teenage entrepreneur, cope with your failure and even turn it into success?

Change your perspective by not seeing failure as the end of your road but rather simply as a setback. Analyzing your failure can help you do this. What went wrong? Which factors led to the setback? Did you miscalculate or make poor decisions? If you understand the causes, you can avoid similar problems in the future.

How Emma Managed to Overcome Her Business Challenges

Emma launched her custom-made jewelry store at the age of 16.

Emma wanted to craft unique, handcrafted jewelry that could tell a story. She spent hours designing and creating each piece, and she hoped her customers would like it.

Emma faced the same challenges and obstacles as any startup. At first, her business received only a few orders. Despite her belief that her product was unique, the market was saturated with similar products, and it was difficult to stand out. She was working hard, but felt she wasn't gaining anything from it.

Then she experienced her first major setback. A larger jewelry company released a similar product, and they could afford to market it aggressively. Her sales fell further, and Emma felt as if her dream was slipping away from her.

However, she wasn't one to give up that easily. Instead, she saw this setback as an opportunity for growth, and took the opportunity to figure out her business model, and how she could bounce back stronger. She sought advice from other entrepreneurs who shared their insights and experiences with her.

Emma realized that her business needed a unique selling point. She revamped her designs to focus on eco-friendly, sustainable materials, appealing to a niche market of environmentally conscious consumers. She also used social media to show how committed she is to sustainability and to spread the word about her creations.

Emma relaunched her business with renewed passion. She used recycled materials for her jewelry and highlighted the importance of ethical and environmentally friendly practices. Emma's brand now stood for making a positive impact on the planet.

The response was more than she had been hoping for. People who shared Emma's values flocked to her online store. They admired her dedication to sustainability and her beautifully handcrafted jewelry. Her unique selling point set her apart from the competition and gained her a loyal customer base.

Emma's passion for sustainability was clear in her creations, and her customers appreciated the craftsmanship behind each piece.

Emma realized that her failures had taught her the resilience, adaptability, and determination she needed to be successful in the competitive business world.

How to Become a High Achiever

Becoming a high achiever in life is a journey that can start in your teenage years. This is the time you can get ahead by setting big goals, working hard, and developing important life skills.

As a teenager, you're still exploring your passions and interests, which will help you find your purpose. For example, if you're passionate about the environment, you can engage in local conservation projects or start an eco club at school. Your greater purpose could be to make a positive impact on the planet.

Be enthusiastic about pursuing your dreams. Let's say you're passionate about music and your goal is to learn a musical instrument and play in a band. Being passionate means practicing your instrument not because you have to but because you love it. It's about jamming with friends, writing songs, and dedicating time to your musical dream.

It's important to embrace lifelong learning while you're still young. For example, if you want to become a skilled basketball player, practice is essential. It's like shooting hoops for hours, working on your dribbling skills, and participating in pick-up games. You have to understand that making mistakes is part of practice, and it's how you grow.

You might be scared of trying new things, like joining a debate club or auditioning for a school play. Having the courage to try means stepping out of your comfort zone, even if you're nervous. When you audition for the school play you'll realize that the stage isn't as scary as you thought.

Never give up on what you want, even when the going is tough. Imagine you're working on a challenging science project, and you're tempted to quit. Perseverance means pushing through the tough parts, looking for help when you need it, and completing the project. You understand it's okay to struggle, but that doesn't mean you should give up.

You need to develop the ability to bounce back from setbacks. In your teenage years, you might face setbacks like not making the sports team you wanted. Resiliency is about bouncing back, trying again next year, and using the experience to improve. It's understanding that failures are opportunities to grow stronger.

For teenagers, becoming a high achiever means embracing your passions, having the courage to try new things, and understanding that practice and perseverance are the keys to success. If you adopt these steps you can set a strong foundation for your future achievements.

Resilience Building Activities And Strategies

The following activities can help you develop resilience.

Mindfulness Meditation

Mindfulness meditation can help you stay grounded and reduce stress. Regular practice can help you become better at emotional regulation, and also more focused.

Goal Setting

Set achievable goals. This can help you stay motivated when you have to deal with obstacles.

Physical Activity

Social Support

Building strong relationships with friends, family, or mentors can provide a support system during tough times.

Problem-Solving Skills

Develop effective problem-solving strategies. This includes breaking challenges into smaller steps and finding solutions.

Gratitude Practice

Regularly reflecting on the things you're grateful for can improve your outlook on life and help you focus on the positive.

Resilience Stories

Read motivational stories of resilience from other teenagers.

Role-Playing Scenarios

Engage in role-play activities where you can practice handling difficult situations such as conflicts or peer pressure.

Stress Management Techniques

Practice stress reduction techniques like deep breathing, progressive muscle relaxation, or time management.

Volunteer Work

Volunteering can give you a sense of purpose and a broader perspective on life's challenges.

Creative Outlets

Express yourself creatively through art, music, or writing.

Emotional Regulation Skills

Identify and manage your emotions, such as anger, frustration, or anxiety.

Positive Role Models

Look up to positive role models who have demonstrated resilience in their lives.

Coping Strategies Toolbox

Create a toolbox of coping strategies. When you encounter adversity, you can choose from this toolkit.

Support Groups

If you're facing specific challenges like loss or addiction, consider support groups that provide a safe space to connect with others who understand.

Encourage Independence

Take responsibility for your decisions and learn from both your successes and mistakes.

Healthy Lifestyle Choices

Get enough sleep, maintain a balanced diet, and limit substance use.

Seek Professional Help

If you're struggling with a severe mental health issue, you should seek help from mental health professionals.

Should You Continue Your Studies or Just Focus on Your Business?

If you're almost at the end of your school career, you're probably faced with the choice of continuing your studies or just focusing on your business. So, how do you decide? We'll look at some points that can help you make up your mind.

Advantages of Continuing Studies

There are various advantages to further studies, even though you might feel that it's going to take up a lot of your time.

Higher education can broaden your skill set, which will be valuable for your business. You might learn about finance, marketing, and management, among other skills.

College or university provides a unique environment for building connections. You can meet potential partners, mentors, or even customers. However, make sure that you always stay true to your authentic self, and connect to people whose values are the same as yours.

Education can serve as a safety net. If your entrepreneurial venture faces challenges, having a degree to fall back on can be reassuring. Many entrepreneurs have faced several business failures and have only really achieved success after several attempts. A degree at least gives you the option of finding a job while you're working on your future business ideas.

Some institutions offer programs and resources specifically designed for budding entrepreneurs. These can help you refine your business skills.

Advantages of Focusing on Your Business

On the other hand, your own business provides hands-on experience that no classroom can replicate. You'll encounter real challenges and learn to adapt. You'll often find you learn better from practical experience than from the theory you find in books.

A business often demands a significant amount of time and energy. By focusing exclusively on it, you can accelerate its growth and development. It can be extremely challenging to split your energy between several endeavors.

Studying at a college or university can be expensive. If you're managing a business, you might prefer to reinvest the money you earn into your business. However, if you're already running a profitable business before you leave school, this may enable you to study without taking expensive study loans.

Factors to Consider

There are certain factors you need to consider when it comes to studying or focusing on your business.

Consider the stage of your business. If it's in the early stages and needs significant attention, it might be the better option to prioritize it for the moment.

Assess your financial situation and funding requirements for both your business and education. This will also affect your decision.

Think about your long-term goals. What do you want to achieve with your business, and how does education fit into that vision? While you don't need the qualification at the moment, might you possibly need it in the future?

It's possible to balance education and entrepreneurship, but it can be challenging. If you're up for the challenge, part-time or online courses might be a compromise. Over the past few years, many universities have made online options available, which gives you the option of working and studying at the same time.

Ultimately, your decision should align with your aspirations and the specific circumstances of your business. It's important to weigh the pros and cons carefully and ask mentors who can help you make an informed choice for advice.

Worksheet: Building Resilience

This worksheet will help you build resilience, which is the ability to bounce back from adversity, grow stronger through challenges, and adapt to life's ups and downs. Do the following exercises in your journal.

Self-Reflection

- Think about challenging situations you've faced in the past. It could be an academic setback, a fight with a friend, or any other challenge. Write a brief description of the situation, how you felt, and how you handled it.

_____

_____

_____

Positive Thinking

- Think about the situation you described in the previous step. Identify any negative or self-critical thoughts that emerged during that time. Write them down.

_____

_____

_____

- Now, challenge your negative thoughts with positive and more realistic perspectives.

_____

_____

_____

Understanding Emotions

- Reflect on how you felt during the challenging situation. Did you feel angry, sad, or frustrated?

_____

_____

_____

- What physical sensations did you feel, such as your heart beating fast?

_____

_____

_____

- Acknowledge that it's natural to feel these emotions and that it's a normal stress response. You can write an affirmation to help you if you'd like.

_____

_____

_____

Building a Support System

- List three people you can turn to for support when facing challenges. These could be friends, family members, teachers, or mentors.

_____

_____

_____

- Reflect on how you can communicate your feelings to these people and ask for their guidance or encouragement.

_____

_____

_____

Problem-Solving Skills

- Think about the challenging situation you've faced. What were some practical steps you could have taken to address it or reduce the impact of your problem?

_____

_____

_____

- Write down at least three potential solutions or strategies for handling similar challenges in the future.

_____

_____

_____

Resilience Stories

Find a story of resilience from someone you admire or even a historical figure who faced significant adversity. Summarize their story and the key lessons you can draw from it.

_____

_____

_____

Coping Strategies

- List three healthy coping strategies that work for you when dealing with stress and adversity (e.g., deep breathing, mindfulness, physical activity).

_____

_____

_____

- Describe how you make these strategies part of your daily life.

_____

_____

_____

Setting Goals

- Think about a personal goal you'd like to achieve in the future. It could be related to academics, hobbies, or personal growth. Write down the specific goal, a timeline, and a plan for achieving it.

_____

_____

_____

Self-Compassion

Reflect on the idea that it's okay to make mistakes and face challenges. Nobody is perfect. Write a compassionate message to yourself, encouraging yourself to be kind to yourself.

_____

_____

_____

Action Plan

Based on the insights and strategies you've explored in this worksheet, create an action plan for building your resilience.

Outline specific steps you will take to strengthen your ability to bounce back from challenges.

_____

_____

_____

_____

_____

Final Thoughts

Think about how completing this worksheet has helped you understand and build your resilience.

_____

_____

_____

Key Takeaways

- Resilience is the ability to stay positive and strong in the face of setbacks and disappointments.
- Resilience can help you deal with life's challenges.
- Resilience can be developed and strengthened over time.
- Grit and perseverance are the determination and passion that fuel long-term goals.
- Grit can be compared to an engine that drives you toward your aspirations.
- Grit can help you maintain determination when you have to deal with challenges.

- The first step in building resilience is the development of self-awareness and balanced perspectives.
- Practical strategies for building resilience are reframing your thoughts, avoiding all-or-nothing thinking, celebrating successes, and fostering positivity.
- You will also build your resilience if you strengthen your social networks and learn from your mistakes.
- You can cope with failure by changing your perspective, analyzing the causes, and using setbacks as opportunities for growth.
- Emma's story of overcoming challenges in her jewelry business is an example of using failure as a stepping stone to success.
- You can become a high achiever in life by focusing on your passion, practice, courage, perseverance, and resilience.
- If you struggle with severe mental health issues, you should seek professional help.

Strategy 6
Social Media: Your Business's Secret Superpower

"In today's digital age, social media is not an option for businesses; it's a necessity for survival."

— Microsoft's CEO Satya Nadella

Being able to use the power of social media can be a game changer for your business in the digital age. If you use the right strategies, you can create a strong brand, and reach a global audience.

We'll look at the various ways you can use platforms like Facebook, Instagram, Twitter, LinkedIn, and others to enhance your brand and communicate with your audience. Before you jump in and start creating your social media platforms, you need to take the first steps by creating a brand identity for your business.

Creating a Brand Identity

Deciding on an identity for your brand before creating your social media pages is extremely important because it will help you create a consistent presence online. Your brand identity includes your brand's personality, values, mission, and visual elements.

Here's how you can develop your brand identity:

Define Your Brand's Mission and Values

Start by clarifying the purpose of your brand. What problem does your business solve? What values do you stand for?

Determine the core values and principles that guide your brand. These will be the basis for the content you share on social media.

Identify Your Target Audience

Understand who your ideal customers are. What are their demographics, interests, and pain points? If you know your audience well, you can tailor your social media to connect with them.

Create Your Brand Voice

Decide on the tone and personality of your brand. Are you friendly, professional, casual, or authoritative? Your target audience should be able to relate to your brand voice.

Choose Visual Elements

Decide on the visual elements that will represent your brand. This includes your logo, color palette, typography, and any other design elements. Your visuals need to be consistent across all your platforms, as it will make it easier to recognize your brand.

Craft Your Unique Selling Proposition (USP)

What sets your brand apart from your competition? You should use this unique selling point in your social media messaging.

Develop a Brand Story

This can be a powerful way to connect with your audience. Share the story of how your brand was founded, your journey, and the impact you aim to make in your industry.

Create a Brand Style Guide

Develop a brand style guide that explains all the elements of your brand identity. This guide will make sure your social media content is consistent.

Competitive Analysis

Study your competitors and similar brands in your industry. Understand what strategies have worked for them and what you could do differently to make yourself stand out.

Test and Refine

Launch your social media profiles with your chosen brand identity, but be prepared to amend it as you get feedback from your audience and gain more insight.

A Social Media Strategy For Your Business

You probably have personal accounts on different social media platforms that you use to communicate with your friends. It can be fun to share posts and photos of good times you've had with your friends.

Did you know that you can also use social media to grow your business? If you've used different platforms in your personal capacity, you already have a good start.

So, let's take a look at why your business needs a social media strategy.

Social media platforms have billions of active users world-wide. If you have a well-crafted strategy you can make your products more visible to your customers, and also reach more potential new customers.

What does a good social media strategy look like?

It will outline your business's objectives, target audience, and how you will approach your content, and involve creating a posting schedule. You should also be able to measure the success of your marketing campaigns by using tools such as Google Analytics. A good social media plan is a roadmap that guides your social media efforts and makes sure that they not only align with your business goals but that they also have a positive effect on your audience.

Information to Include in Your Strategy

Your well-crafted plan should include the following information:

- Define specific, measurable, and time-bound objectives. Do you want to increase awareness of your brand, drive traffic to your website, boost sales of your products and services, or improve customer engagement?
- You need to know your target audience, and who your ideal customers are. Understand their demographics, interests, and behaviors. This information will help you create the best content to make an impact on them.
- Choose the social media platforms that align with your business goals, but that are also used by your target audience. Each platform has unique characteristics and user demographics. For example, if you want to reach mostly young people, you can look at marketing on TikTok.

- Does your business have competitors? Study their social media and try to figure out what they're doing well. What can you do better? Once you have an understanding of this, you can amend your social media strategy.
- You'll also need to think about the type of content you'll create and share. This can include blog posts, videos, infographics, user-generated content, and more. Create a content calendar to plan your posts in advance.
- Establish a consistent posting schedule based on the platforms you're using. Different platforms have optimal posting times, so you need to do some research and then schedule your posts according to this.
- Figure out how you're going to interact with your audience on social media. Respond to comments and messages, and take part in conversations relevant to your industry. How will you manage negative comments and deal with social media trolls?
- If you have some money for paid advertising, you can look at platforms like Facebook Ads or Instagram Ads.
- If you know someone who is an influencer on social media and has lots of followers, they can also help you promote your products and services. A social media influencer is a person with credibility and a dedicated following in a specific niche or industry on social media platforms. They use their online presence to impact the opinions, behaviors, or decisions of their audience through content, endorsements, and recommendations.

- Research and use relevant hashtags to increase the visibility of your content. A hashtag is a keyword or phrase preceded by the "#" symbol (e.g., #Travel, #Foodie). It is used on social media platforms to categorize and group content that's about a specific topic or theme. Hashtags make it easier for users to discover and interact with posts, discussions, and trends.
- Define your brand's voice and tone on social media. Are you friendly and casual or formal and informative? You have to be consistent across all the platforms you use.
- Develop a crisis management plan for handling negative comments, reviews, or other PR issues. The reality is that you may have to deal with cyberbullying and trolls. You may even have to deal with "concern trolls" who don't seem so harmful at first. A concern troll pretends to be genuinely concerned about a specific topic, issue, or group, but they really want to provoke or criticize. Concern trolls often engage in online discussions or forums under the guise of offering helpful advice or expressing worry, but their underlying motive is to turn people against each other. They challenge opinions or undermine the credibility of those they're engaging with.
- You need to define key performance indicators (KPIs) to track the success of your strategy. Common metrics include engagement rate, reach, website traffic, leads generated, and sales conversion.

- Create a schedule for reviewing and reporting on your social media performance. Regular assessment can help you change and improve your strategy.
- You must make sure that your social media activities adhere to legal and regulatory guidelines relevant to your industry.
- A well-crafted social media strategy is not static. It will have to be amended as your business grows and as the social media landscape changes.

The Benefits of a Social Media Strategy

There are many benefits to having a social media strategy for your business.

Social media platforms are rich sources of data. Your strategy can involve monitoring and analyzing customer interactions, which will give you insight into market trends, preferences, and competition.

Social media is a cost-effective and fast marketing tool. You can create targeted ad campaigns to reach specific demographics, boosting the visibility of your products or services around the globe. It's no longer necessary to spend a lot of money on printed marketing material.

Consistent and meaningful interactions on social media can help you build a loyal customer base. By sharing valuable content and addressing customer needs, you can turn one-time buyers into your loyal supporters.

A social media strategy helps you respond quickly to any negative developments or crises that may affect your business. You can address issues transparently and manage your business reputation effectively.

Social media can drive traffic to your website. Sharing blog posts, product pages, or other content can send users to your website where they can learn more and make purchases. If you don't have a business website, you should consider creating one or getting someone to help you create one. We'll take a look later on in this book on how you can create a website quickly and almost effortlessly. This is also an opportunity to gain useful computer skills that can help you later on in your career. Who knows, you could even set up a side hustle as a web designer.

A strategy will help you to set goals and metrics for tracking your social media success. You can use analytics to measure the performance of your social media efforts and adjust your strategy accordingly.

Social media allows you to gather useful and almost instant feedback from customers. You can learn what they like or dislike about your products and services and make improvements. For example, customers can leave you feedback in the comments they add to your social media platforms.

Best Social Media Platforms For Teen Entrepreneurs

The platform you will use will depend on different factors. You will need to consider the type of audience you want to target, and also what your content strategy is going to be.

Here are some social media platforms that are popular with teenagers and that can also be a good fit for you as a teenage entrepreneur:

- Instagram is a visual platform that's popular with younger people. You can show your products and share behind-the-scenes content. You should also use Instagram Stories for engagement.
- TikTok is popular among teenagers and is known for its short, engaging videos. It can help you create creative content, tell your brand story, and connect with your peers.
- Snapchat is another platform preferred by teens. It's ideal for sharing time-sensitive content, offering flash deals, and connecting with younger people.

- You can also use YouTube to share video content, and use it for tutorials, vlogs, product reviews, and more. A vlog, which is short for "video blog," is a type of online content that involves the creation and sharing of videos. The video is usually diary-like or in a documentary style and conveys personal experiences, opinions, or information to an audience.
- Twitter allows for real-time engagement and quick updates. You can share industry news and participate in trending conversations about your industry.
- Facebook is useful if you want to reach a wider audience, especially when offering products or services that appeal to a broader age range.
- If your business is focused on professional services or B2B products, LinkedIn can help you network and show others your expertise.
- If you're involved in creative niches like fashion, art, or crafts, Pinterest can help you share visual content and drive traffic to your website or online store.
- Etsy is a popular e-commerce platform if you want to sell handmade items.
- Creating a personal blog or website can be an effective way to share knowledge and expertise and promote products or services.

Creating a Professional Profile

If you want to get attention for your business on social media, you need to know how to create a professional profile that will keep your readers coming back for more. An unprofessional profile full of mistakes and bad-quality photos will just give your business a bad name, which won't attract anyone to read more about your business.

Remember that you can also use your social media to funnel or attract customers to your website if you have one.

Creating a profile on social media is something that can take a lot of time, especially if it needs to convey a professional image.

Here are the steps to create an effective profile:

Profile Picture

Choose a clear, high-resolution image of yourself or your business logo. For personal branding, a professional head-shot is ideal, while for a business, the logo is suitable.

Ensure that the image is well-lit and free from distractions.

Use the same profile picture across all social media platforms to make sure your brand is consistent.

Cover Photo

Your cover photo should complement your profile picture and reflect your brand or business theme.

It can be an image related to your products or services, a professional banner with your business name and tagline, or a visually appealing landscape relevant to your niche.

Make sure your photo has high resolution and is well composed. For example, you won't photos where you're at a party with your friends or you're enjoying a day at the beach.

Bio/About Section

Write a concise and informative bio that captures your business identity and value proposition. Use keywords relevant to your niche.

Include the necessary information such as your business name, location, website link, and a brief overview of what you offer.

If applicable, mention your unique selling points or what sets your business apart.

Use a consistent tone and style that aligns with your brand's identity.

Contact Information

Provide accurate and up-to-date contact information. This may include your email address, phone number, and physical address if you have a physical location. Use a professional email address.

Call to Action (CTA)

Some platforms allow you to include a call to action button on your profile. Use this to encourage your visitors to take specific actions, such as "Contact Us," "Learn More," or "Shop Now."

Highlights and Stories

If the platform supports highlights or stories, use these to share updates, promotions, or behind-the-scenes glimpses of your business. This can be useful if you want to show how you make certain things, e.g. craft products or baking cakes.

Credentials and Achievements

If you or your business have received awards, recognition, or certifications, consider mentioning them in your profile to build credibility.

Keywords and Hashtags

Incorporate relevant keywords and hashtags in your bio to make yourself more discoverable. For example, if you're a writer, use terms such as "creative writer" or "romance fiction."

Consistency

Make sure you use the same profile image, cover photo, and branding elements across all your platforms to help people recognize your brand.

Privacy Settings

Review and adjust privacy settings to suit your preferences. Some information may be set to public, while you might prefer to keep other details private.

Regular Updates

Always keep your profile information up to date. Update it whenever there are significant changes to your business, such as new services, products, or contact details.

Your social media profile is often the first impression potential customers will get of your business. Put some time into creating a profile that will appeal to your target audience.

Paid Social Media

Paid social media is another good option for your business, especially if you're concerned about keeping trolls off your pages. However, it won't entirely keep them out, but it can help lessen their impact. If you haven't heard about trolls before (most of us have) they're people who enjoy posting offensive or disruptive content on social media. For example, if there are people who don't like you for some reason, they may post negative content about your products and services, encouraging others not to use them.

When you run paid advertising campaigns on platforms like Facebook or Instagram, you have more control over who sees your content because you can specify your target audience. Other paid social media platforms like Patreon could also be a good option.

Paid campaigns also allow you to exclude certain demographics or target a more specific group to reduce exposure to trolls.

To deal with trolls, you can also use community management strategies to monitor and moderate comments on your posts. You can hide or delete inappropriate comments, block or report users, and encourage a more positive online community.

What is Patreon?

So, let's take a look at Patreon, which is a paid platform. Patreon might be a great option for you if you run an online content creation business. It's an online platform that allows content creators to receive financial support directly from their fans or patrons. On Patreon, you can set up your account according to various membership tiers or subscription levels for your fans. In return for supporting you, your followers gain access to exclusive content and certain perks that aren't available to everyone. For example, they can be the first to view your exclusive new content.

If you're a YouTuber, podcaster, musician, artist, writer, or any other type of content creator you could use Patreon to offer different membership levels, each with its own set of rewards. These rewards can include early access to content, exclusive live streams, private community forums, or even physical merchandise like posters or T-shirts.

Patreon operates on a monthly subscription model, so your fans can support you with a recurring monthly payment. This can create a regular income to help you sustain your work and often provides a more stable and predictable source of revenue. You won't only have to rely on advertising or one-time purchases.

Activity: Social Media Profile Template

Here's a basic social media profile template that you can adapt for various platforms. Keep in mind that each platform has different character limits and features, so make sure your profiles meet the requirements of all the platforms.

Use the template to create your first social media profile.

Profile Picture

[Upload a clear and professional profile picture.]

[Use your logo or a high-quality headshot.]

Cover Photo

[Add a visually appealing cover photo that aligns with your brand or theme.]

Bio/About Section

Name: [Your name or business name]

Location: [Your city or region]

Website: [Your website URL]

Description: [Concise, informative description of your business.]

Contact Information

Email: [Your professional email address]

Phone: [Your contact number]

Address: [Your physical address, if applicable]

Call to Action (CTA)

[Add a CTA button if the platform allows. Choose an appropriate action, e.g., "Contact Us," "Learn More," or "Shop Now."]

Highlights/Stories

[Create and organize highlights or stories to share updates, promotions, or behind-the-scenes content.]

Credentials and Achievements

[Mention any awards, certifications, or achievements your business has earned.]

Keywords and Hashtags

[Incorporate relevant keywords and hashtags to improve discoverability.]

Privacy Settings

[Review and adjust privacy settings to control what is public or private.]

Regular Updates

[Remember to update your profile information as your business grows.]

Change this template to suit your needs on different social media platforms. It's important to keep in mind that character limits and features can be different from platform to platform.

Key Takeaways

- Before you develop a plan for your social media, you need to start with a clear mission and core values for your brand.
- Identifying your target audience and understanding their demographics, interests, and behaviors will make it easier for you to develop social media that is relatable to them.
- Your business needs a unique brand voice and personality.
- Choose visual elements, including logos, color palettes, and typography that fit in with the vision you have for your business's brand.
- Highlight your Unique Selling Proposition (USP). Having a USP means your product or services stand out from that of your competitors. There is something distinctive that sets it apart.
- As your business grows, you will have to adapt your brand identity.
- Define specific, measurable, and time-bound objectives for your business.
- Know your target audience, their demographics, interests, and behaviors.
- Choose the right social media platforms aligned with your business goals and target audience.
- Analyze your competitors and learn from their social media strategies.
- You also need to have a strategy for the content you want to share with your followers.

- Plan your approach to interacting with your audience and handling negative comments or trolls.
- Consider using paid advertising and partnering with influencers.
- Research and use relevant hashtags to boost content visibility.
- Develop a crisis management plan to handle negative comments and PR issues.
- Make sure all your media activities are legal.
- Build a loyal customer base through interacting in a meaningful way on social media.
- Consider Instagram for visual content and Instagram Stories.
- Use TikTok for engaging short videos.
- Create video content on YouTube.
- Engage in real-time conversations on Twitter.
- Facebook can help you reach a broader audience.
- LinkedIn is a great choice if you want to market your specific expertise and you want to network with others in your field.
- Consider Etsy if your business sells handmade items.

Strategy 7
Building Your Epic Business Website

"Your website is the window of your business. Keep it fresh, keep it exciting."

— Jay Conrad Levinson

In today's digital age, your business needs a website, even when you're just starting out. It's your digital storefront, a 24/7 sales representative, and a powerful marketing tool that can connect you with potential customers across the globe.

It's the gateway through which potential customers learn about your business, explore your products or services, and decide if they want to buy from you.

Having a website can help you serve your customers in the most effective and efficient ways.

Why Your Business Needs a Website

A well-designed and attractive website can serve as your business card and digital storefront. It gives the impression that your company is established and professional, and potential customers will be more likely to trust you and buy your services. This gives you an advantage over your competitors.

Your website is also an information hub about your business. You can share details about your products or services, contact information, pricing, and frequently asked questions. If there is a chat functionality, people can also chat with you directly on the site.

Unlike physical stores, your website is available 24/7, and customers can obtain information and buy items when they find it convenient.

Customers also find it convenient to research and shop online. Visiting your website gives them time to browse and compare products. Indecisive people who want a lot of information about products before they decide which one to buy will definitely appreciate this feature.

Websites provide a cost-effective platform for marketing and advertising your business. You can use various digital marketing strategies to reach a broad audience without having to pay a lot of money for traditional marketing.

A website also allows you to grow your customer base and reach more customers—even internationally. It also makes it easier to communicate with your customers through features like contact forms, live chat, social media integration, and email subscriptions. Customers can even communicate with you in real-time if your website has a chat functionality.

You can display your products or services with detailed descriptions, high-quality images, and even videos. This will also give your customers a better understanding of what you have to offer.

A website provides a platform for content marketing. You can create and share valuable content such as blog posts, articles, and guides to show that you're an expert in your industry.

A website also offers you the advantage of collecting data and insights about customer behavior. You can use analytics tools to track user activity, demographics, and preferences, allowing you to refine your marketing strategies.

As your business grows, your website can grow with it. You can add new pages, features, and capabilities to accommodate expanding product lines or services.

A Guide to Creating Your Website

It can be quite a process to create your website, but you need to start out by first deciding exactly what you want to do with it. Once you know its purpose, the rest of the process will become easier.

Define Your Website's Purpose

Decide the main purpose of your website. Is it for e-commerce, providing information, showing your portfolio, or getting clients? It will help you with the design and content if you know your website's purpose.

Choosing Your Domain Name

Select a domain name that reflects your business. Keep it simple, memorable, and relevant to your brand. Consider using your business name if possible.

You will have to purchase your domain name from a domain registrar or web hosting provider.

Choose a Website Building Platform And Hosting Provider

Choose a web hosting provider that suits your needs. Look for hosting services that offer website builders or content management systems (CMS) for easy website creation.

Popular hosting providers include Bluehost, HostGator, SiteGround, and Wix.

Site 123 is an excellent, cost-effective option for beginners. It's a user-friendly and versatile content management platform, which will make it easy for you to create and manage your website. It has an intuitive drag-and-drop interface and a wide range of beautiful templates.

Site123 makes it easy for you to create professional-looking websites without the need for extensive technical knowledge. This platform also provides hosting services, domain registration, and e-commerce capabilities, making it a one-stop solution for those looking to establish a robust online presence. It offers you a hassle-free website-building experience.

Design Your Website

Once you've picked your website builder, you can start designing your site.

Use the chosen website builder to design your site. Most platforms offer pre-designed templates that you can select and change as you want them to be.

Focus on creating a visually appealing, user-friendly, and responsive design that works well on both desktop and mobile devices. Make sure that you keep your branding consistent with your logo, colors, and style.

Basic Website Design Tips

Whether you're going to design your website yourself or get someone else to help you design it, you will find the following tips useful.

Firstly, your website needs user-friendly navigation. Make sure that your menu structure is intuitive and easy to navigate. Use clear labels and organized menus to help visitors find what they're looking for quickly. People are much more likely to come back to your website and even buy your products and services if your website is user-friendly.

Ensure your website is mobile-responsive, so it looks and functions well on different digital devices, such as smartphones and tablets.

When it comes to the visual elements of the design, branding such as your logo, color schemes, and typography need to be consistent throughout your website. This will help your brand identity become even stronger.

You can make sure your website loads fast by making sure your images are small enough, minimizing unnecessary scripts, and making sure you're using a reliable provider to host your website.

Use high-resolution images and graphics that enhance your content and support your brand. Pixelated and low-quality visuals will just create a negative impression of your business, and people might think that you're not delivering a professional product or service.

The fonts on your website need to be readable and consistent throughout your site. For example, if your font is too small, people might not be able to read it and they will just move on to the next website.

Effective use of whitespace (empty space) can also help you improve the readability of your website. Avoid cluttered layouts.

Organize content logically, with headings, subheadings, and bullet points. Use relevant categories and tags for blog posts and articles. If your website includes forms, keep them simple and easy to fill out. Minimize the required fields to encourage submissions.

Ensure your website is accessible to all users, including those with disabilities. This includes using alt text for images and providing captions for videos.

Avoid excessive pop-ups, animations, and distracting elements that may overwhelm or annoy visitors. Focus on what's essential. It's useful to have loading animations and progress bars to keep your visitors engaged while your content is loading. This will prevent them from leaving your site and becoming frustrated.

Also make sure you include social media icons and share buttons, which will make it easier to access your website through your social media accounts.

The Search Engine Optimization (SEO) Side of Web Design

Search Engine Optimization (SEO) is like the magic behind getting your website to show up on Google when you search for something. It will make your website easier to find.

SEO involves picking the right words (keywords) that people use in their searches and putting them in your website's content. You also need other websites to talk about you and say how great your site is (linking to you). The more links you have, the more Google thinks you're important, and the higher you'll show up in search results.

You also need to incorporate optimized meta tags and descriptive URLs.

An optimized meta tag is a specific type of HTML tag that is used to provide information about a web page's content to search engines and website visitors. The two most common types of meta tags are the "title" and "meta description" tags.

This is a critical meta tag that provides the title of a web page. It appears as the main clickable link in search engine results. An optimized title tag should be concise, relevant to the page's content, and contain targeted keywords to improve search engine ranking and attract user clicks.

The meta description tag provides a brief summary or description of the web page's content. An optimized meta description should be engaging and informative and include keywords to encourage users to click on the link in search results. While it doesn't directly impact search rankings, a well-crafted meta description can improve click-through rates.

```html
<div class="container">
  <div class="row">
    <div class="col-md-6 col-lg-8"> <!--          BEGIN NAVIGATION
      <nav id="nav" role="navigation">
        <ul>
          <li><a href="index.html">Home</a></li>
          <li><a href="home-events.html">Home Events</a></li>
          <li><a href="multi-col-menu.html">Multiple Column Men
          <li class="has-children"> <a href="#" class="current"
            <ul>
              <li><a href="tall-button-header.html">Tall But
              <li><a href="image-logo.html">Image Logo</a></
              <li class="active"><a href="tall-logo.html">Ta
            </ul>
          </li>
          <li class="has-children"> <a href="#">Carousels</a>
            <ul>
              <li><a href="variable-width-slider.html">Variab
                        html">Testimoni
```

A descriptive URL, also known as a "user-friendly URL" or "clean URL," is a web address that is designed to convey the content or purpose of a web page in a way that's easy to understand. Descriptive URLs typically include keywords or phrases related to the page's content, which makes it easier for other users and search engines to navigate your website.

Regular updates to your website is also good SEO practice. Keep your website up-to-date with fresh content and regular maintenance. An outdated website won't get you any visitors and you'll lose out on sales.

Make sure you implement security features such as SSL certificates to protect user data and build trust. Your web hosting provider should be able to help you with this.

So, how will you know if visitors find your website useful? User testing can help you gather feedback and determine if there are areas where your website needs to be improved.

During user testing, a selected group of participants complete specific scenarios or tasks on the website and they provide feedback about their experiences.

Web developers analyze the results and implement recommended improvements. They can ensure that the site is user-friendly, efficient, and tailored to meet the needs of its audience, which will help you create a more effective online presence for your business.

Creating Content

Creating relevant content for your website is kind of like curating your Instagram feed. It's all about showing your best side and giving your audience what they want to see. It's quite simple really, and you don't have to be able to write like Shakespeare. In fact, you're actually better off if you don't write like a famous literary writer.

Here's how to do it:

- Your website is like your personal online diary. The "About Us" page is your chance to introduce yourself and share your journey. Why did you start your business? What do you love about it? Tell your visitors more about yourself so that they can get to know you.
- Imagine your website as a virtual store. The "Products/Services" page is like your display window. Use fantastic images and videos to showcase what you're offering.
- You should make it easy for people to contact you on your website. Make it easy with a "Contact" page. Provide your email or a contact form so visitors can reach out.
- If you're into blogging, you can have your own space to share your thoughts. It's like a social media feed, but it's all you. Write about what you're passionate about, and your readers will keep coming back.

The trick is to think of your website as your online showcase. Fill it with great content and you'll keep your audience interested and coming back for more!

Hiring External People to Help You Create Your Website

Hiring external professionals to create your website can be a wise decision, especially if you don't have the time or the skills to do it yourself. However, keep in mind that this might take a large chunk of your budget. Set a realistic budget and discuss it with the professionals. Be prepared for additional expenses that may arise during the project.

You'll have to be clear about your needs. Clearly communicate your website's design and the features and functionality you want. The more precise your instructions, the smoother the development process.

It's important that you work actively along with the people who will be designing your website. Make sure you respond to their inquiries and provide them with regular feedback.

Keep the work going by establishing a project timeline with milestones and deadlines.

Also, discuss ongoing maintenance and support. You need to understand who will handle updates, security, and troubleshooting after the website is live. Determine ownership and hosting details and clarify domain ownership.

Regularly review the website during development to provide feedback and ensure it aligns with your vision. Once the site is live, you also need to check if it aligns with what you initially had in mind for it.

Make sure you know how to maintain the website once it's live, otherwise, you will have to ask the design agency to train you on how to do so.

Hiring professionals to create your website can save you time and lead to a high-quality result while maintaining clear communication.

An E-Commerce Section For Your Website

If you're going to be selling items, you will have to set up an e-commerce section on your website. This will be like opening your own online store.

Imagine your website as a mall, and your e-commerce section is your shop. This is where you can display all your amazing products for the world to see.

Just like Instagram pics, use high-quality images to show your products. Good photos will entice people to buy them.

Think of your website's checkout process as a quick and easy transaction at your favorite snack bar. Ensure it's hassle-free, with secure payment options so customers can pay with confidence.

When someone clicks "Add to Cart," it's like ringing up their order at the cash register. Make sure everything is smooth and efficient, just like when you're checking out at your favorite online stores.

So, setting up your e-commerce section is like having your own online shop—just make sure it's as appealing and user-friendly as your go-to online stores. Your products deserve the spotlight, and your customers deserve a seamless shopping experience.

Registering Your Website With Search Engines

When your website is ready to be launched, you don't just want it hanging out there; you need your potential customers to be able to find it. Registering your site with search engines will put your business on the map in the digital world.

Just like how you'd want your favorite hangout spot to appear on the map app on your phone, you need your website to show up when people search for your business. This is where the search engines like Google, Bing, and Yahoo come into play. You register your website with them. It's almost like adding your business to a directory. This way, when someone types in keywords related to your business, your website will have a better chance of showing up in the search results.

You have to submit a site map when you register your website. Your sitemap is almost like a menu of all the items you offer your customers. On your website, a sitemap is like a list of all the pages and content it contains. By submitting this sitemap to search engines, you're basically telling them to check out all the great stuff on your websites. It makes it easier for search engines to explore and index your site. So when someone's searching for something specific, your site is more likely to pop up in their search results.

How do You Create a Sitemap?

Creating a sitemap for your website is essential for improving its discoverability by search engines. Here's how to create a sitemap.

Manual Sitemap Creation

This method is suitable for smaller websites with a limited number of pages:

- You can create a sitemap manually by listing all the pages on your site.
- Open a text editor or a spreadsheet program like Microsoft Excel or Google Sheets.
- Create a table with two columns: one for the page URL and one for the last modification date.
- List all the pages of your website in the first column, starting with the homepage. You can also add the last modification date for each page.
- Save the file with a name that's easy to recognize, such as "sitemap.xml."

Online Sitemap Generators

For larger websites with many pages, it can take too much time to create a sitemap manually. Online sitemap generators can help you with this process.

- Use a free online sitemap generator like XML-sitemaps.com, Screaming Frog, or Yoast SEO (if you're using WordPress).
- Enter your website's URL.
- You can customize your settings if you want to do so, such as by selecting specific pages.
- Click the "Generate Sitemap" button.
- The tool will create an XML sitemap for your website.

- Download the generated sitemap and save it in your website's root directory.

Content Management Systems (CMS)

If your website is built using a content management system like WordPress you can use plugins to generate and manage your sitemap.

Install and activate an SEO plugin like Yoast SEO or All in One SEO Pack.

When you configure the plugin's sitemap settings it will automatically generate a sitemap for your website.

Once you've created your sitemap you should submit it to major search engines like Google, Bing, and Yahoo using their respective webmaster tools. This will help them index your website's content more efficiently, making it more visible to the different search engines.

Registering Your Website With Google, Bing And Yahoo

Follow these steps to register your website.

Google Search Console

- Go to Google Search Console.
- Sign in with your Google account. If you don't have one, you'll need to create it.
- Click on the "Add URL Prefix" button.
- Enter your website URL and click "Continue."
- Choose a verification method. The easiest way is to use the HTML tag option.

- Copy the provided HTML tag.
- Go to your website's source code and paste the HTML tag within the <head> section.
- Go back to Google Search Console and click "Verify."
- Once verified, you can submit your sitemap to Google.

Bing Webmaster Tools

- Go to Bing Webmaster Tools.
- Sign in with your Microsoft account or create one if you don't have it.
- Click "Add a Site" and enter your website URL.
- Verify ownership by selecting one of the verification methods (e.g., adding a meta tag to your website's home page).
- Once verified you can submit your sitemap to Bing.

Yahoo (via Bing)

Since Yahoo's search results are powered by Bing you don't need to submit your site separately to Yahoo if you've already done so through Bing Webmaster Tools.

Remember to create and submit a sitemap for your website through these tools. A sitemap is like a roadmap for search engines, helping them index your website's pages more effectively.

By registering your website with these major search engines and submitting a sitemap, you'll increase your site's chances of appearing in search results when people look for content related to your business or interests. This is an important step in getting your website noticed on the web.

Testing, Launching, and Maintaining Your Website

Before launching, thoroughly test your website to check for functionality, broken links, and responsive design. Make sure it works well on different web browsers and devices.

You'll also have to implement security measures to protect your website from cyber threats. Regularly update your website's software and plugins. Use SSL certificates to encrypt data transmission and set up strong passwords for site access.

Once everything is in place and you've tested everything, you can launch your website for the world to see. Promote it on your social media accounts and to your network.

Regularly update your website with fresh content, product listings, and information. Make sure you stay informed about website security and SEO best practices.

Monitor your website's performance with analytics tools like Google Analytics. Also, ask your users and customers for feedback which will help you continuously improve your website.

Worksheet: Teenage Entrepreneur Website Development

Completing this worksheet will help you get started on planning your website.

Name:

_____

Business Idea: [Briefly describe your business or project]

_____

Goal: [What do you want to achieve with your website?]

_____

_____

_____

Define Your Website's Purpose

Why are you creating this website? [E.g., To sell my products and services]

_____

_____

_____

Choose a Domain Name

What are your top domain name choices?

_____

_____

_____

Select a Website Building Platform

Which website builder are you considering? [E.g., Site123, Wix, WordPress]

_____

_____

_____

List the features that are important for your website. [E.g., e-commerce capabilities, blogging, gallery]

_____

_____

_____

Website Design

Describe the style and design you envision for your website. [E.g., colorful and playful, minimalist and modern]

_____

_____

_____

What should your website's color scheme be? [E.g., red and white, blue and green]

_____

_____

_____

Do you have a logo? [Yes/No]

_____

_____

_____

Navigation and Layout

Create a sitemap of your website's menu structure. [E.g., Home, About, Products, Contact]

_____

_____

_____

What elements will be on the homepage? [E.g., banner image, introduction]

_____

_____

_____

Mobile Responsiveness

How important is it that your website looks good and functions well on mobile devices? [Very important, somewhat important, not very important]

_____

_____

_____

What elements would have to be optimized for mobile?

_____

_____

_____

Branding

Describe your branding elements (e.g., logo, colors, fonts).

_____

_____

_____

How will you ensure consistency throughout your website?

_____

_____

_____

Content Creation

What content will you create for your website? [E.g., product descriptions, blog posts, customer testimonials]

Who will be responsible for creating content? [You, a friend, a professional]

SEO Strategy

What are some keywords relevant to your business? [E.g., handmade cupcakes, art prints, English tutoring]

How will you incorporate these keywords into your content?

User Testing

Who will be the user testers for your website? [E.g., friends, family, potential customers]

_____

_____

_____

What tasks should they complete during testing? [E.g., buy a product or service, submit a contact form]

_____

_____

_____

How will you gather and analyze feedback from user testing?

_____

_____

_____

Marketing and Promotion

List some ideas for promoting your website and business. [E.g., social media advertising, email marketing, word of mouth]

_____

_____

_____

Security and Data Protection

How will you protect your website and user data? Do you have strong passwords?

_____

_____

_____

Ongoing Maintenance

Who will be responsible for maintaining your website? [You, a web developer]

_____

_____

_____

How often will you update your website's content? Do you have a publishing plan in place?

_____

_____

_____

Feedback and Improvements

How will you gather feedback from website visitors?

_____

_____

What are some possible improvements or additional features you might consider for your website in the future?

_____

_____

_____

Launch Plan

When do you plan to launch your website?

_____

_____

_____

How will you announce the launch to your target audience?

_____

_____

_____

Budget

Create a budget for your website project. Include costs for domain registration, hosting, web development, marketing, and any other expenses.

_____

_____

Next Steps

List the immediate steps you need to take to start building your website.

_____

_____

_____

Deadline

Set a deadline for completing your website development project.

_____

_____

_____

Key Takeaways

- A website is a vital tool for any business in the digital age, functioning as a 24/7 digital storefront and a platform for connecting with customers worldwide.
- It's essential for customers to be able to learn about your business, explore your products/services, and decide whether to buy from you.

- A well-designed and attractive website creates a professional and trustworthy image, setting you apart from competitors.
- Your website serves as an information hub, sharing details about your offerings, contact information, pricing, and FAQs.
- Unlike physical stores, your website is available around the clock, allowing customers to access information and buy your products and services at times that are convenient to them.
- Convenience is important, as customers prefer researching and shopping online. Websites enable product browsing and comparison.
- Websites offer a cost-effective way to market and advertise your business, and you can use digital strategies to reach a broad audience.
- Detailed product or service descriptions, high-quality visuals, and videos enhance customer understanding.
- Websites support content marketing, demonstrating your expertise in your industry through blog posts, articles, and guides.
- As your business expands, your website can grow with it, accommodating more pages, features, and capabilities.
- To create a website, start by defining its purpose, selecting a domain name, choosing a website builder and hosting provider, and designing a user-friendly and responsive layout.

- Consider user-friendly navigation, mobile responsiveness, brand consistency, fast loading times, high-resolution visuals, readable fonts, effective use of white space, and accessible content.
- Avoid excessive pop-ups and prioritize essential elements. You should also incorporate social media icons and share buttons.
- For better search engine visibility, focus on SEO practices by optimizing meta tags, descriptive URLs, regular content updates, and security measures.
- Sitemaps are essential for search engine indexing; they can be created manually, with online generators, or through content management systems.
- Register your website with search engines like Google, Bing, and Yahoo to help them become more discoverable, and submit your sitemap to help them index your content.
- Before you launch your website, test it for functionality, responsive design, and security. Regularly update and maintain it, and use feedback from users to improve it.

Strategy 8

Money Mastery For Your First Business

"Formal education will make you a living. Self-education will make you a fortune."

— Jim Rohn

S tarting your own business as a teen is like leveling up in the game of life. You're already way ahead of your peers if you're an entrepreneur. It's all about taking your cool ideas and turning them into real-life moneymakers. You've worked on your marketing strategy, and you have established a social media platform and a website, so the word about your business is officially out there. But there's another secret weapon you need for this epic adventure: financial management.

We're going to show you the key tricks and tips to kick-start your business, manage your money, and become a financial wizard. From creating your money plans to understanding how it flows in and out, setting your prices, and even building a shield for unexpected surprises, we'll guide you on this awesome journey of success in the entrepreneurial world.

Kickstarting Your Financial Management Journey

Starting a business as a teenager can be an exciting and educational experience. However, effective financial management is crucial for the success and sustainability of your business, and that can be tricky and scary when you're just starting out. Here are some financial management tips tailored to a teenager starting their first business:

Create a Budget

Begin by creating a comprehensive budget that sets out your expected income and expenses. This will help you understand your financial needs and limitations.

Open a Business Bank Account

Open a separate business bank account. If you have a separate account for your business and personal expenses, it makes it easier to track your business finances and it will be easier to work out the tax that your business needs to pay.

Record Keeping

Maintain organized records of all your financial transactions. This includes invoices, receipts, and statements. Using accounting software or a spreadsheet can also help you with this process.

Set Clear Financial Goals

Establish clear financial goals for your business, including revenue targets, expense limits, and profit margins. Having specific objectives will help you stay focused and become more successful in the long term.

Monitor Cash Flow

Regularly track your cash flow, which is the money coming in and going out of your business. Cash flow management is important to cover your day-to-day expenses.

Cost Control

Be frugal and find ways to minimize expenses. Consider purchasing second-hand equipment or finding cost-effective suppliers. Avoid unnecessary spending such as spending money on transport by holding most of your meetings online. In the past, businesses used to spend a lot of money on transport and food for meetings, and this cost can be avoided when meetings are held virtually.

Pricing Strategy

Carefully set your prices to cover your costs and make sure you can generate a profit. Research your competitors' pricing to ensure your rates are competitive.

Invoicing and Payment Terms

Create clear and professional invoices for your customers. Set reasonable payment terms, and follow up on unpaid invoices promptly.

Savings and Emergency Fund

Set some of the money you make aside for emergency expenses. If your business faces hard times at some stage, you still want to be able to forge ahead.

Taxes

You need to understand how your tax situation will work, and how you can set some money aside to pay your taxes. A tax professional and accounting software can help you deal with this.

Financial Education

Invest time in learning about basic financial concepts, including profit and loss, balance sheets, and cash flow statements. This knowledge will you make informed financial decisions. Take some classes in accounting to learn more.

Seek Advice

Ask mentors for advice, as well as experienced entrepreneurs, or even family members who have financial expertise.

Invest in Learning

Consider taking courses or attending workshops related to financial management for small businesses. There are many courses and other resources available online that can help you.

Track Your Business Performance

Regularly review your financial statements, assess your business's performance, and adjust your strategies as needed.

Useful Accounting Software

Maybe you think accounting software sounds boring, but it can save you a lot of time and effort and contribute to your business's success.

You might even wonder if you really need this type of software. Well, imagine this: you're running your own business, selling the products and services you've designed and things are taking off. Money's coming in, but where is it going? How much profit are you really making? That's where accounting software can be your secret weapon. It's like having a financial sidekick that helps you keep track of every dollar and cent so you can focus on doing business.

So, how can accounting software help you?

Accounting software isn't some boring number-crunching tool. It can help you figure out your sales, expenses, and profits pretty quickly, and you don't have to spend forever trying to figure out the math by scribbling numbers on paper. You can focus on what's really important to you, while still feeling like a financial wizard.

As a teenpreneur, your days are probably already jam-packed. You're working on your business, studying, and also trying to run a social life. Accounting software saves you time by automating tasks like invoicing and tracking expenses. That means more time for doing the stuff you really enjoy doing.

Want to buy a new gadget or save up for tickets for that awesome concert you want to attend? Accounting software helps you create budgets and stick to them. You can set goals and track your progress without having to worry about complicated ways of doing it.

Most accounting software is super user-friendly and visually appealing. It's designed to be intuitive, making it easy for you to understand your financial picture.

If you have a team or partners in your business, you can invite them to collaborate on the software. It's like working together on a digital project, which is way cooler than spending all your precious time doing boring spreadsheets.

With accounting software, you can plan for the future. It helps you make smart decisions by providing insights into what's working and what's not. It can help you see how to bring your business into the future.

Many accounting software options have mobile apps. You can check your finances on the go, whether you're at a friend's house or waiting for the bus. Your business is in your pocket!

Accounting software can teach you valuable financial skills. You'll learn about cash flow, financial health, and how to manage money like a pro. These skills will serve you well, no matter where life takes you.

You're probably wondering, what is the best type of accounting software for teenage entrepreneurs? There are a number of options available.

When you choose software for your business, you need to consider the following factors:

When choosing accounting software, consider the following factors:

- What specific accounting tasks do you need to perform? Choose software that will make it easier for you to run your business.
- Look for software with an intuitive and user-friendly interface, especially if you're new to accounting. You don't want to waste your precious time trying to figure out how a program works, and then getting nothing else done.
- Many accounting software options offer free trials or have free versions, making them accessible to teenage entrepreneurs. Consider your budget and choose software that fits your budget.
- If you need to access your financial information while rushing through your busy life, you can choose software with a mobile app.
- Consider whether the software can grow with your business. If you plan to expand, you need to choose software that can accommodate your future needs.
- Check if the software provider offers customer support and educational resources to help you get the most out of the software.

Some of the following options might be suitable for your business:

- QuickBooks has a user-friendly interface and a range of features. It's a great choice for small businesses and startups. It offers a free trial, which means it's accessible to you if you're just looking to get started with this type of software.

- Wave is a free accounting and invoicing software that's perfect for small businesses and freelancers. It offers a user-friendly interface and features like income and expense tracking, invoicing, and financial reports.
- Zoho Books is an affordable, cloud-based accounting software that offers invoicing, expense tracking, and basic accounting features.
- FreshBooks is user-friendly and designed for self-employed people and small business owners. It offers features like invoicing, expense tracking, and time tracking.
- Xero is a more advanced accounting software suitable for small to medium-sized businesses. It offers a wide range of features, including multi-currency support, inventory management, and the ability to handle multiple businesses.

A Story About Teen Financial Wizards

A group of high school friends decided to start a business together. Max, Emma, Olivia, and Liam shared a passion for creating custom-designed phone cases and T-shirts. It started as their hobby, but they managed to turn it into a successful business.

As their business grew, so did their ambition to manage their finances more efficiently. They knew they needed a tool that could help them understand the money side of things. Then

Emma had an idea that would change their entrepreneurial journey forever.

She told the others that they needed accounting software to help them keep track of their money, as it would make their lives much easier and give them the time to focus on what's really important.

The others agreed, and they decided to embark on this financial adventure together. They spent days researching different accounting software options and ultimately found one they liked and that was easy to use.

With their newfound tool, the Teenpreneurs began to understand their business's financial health better than ever before. Max, the creative genius, continued to design and print their products. Olivia, the tech-savvy member of the team, took charge of setting up the software and connecting it to their bank accounts. Liam tracked and categorized their expenses. Emma, the communicator, managed customer invoices and payments. Everyone had a role to play.

As they delved into their financial records, they gained a better understanding of their profits, costs, and sales patterns. The colorful charts and graphs helped them visualize their financial progress, and the entire process became even more exciting to them.

One day, Olivia discovered that their line of phone covers was their most profitable product. Armed with this knowledge, they decided to invest more time and resources in that area. They also noticed that spending on promotional materials wasn't getting them the results they desired so they reevaluated their marketing strategies.

Their accounting software became their financial compass, helping them set and achieve their goals. They established a budget for their next product launch and tracked their spending closely. The software alerted them when their expenses exceeded the budget, acting like a responsible guardian of their treasure.

The friends' business flourished. With their strong financial knowledge and the insights gained from their accounting software, they expanded their product line and even attracted international customers. They were savvy business owners who managed to turn their hobby into a successful business.

Budgeting For Your Startup—A Step-By-Step Guide

Budgeting is one of the most important things you can do when starting your new business. You can use this step-by-step guide to make things easier for yourself.

Look at Your Finances

Look at how much money you have available to spend on your business. This will include money you get from your parents and possibly other people who want to invest in your business. Perhaps you have held part-time jobs such as delivering newspapers, or you've worked as a waitress. If you've managed to save some of this money, you can also use this for your business.

Set Clear Goals

Define your short-term and long-term financial goals. This could include startup costs, the monthly costs of operating your business, and how much profit you want to make.

Create a Business Budget

Separate your business and personal finances. Develop a detailed budget for your business that covers all expenses, including:

- Your costs for starting the business. This would be one-time expenses like equipment, licenses, and initial marketing.
- The money you will spend to keep your business operating. This will include ongoing costs such as rent, utilities, salaries, and materials.
- Estimate how much your income will be, based on sales, pricing, and market research.

Emergency Fund

You should also build an emergency fund that can help your business during tough times. This savings buffer can help you cover unexpected business or personal expenses. For example, if you run a business that bakes healthy snacks, and the cost of your ingredients suddenly goes up due to an increase in inflation.

Track Expenses

Make sure you keep track of how much money your business spends, as this will directly influence your profit. The accounting software that we discussed can also help you with this.

Monitor Cash Flow

You also need to keep track of how much money you spend in your business, as you could potentially suffer losses if you spend too much money.

Prioritize Expenses

Identify your essential business and personal expenses. Once you've prioritized expenses, you'll also be better able to see where you can do cost-cutting, when you need to do so.

Save for Taxes

It's important to set some money aside for taxes. Consult with a tax professional to understand your tax obligations and ensure compliance.

Invest Wisely

When you make money, make sure you invest it wisely. Invest at least some of it back into your business.

Review and Amend Your Budget

Regularly review your budget to track your progress, make adjustments, and ensure you're on track to meet your financial goals.

Maintain Discipline

Stick to your budget and avoid unnecessary expenses and impulse spending that could cause you financial trouble in the long run.

How Can You Get External Financing For Your Business?

If you prepare well, and you have business strategies in place, you should be able to get funding for your business like any other adult entrepreneur.

Here's how you can explore external funding options.

It is often best to start out by seeking support from family and friends who believe in your business idea. Be clear about the terms, repayment plans, and potential risks to maintain healthy relationships. You don't want to burn your bridges and find yourself in a situation where people don't trust you anymore because you owe them money.

Grants

Another option is to look for business grants and competitions specifically designed for young entrepreneurs. Organizations, schools, and government agencies often offer such opportunities. These grants can be a source of non-repayable funding.

Angel Investors

Then you get the wonderful people called angel investors.

Angel investors are rich people who invest in startup businesses in exchange for ownership equity or convertible debt. They are typically early-stage investors, providing vital financial support and often offering valuable mentorship and industry expertise.

Many of them are prepared to take risks, and they're willing to invest in high-potential startups. Their investment amounts can vary widely, and they often expect a return on their investment through an exit strategy, such as a merger, acquisition, or initial public offering in the future. Angel investors can operate individually or join investment groups, and their contributions can be a significant source of capital for entrepreneurs.

Some angel investors are open to investing in teen-owned businesses, especially if they see potential in your idea. Be prepared to pitch your business confidently and professionally.

Crowdfunding

Platforms like Kickstarter and Indiegogo allow you to raise funds from a crowd of supporters who believe in your project. Crowdfunding can be an effective way to fund product development or a specific project.

Mentorship and Networking

Connect with experienced entrepreneurs, mentors, and local business organizations. They can provide guidance, connections, and, in some cases, financial support.

Business Incubators and Accelerators

Some incubators and accelerators, such as the Young Entrepreneur Council (YEC) programs, cater to teen entrepreneurs. These programs often provide funding, mentorship, and resources in exchange for equity or a fee.

Microloans

Look at microloan programs tailored for young entrepreneurs. These loans, often provided by nonprofit organizations, can be used for various business needs.

Online Lenders

Consider online lending platforms that may have more flexible requirements than traditional banks. Some of these lenders are open to working with younger business owners.

Competitions and Scholarships

Search for entrepreneurship competitions and scholarships that offer financial prizes to young entrepreneurs. These can provide both funding and recognition for your business.

Educational Institutions

Some schools or universities have entrepreneurship programs that offer funding, resources, and support to student entrepreneurs. Check if your school or college doesn't have such opportunities.

Local Business Grants

Investigate local or regional grants and funding programs aimed at supporting small businesses. Your location may offer opportunities for funding.

Small Business Associations

National or regional small business associations may have programs or grants designed to support young entrepreneurs. Check with organizations like the Small Business Administration (SBA).

When you're looking for external funding, you need to do the following:

- Develop a strong and professional business plan.
- Be clear and explain how you will use the funds and the potential return on investment.
- Ask experienced entrepreneurs what you can do to improve your pitch and strategy.
- Demonstrate your passion and commitment to your business idea.
- Interact in a professional way with potential investors or funders.
- If you're well prepared and confident when you do your proposition, it will increase your chances of obtaining the funding you need to launch and grow your business.

Worksheet: Business Funding Proposal

Here's a worksheet that outlines the key elements to include in your funding proposal. You can base your proposal on the template below.

Cover Page

Title: Your Business Name

Your Name

Contact Information (Address, Phone, Email)

Date

Executive Summary

Provide a brief overview of your business idea.

Describe the amount of funding you are seeking and how you plan to use it.

Highlight what makes your business unique and its growth potential.

Business Description

Provide a detailed description of your business, including its mission, vision, and goals.

Explain your target market and your products or services.

Share your business's legal structure (e.g., sole proprietorship, LLC) and location.

Market Research

Summarize your market research findings, including market size, trends, and competition.

Demonstrate a clear understanding of your target market and its needs.

Financial Projections

Present your financial projections, including income statements, cash flow statements, and balance sheets for at least the next two years.

Describe and show how the funding will impact your business's financials and profitability.

Use of Funds

Detail your plan to use the requested funding. Include a breakdown of expenses, such as marketing, product development, equipment, or hiring.

Business Plan

Provide an overview of your business plan, including strategies for growth and business expansion.

Explain how the funding will help you achieve your business goals.

Marketing and Sales Strategy

Describe your marketing and sales strategies to get and keep customers.

Highlight any innovative approaches or advantages you have in the market.

Management Team

Introduce your management team, including their backgrounds and roles.

Emphasize any unique skills, experience, or expertise that sets your team apart. If you're the only person working in the business, describe your skills and experience.

Competitive Analysis

Analyze your competitors and explain your competitive advantage.

Address how you plan to maintain or strengthen your position in the market.

Exit Strategy

Provide a timeline for when investors can expect returns on their investment.

Risks and Mitigation

Identify potential risks and challenges your business may face.

Explain how you plan to mitigate these risks and uncertainties.

Request for Funding

Specify the exact amount of funding you need from investors.

Provide details about the type of funding (e.g., equity investment, convertible note, loan) you are open to.

Appendix

Include any supporting documents, such as resumes, market research data, product images, or testimonials.

You can adapt this worksheet to suit your business and its unique characteristics. A well-prepared funding proposal is essential to convince potential investors of the viability of your business.

Key Takeaways

- Financial management is a crucial aspect of starting a business.
- Key financial management tips for teenage entrepreneurs include creating a budget, opening a separate business bank account, maintaining organized records, setting clear financial goals, monitoring cash flow, controlling costs, setting pricing strategies, managing invoicing and payment terms, saving for emergencies, understanding taxes, investing in financial education, seeking advice from mentors and experts, and tracking business performance.
- Accounting software can be a valuable tool for teenage entrepreneurs, helping them manage their finances efficiently and make informed decisions. It automates tasks, saves time, helps with budgeting, offers user-friendly interfaces, and provides insights for future planning.
- When choosing accounting software, consider factors such as your specific accounting needs, user-friendliness, cost, mobile accessibility, scalability, customer support, and educational resources.

- Teen entrepreneurs can explore external funding options for their businesses, including seeking support from family and friends, applying for grants and scholarships, attracting angel investors, using crowdfunding platforms, building mentorship and networking relationships, participating in business incubators and accelerators, accessing microloans, working with online lenders, and participating in business competitions.
- To secure external funding, teenage entrepreneurs should prepare a professional business plan, clearly explain how the funds will be used, demonstrate passion and commitment, and interact professionally with potential investors or funders.
- A well-prepared funding proposal is essential for convincing potential investors of the viability and potential of your business.

Conclusion

In the closing chapter of this book, we empower you, teens, to balance entrepreneurship and a healthy lifestyle. We offer you practical strategies, resources, and motivation to help you get started on your journey to becoming successful and healthy entrepreneurs.

We've looked at the following strategies:

- **Goal Setting:** The importance of setting clear and achievable goals for both their business and personal well-being.
- **Time Management:** Helping you manage your time effectively will ensure that you can balance your entrepreneurial endeavors with self-care.
- **Financial Literacy:** Educating you on the fundamentals of financial management and wealth-building.

- **Mental Health:** Highlighting the significance of mental health and providing you with tips on how to maintain a healthy mindset while pursuing entrepreneurship.
- **Networking:** We encourage you to build a strong network to support your entrepreneurial aspirations.

Resources For Your Further Learning And Development:

- **Nomads with a Purpose:** Offers guidance on teaching entrepreneurship to teens. (https://www.nomadswithapurpose.com/teaching-entrepreneurship-to-teens/)
- **Career Addict:** Provides insights and advice for teen entrepreneurs. (https://www.careeraddict.com/teen-entrepreneurs)
- **PlanStreet Inc:** Explains the importance of mental health and well-being. (https://www.planstreetinc.com/top-ten-reasons-why-mental-health-is-so-important/)

While becoming a healthypreneur may seem daunting, it's entirely doable if you take it one step at a time. The key is to balance entrepreneurship with a healthy lifestyle, and the book offers you tools to achieve this.

Finally, the key takeaway is that you can achieve both entrepreneurial success and a healthy lifestyle by setting clear goals, managing time effectively, mastering financial literacy, prioritizing mental health, and building a strong network of support.

So, don't wait any longer to start building wealth and become an entrepreneur, all while maintaining your health. Take action now, as outlined in this book.

As we close this chapter and set forth on your healthypreneurial journey, remember this: "You, as a teenage healthypreneur, are on the cusp of something extraordinary. The world is yours to shape, not just in terms of wealth, but in terms of well-being, wisdom, and impact. The journey is yours to chart, and I have no doubt that it will be nothing short of remarkable."

If you've found this book to be a helpful companion, I invite you to share your thoughts with a review. Your feedback can serve as a guiding light for other teens embarking on a similar path to success and well-being. And while you're exploring, remember to check out my other books, "The Teenage Wealthypreneur" and "Ink of Tears: Echoes of Shattered Souls Poetry Collections," where you'll find additional inspiration and guidance for your remarkable journey in life!

References

Alaska Business. (2019, November 7) *Research Shows 41 Percent of Teens Would Consider Starting Business as Career Option..* Alaska Business Magazine. https://www.akbizmag.com/monitor/national-entrepreneur ship-month-research-shows-41-percent-of-teens-would-consider-start ing-business-as-career-option/

Barrett, B. (2023, January 30). *Lessons from a young entrepreneur | Ep 422.* ChooseFI. https://www.choosefi.com/lessons-from-a-young-entrepreneur-ep-422/

Baskin, K. (2019, December 31). *The 7 superpowers of resilience.* MeQuilibrium. https://www.mequilibrium.com/resources/the-7-super powers-of-resilience/

Career Addict. (2018, November 14). *The 9 Most Successful Teen Entrepreneurs in the World.* CareerAddict. https://www.careeraddict. com/teen-entrepreneurs

Daniel, Farrah, & Hardy, Adam. (2021, April 13). *How to make a website for your brand or small business.* Forbes. https://www.forbes.com/advisor/ business/how-to-make-a-website-for-your-business/

Gabi. (2022, May 21). *Teaching entrepreneurship to teens [Ultimate How-to Guide].* Nomads with a Purpose. https://www.nomadswithapurpose. com/teaching-entrepreneurship-to-teens/

Gordon-Barnes, C. (2014, October 12). *6 fresh ways to find your passion.* Themuse.com; The Muse. https://www.themuse.com/advice/6-fresh-ways-to-find-your-passion

Greenberg, M. (n.d.). 8 Ways to Bounce Back After a Disappointment | Psychology Today. Www.psychologytoday.com. https://www.psychologytoday.com/ us/blog/the-mindful-self-express/201506/8-ways-bounce-back-after-disappointment

Hussain, A. (2018). *7 habits of highly effective people [Book Summary].* Hubspot.com. https://blog.hubspot.com/sales/habits-of-highly-effec tive-people-summary

Lodge, M. (2019, October 25). *10 successful young entrepreneurs. Investopedia.* https://www.investopedia.com/10-successful-young-entrepreneurs-4773310

Macready, H. (2022, November 7). *How to use social media for small business: 11 simple tips.* Hootsuite Social Media Management. https://blog.hoot suite.com/social-media-tips-for-small-business-owners/

Page, M. (n.d.). *5 tips to better your time management | Michael Page US.* Michael Page. https://www.michaelpage.com/advice/career-advice/growing-your-career/5-tips-better-your-time-management

Panel, E. (n.d.). *Council post: 10 ways to live a healthier lifestyle as an entrepreneur.* Forbes. Retrieved October 27, 2023, from https://www.forbes.com/sites/theyec/2021/08/12/10-ways-to-live-a-healthier-lifestyle-as-an-entrepreneur/?sh=3e83c1046de6

Parker, T. (2020, June 17). *The basics of financing a business.* Investopedia. https://www.investopedia.com/articles/pf/13/business-financing-primer.asp

Rebic, D. (2022, August 15). *5 lessons we learned from the body keeps the score.* Myndlift. https://www.myndlift.com/post/5-lessons-we-learned-from-the-body-keeps-the-score

Shopify Staff. *What is entrepreneurship? Definition and guide for 2022.* (n.d.). Shopify. https://www.shopify.com/ca/blog/what-is-entrepreneurship

Stowers, J. (2019). *A step by step guide to starting a business.* Business News Daily. https://www.businessnewsdaily.com/4686-how-to-start-a-business.html

·